BEACON
BIBLE
EXPOSITIONS

BEACON BIBLE EXPOSITIONS

1. Matthew
2. Mark
3. Luke
4. John
5. Acts
6. Romans
7. Corinthians
8. Galatians, Ephesians
9. Philippians, Colossians, Philemon
10. Thessalonians, Timothy, Titus
*11. Hebrews, James, Peter
12. John, Jude, Revelation

BEACON BIBLE EXPOSITIONS

VOLUME **11**

HEBREWS
JAMES
PETER

by
W. T. PURKISER

Editors
WILLIAM M. GREATHOUSE
WILLARD H. TAYLOR

BEACON HILL PRESS OF KANSAS CITY
Kansas City, Missouri

Copyright, 1974
Beacon Hill Press of Kansas City
ISBN: 083-410-3222

Printed in the United States of America

Permissions to quote from copyrighted versions of the Bible are acknowledged as follows (code letters indicated in parentheses):

New American Standard Bible (NASB), copyright © The Lockman Foundation, 1960, 1962, 1963, 1968, 1971.

The New English Bible (NEB), © The Delegates of the Oxford University Press and the Syndics of the Cambridge University Press, 1961, 1970.

New International Version (NIV), copyright © 1973 by New York Bible Society International.

The New Testament in Modern English (Phillips), copyright © by J. B. Phillips, 1958. Used by permission of the Macmillan Co.

Revised Standard Version of the Bible (RSV), copyrighted 1946 and 1952.

Today's English Version of the New Testament (TEV), copyright © American Bible Society, 1966.

Weymouth's New Testament in Modern English (Weymouth), by Richard Francis Weymouth. By special arrangements with James Clarke and Co., Ltd. By permission of Harper and Row, Publishers, Inc.

The New Testament in the Language of the People (Williams), by Charles B. Williams. Copyright 1937 by Bruce Humphries, Inc.; assigned 1949 to Moody Bible Institute, Chicago.

The Modern Language Bible (Berk.)—the New Berkeley Version in Modern English, copyright © 1945, 1959, 1969 by Zondervan Publishing House.

The Amplified New Testament (Amp.), copyright 1958 by the Lockman Foundation, La Habra, Calif.

The Bible: A New Translation (Moffatt), by James Moffatt. Copyright 1954 by James Moffatt. By permission of Harper and Row, Publishers, Inc.

The Bible: An American Translation (Goodspeed), by J. M. Powis Smith and Edgar J. Goodspeed. Copyright 1923, 1927, 1948 by the University of Chicago Press.

The Living Bible (TLB), copyright © 1971, Tyndale House Publishers, Wheaton, Ill.

Quotations from the *American Standard Version* are coded (ASV) and from the *Twentieth Century New Testament* (TCNT).

Contents

Editors' Preface	7
The Epistle to the Hebrews	9
The Epistle of James	123
The First Epistle of Peter	167
The Second Epistle of Peter	209
Reference Notes	227
Bibliography	230

Editors' Preface

No Christian preacher or teacher has been more aware of the creating and sustaining power of the Word of God than the Apostle Paul. As a stratagem in his missionary endeavors, he sought out synagogues in the major cities where he knew Jews would gather to hear the Old Testament. No doubt he calculated that he would be invited to expound the Scriptures and so he would have a golden opportunity to preach Christ. That peripatetic preacher was confident that valid Christian experience and living could not be enjoyed apart from the Word of God, whether preached or written. To the Thessalonians he wrote: "And we also thank God constantly for this, that when you received the word of God which you heard from us, you accepted it not as the word of men but as what it really is, the word of God, which is at work in you believers" (1 Thess. 2:13, RSV). Strong Christians—and more broadly, strong churches—are born of, and nurtured on, authentic and winsome exposition of the Bible.

Beacon Bible Expositions provide a systematic, devotional Bible study program for laymen and a fresh, homiletical resource for preachers. All the benefits of the best biblical scholarship are found in them, but nontechnical language is used in the composition. A determined effort is made to relate the clarified truth to life today. The writers, Wesleyan in theological perspective, seek to interpret the gospel, pointing to the Living Word, Christ, who is the primary Subject of all scripture, the Mediator of redemption, and the Norm of Christian living.

The publication of this series is a prayerful invitation to both laymen and ministers to set out on a lifelong, systematic study of the Bible. Hopefully these studies will supply the initial impetus.

—WILLIAM M. GREATHOUSE AND
WILLARD H. TAYLOR, *Editors*

The Epistle to the
HEBREWS

Topical Outline of Hebrews

Introduction

The Preface: God Has Spoken in His Son, 1:1-4

The Person of Christ, 1:5—4:16
- The Deity and Eternity of the Son, 1:5-14
- Our Responsibility to Hear God's Son, 2:1-4
- The Humanity of the Redeemer, 2:5-9
- Christ's Identification with His People, 2:10-13
- The Reasons for the Incarnation, 2:14-18
- The Builder and the House, 3:1-6
- Warning Against Disobedience, 3:7-19
- Promise of a Greater Rest, 4:1-10
- The Searching Word of God, 4:11-13
- The Support of Our Great High Priest, 4:14-16

The Priesthood of Christ, 5:1—7:28
- The Qualifications of the High Priest, 5:1-4
- The Special Qualifications of Jesus, 5:5-10
- The Immaturity of the People, 5:11-14
- Failure to Go On to Perfection, 6:1-8
- Things That Accompany Salvation, 6:9-20
- Melchisedec, the Type of Christ, 7:1-10
- Changing Priesthoods Imply Changing Law, 7:11-14
- The Total Superiority of the New Priesthood, 7:15-28

The Ministry of Christ, 8:1—10:39
- Christ Ministers in a Better Tabernacle, 8:1-5
- Christ Ministers Under a Better Covenant, 8:6-13
- The Heavenly Sanctuary, 9:1-14
- Christ's Blood Seals the New Covenant, 9:15-22
- Christ's Atonement Is Spiritual and Eternal, 9:23-28
- Repeated Sacrifices Show Their Inadequacy, 10:1-4
- Christ's Supreme Sacrifice His Surrendered Will, 10:5-10
- Christ's Finished Work, 10:11-18
- Acting on the Promises, 10:19-25
- The Hopelessness of Apostasy from Christ, 10:26-31
- Past Loyalty Yields Future Hope, 10:32-39

The Life in Christ, 11:1—13:19
- The Definition of Faith, 11:1-3
- Examples of Faith: Abel to Noah, 11:4-7

Abraham, the Obedience of Faith, 11:8-12
Faith and the Pilgrim Life, 11:13-16
Faith's Supreme Test, 11:17-19
Faith's Farsightedness, 11:20-22
Moses, the Choice of Faith, 11:23-28
Faith That Conquers All Odds, 11:29-31
The Contrast in Faith's Consequences, 11:32-38
A Better Faith for Us, 11:39-40
The Supreme Example of Faith, 12:1-4
The Discipline of Our Faith, 12:5-13
Exhortation to Peace and Holiness, 12:14-17
The Christian's Privilege in Worship, 12:18-24
The Unshakable Kingdom, 12:25-29
The Christian's Moral Obligations, 13:1-6
Following the Changeless Christ, 13:7-16
Respect for Leadership, 13:17
Prayer for Leadership, 13:18-19

A Benediction and Concluding Remarks, 13:20-25

A Benediction, 13:20-21
Concluding Remarks, 13:22-25

Introduction

The one word that best describes the Book of Hebrews is *unique*. It is one of a kind. There is no other quite like it in the Bible in either form or content. It is not a typical New Testament letter, although it ends like one. Archibald Hunter described it as "three parts tract and one part letter."

Hebrews is most like an ancient sermon—a doctrinal discussion with a practical purpose. Yet it is marked by the literary style of an unusually articulate essay, carefully thought out and logically organized.

The Book of Hebrews is a largely neglected book. Part of this is due no doubt to the strangeness of its subject matter. It talks about events in Hebrew history, about the Tabernacle, its altar, its utensils, its veil, its sacrifices, its priestly ministries, its laws, and its covenants. It speaks of types and symbols that are strange to modern ears.

Yet its strangeness is its strength. It deals with subjects as important to modern Christians as to those of the first century.

These subjects will be seen in detail throughout this exposition. In this introduction, it is important to see them in perspective.

The Old Testament and the New

Hebrews tells us two things about the Old Testament: it is authentically the Word of God, and it is not God's last word.

That "God spoke to our forefathers through the prophets at many times and in various ways" (1:1, NIV) is stated without qualification. That "in these last days he has spoken to us by his Son" is just as certain.

There are a number of ways the relationship of the Old Testament to the New might be described. The writer of the Book of Hebrews sees it chiefly in terms of type and fulfillment.

Possibly nothing about Old Testament study goes quite so counter to modern ways of thinking as what have classically been called its types. Many of us have encountered typology in some of its wilder forms. We have heard the two humps on Eliezer's camel described as the first and second blessings. Some of us have cringed when we remembered that while a camel has two humps its cousin the dromedary has only one. As E. Stanley Jones said of divine healing, so of typology, we have let "the queer queer it for us."

But the author of Hebrews sees in Old Testament events and ritual shadows that could be cast only by substance. Earthly events, like parables, have heavenly meanings.

Never does the author lose the forest in the multitude of its trees. He never concerns himself with irrelevant detail, as have some typologists of more recent vintage. But he shares with us his practical certainty not only that the Old Testament is a sort of prelude to the New but that it reflects, however dimly, the same eternal reality that blazes in glory in the face of Jesus Christ.

In this, the Book of Hebrews can be an important lesson in hermeneutics (the art of biblical interpretation) for students of the Old Testament. We must never lose sight of the value of the history itself as a mode of God's self-revelation. Neither should we ever forget that in the events of the history there are symbols that stand for a greater reality.

The Priesthood of Jesus

Hebrews is the great New Testament presentation of the priesthood of Jesus. Other New Testament writers speak of Christ's intercession; Hebrews presents it as the mediatorial ministry of the great High Priest.

In this are brought together the two essential strands in New Testament Christology. By virtue of His deity, Christ Jesus ministers in the true and heavenly tabernacle.

By reason of His complete humanity, Jesus is able to be our perfect Representation in God's holy presence.

Priesthood was long known and well understood among the Jewish people. But it was equally a part of Gentile religious life. The essential idea in priesthood is representation. The priest stands in the place of those unworthy or unable to stand for themselves in the presence of God. The priest himself must be qualified by God's authorization to appear before the Majesty on high. But he also must be one in nature with those in whose place he stands.

No one, Jew or pagan, could ever fulfill the idea of priesthood as Jesus did. He was "made like his brothers in every way" (2:17, NIV). At the same time, He was "the radiance of God's glory and the exact representation of his being" (1:3, NIV).

Yet beyond anything any other could ever conceivably be, Jesus was not only Priest but Sacrifice as well. Other priests, Jewish and pagan, offered the blood of animal sacrifices and thereby gained ritual purity. Our great High Priest offered His own blood to "cleanse our consciences from acts that lead to death, so that we may serve the living God!" (9:13-14, NIV).

The Finality of the Gospel

The key word to much of the Book of Hebrews is *better*. Christ is a better Mediator of truth than angels. He is a better Leader than Moses and Joshua. He is a better Priest than Aaron. He is a better Sacrifice than the bulls and goats of the Tabernacle and Temple altars. He brings in a better covenant, based on a better law, leading to a better faith and a better life.

But *better* finally drops out of the vocabulary of the writer. The comparative gives way to the superlative. Christ Jesus is not just a better way. He is the only Way.

The issue becomes sharp and clear. Those who follow Christ must follow Him outside the gate, without the camp (13:12-13). What stands out unmistakably is the conclusion. That is the absolute finality of Christ only as "the way, the truth, and the life" (John 14:6).

This fact has two meanings. Historically, the Book of Hebrews stands as a Christian emancipation proclamation from subservience to Judaism. It is hard for us to imagine now how easily Christianity might have become just another Jewish sect like those of the Pharisees, the Sadducees, or the Essenes. Christianity could have been smothered in its Jewish swaddling clothes. We owe it to men like Stephen, Paul, and the writer to the Hebrews that the Christian faith is known today for what it really is, one faith for one world.

In no way could we say that God caused the rejection of their Messiah by the chosen people. That rejection, as Paul makes abundantly clear in Romans 10, was the result of disobedience and unbelief. But what God does not cause, He uses. The rejection of their Messiah by the chosen people had the practical effect of opening the door of the gospel to the Gentiles on equal terms with the Jews. Like Paul, we cherish the hope that Gentile benefactors of the gospel may take it back to those through whom it originally came (Romans 11).

But in the meantime, the new covenant and the new sacrifice replace the old. Those who have the new cannot longer find salvation in the old. The better way is in truth the only way. "There is no other name under heaven given to men by which we must be saved" (Acts 4:12, NIV).

This truth not only has a historical meaning. It has also a present, practical meaning. We do well to see it today. Ours is a day of permissiveness in morals and "tolerance" in religion. Syncretism—putting together elements from all sorts of religions—is the mood of our times.

But the truth of God is not indifferent. The Ten Commandments cannot become the "Ten Amendments." Christ Jesus alone is "the same yesterday, and to day, and for ever" (13:8). It is eternally true that no man comes to the Father but by Him. It is this we will learn in all its rich variety of illustration and application as we turn the pages of the letter to the Hebrews.

The Dynamic of Inspiration

A quick look at the introduction to the Book of Hebrews in practically any commentary will show that the number one "critical" problem in the book is the question of its authorship. Paul, Apollos, Barnabas, Aquila and Priscilla, and Luke have all been named.

This is no recent cavil. Origen in the third century of the Christian era wrote: "If I were setting forth my own judgment I should say that the thoughts are the Apostle's [Paul's] but the diction and composition are due to some one who had taken notes of the master's teaching. If then any Church holds this Epistle as Paul's, it may be left happily in that belief: for it was not at random that ancient tradition attributed it to him: but who it was who wrote it God knows."

Probably we should be as wise as Origen and leave the matter of authorship there: "who it was who wrote it God knows," and He alone with certainty. It is never a mistake to honor the silence of the Holy Spirit and accept the anonymity in which He left the letter. As William Neil says, "The fact that some New Testament books, which were thought at one time to be written by an apostle, turn out to be . . . anonymous, makes us rather realize how much richer the early Church was in theologians than we imagined."

Yet the curious paradox of it all is the contrast that exists between the uncertainty of authorship and the certainty of the inspiration and value of Hebrews. Here is a marvellous instance of the "self-authenticating" character of divine inspiration. We know that Hebrews is inspired because through its lines the Holy Spirit inspires within us a new look at and love for our Lord Jesus Christ, and His and our God and Father.

HEBREWS 1

The Preface: God Has Spoken in His Son
Hebrews 1:1-4

No book in all scripture opens with a greater sweep of truth than is given in these words which preface the Epistle. In one tremendous statement, the author establishes the divine authority of the Old Testament and affirms the superiority of the New.

Hebrews 1:1-4

> 1 God, who at sundry times and in divers manners spake in time past unto the fathers by the prophets,
> 2 Hath in these last days spoken unto us by his Son, whom he hath appointed heir of all things, by whom also he made the worlds;
> 3 Who being the brightness of his glory, and the express image of his person, and upholding all things by the word of his power, when he had by himself purged our sins, sat down on the right hand of the Majesty on high;
> 4 Being made so much better than the angels, as he hath by inheritance obtained a more excellent name than they.

1. God spoke through the prophets of the Old Testament. The author uses the preposition *en*, "in," not *dia*, "through"; for the prophets were not passive instruments. God dwelt in them by His Spirit, controlling and illuminating them, in order to reveal himself to men of old. Peter put the same truth in slightly different terms: "For the prophecy came not in old time by the will of man: but holy men of God spake as they were moved by the Holy Ghost" (2 Pet. 1:21).

a. In many parts. The Greek is literally, "In many parts and various ways, God spoke of old to our fathers." The word *part* is used in comparison with the whole. It suggests the stages through which the Old Testament revelation of God moved: the Law, the Prophets, and the Writings.

This is "progressive revelation." But we must always remember that the progress is not from the false to the true. It is from the part to the whole, from promise to fulfillment. We still need the Old Testament just as higher mathematics still needs the multiplication table. There is much more in mathematics than "two times two equals four." But higher forms of mathematics do not contradict arithmetic; they build on it. Christ came to "fulfil" the law—and "law" is a term that comes very close to meaning the whole Old Testament truth about God and man. He did not come to destroy it.

b. In various ways. God revealed himself in the Old Testament in different ways. He made himself known through His mighty acts in history. In the Bible, history is literally "His story." He spoke through prophets and seers. He used visions. He appeared as "the angel of the Lord." In recording it all, He so guided His inspired penmen that Paul could write, "All scripture [in direct reference to the Old Testament] is given by inspiration of God, and is profitable for doctrine, for reproof, for correction, for instruction in righteousness: that the man of God may be perfect, throughly furnished unto all good works" (2 Tim. 3:16-17).

c. In olden times. The word here used, *palai,* does not merely mean formerly. It describes something completed in the past. The writer is getting ready to say that the partial and varied revelation of the Old Testament has been surpassed. It is the finished foundation upon which the building has been erected. A decisive turning point has been reached. The old has been established that the new might be made known.

2. *In these last days* the God of the Old Testament has spoken—as the passage literally says—"in His Son" or "in Son." *Last days* is the special biblical term for the age of the Messiah. The New Testament consistently speaks of our dispensation as "the last days" (Acts 2:17; 2 Tim. 3:1; Jas. 5:3; 1 Pet. 1:20; 1 John 2:18). The Greek may be translated, "In the end of these days."

New Testament writers lived in the conviction that the end of time was approaching very rapidly. Probably all of them expected Christ to come again in their lifetimes. Yet the deeper meaning of such words as the writer uses here is that God has spoken with finality—"for the last time." What had before been grasped only in part and imperfectly is now fully revealed in the Son, who is the eternal Word and, coming from the bosom of the Father, fully declares His grace and truth (John 1:1-5, 14-18).

a. The person of the Son. In contrast to the prophets stands the person of the Son. Oscar Cullmann has written: "Jesus' deity is more powerfully asserted in Hebrews than in any other New Testament writing, with the exception of the Gospel of John. Hebrews understands 'Son of God' to mean 'one with God,' just as does John 10:33, 36. The Old Testament psalms (for example Pss. 45:6 f.; 102:25 ff.) are applied to Jesus so that he can be addressed directly as 'God' (Heb. 1:8 f.), and the creation of the world ascribed to him (Heb. 1:10 ff.). . . . 'Son of God,' then, means complete participation in the Father's deity."

(1) Christ is the *appointed heir of all things* (2). All things belong to Him because He created them and because He redeemed them.

This dual ownership is illustrated by the story of the junior boy who carved out a small sailboat with great care. It was his pride and joy. One day, as he was sailing it on the river near his home, the string slipped from his fingers. The current carried the boat downstream out of sight and beyond recovery.

Some weeks later, passing a secondhand store in town, the lad saw his boat in the window for sale. He went in and claimed it. The merchant said, "I'm sorry, Son; but I paid good money for that boat to the boy who found it. If you want it, you'll have to buy it."

Saving his allowance, the young boat builder bought back the boat he had made and lost. As he left the store with his prize cradled in his arms, he said, "You're mine! You're twice mine! You're mine because I made you, and you're mine because I bought you!"

(2) Christ is the Agent of the Father in creation. *The worlds (tous aionas)* is literally "the ages." The reference is to the universe as temporal. John and Paul both express this same general truth: "All things were made by him; and without him was not any thing made that was made" (John 1:3); "By him were all things created, that are in heaven, and that are in earth, visible and invisible, wheth-

er they be thrones, or dominions, or principalities, or powers: all things were created by him, and for him" (Col. 1:16; cf. 1 Cor. 8:6; Eph. 3:9).

(3) Christ is *the brightness* (literally, the radiance) *of his glory* (3). These words may mean either that Jesus is the Radiance that streams from God, or that He is the Reflection of God's very being. This is the clearest possible statement of the essential relationship of Father and Son. It is the nature of light to radiate. The radiation may always be traced back to the source from which it comes.

(4) Christ is *the express image of his person.* Rotherham translates this phrase, "An exact representation of his very being." Phillips puts it, "The flawless expression of the nature of God." Marshall's literal translation is, "The representation of the reality of him." F. F. Bruce comments, "What God essentially is, is made manifest in Christ. To see Christ is to see what the Father is like."

Express image is *charakter* (representation, expression) in the Greek. *His person* is *hypostasis* (being, nature, reality). With the preceding phrase, *brightness of his glory,* this is the strongest possible statement of the complete deity of Jesus Christ. The use of these terms, William Barclay notes, "is to state the essential identity of Jesus with God and the essential independence of his being; it is at one and the same time to state his deity and his humanity."

b. The work of the Son. The finality of God's word in Jesus is seen not only in the person of the Son; it is also seen in His work both in nature and providence and in redemption. Three great statements about the work of the Son are added to what has been said about His being:

(1) Christ upholds *all things by the word of his power.* Not only is He the Agent of the Father in creation; He is also God's Agent in the preservation and providence that sustains and controls the universe. *Deism* holds that God created the universe as a self-contained system that runs its own course. *Theism* recognizes that God not only creates, but that He continues to sustain and control the universe moment by moment. If God were to "die" or

cease to be, there would not be a self-sufficient finite universe left as a monument to His past creativity. There would be only chaos and death—or nothing at all.

Paul parallels the statement that Christ sustains the created universe, just as he parallels the statement that Christ is the Father's Agent in creation: "By him all things consist" or cohere (Col. 1:17). He holds all things together —"He sustains and embraces them all" (Goodspeed). Again, the emphasis is on the full deity of the Son.

(2) Christ has *by himself purged our sins.* In practical importance, the work of the Son in redemption overshadows His work in creating and sustaining the universe. *By himself* is actually an anticipation of the truth later definitely stated. It implies that it was by the sacrifice of himself that our sins are put away and we are cleansed. *Purged* is *katharismon,* from which "cathartic" comes. It is the typical New Testament word to describe the cleansing or purification of the believer's heart.

(3) Christ has *sat down on the right hand of the Majesty on high.* "He took His seat at the right hand of God's majesty" (Williams). Typically, the writer to the Hebrews introduces in a preliminary way subjects he intends to develop more fully later. The purging of our sins and our Lord's high priestly ministry at the throne of grace are important themes throughout the rest of the book. Hebrews not only stresses both the deity and the humanity of Christ; it emphasizes both Christ's atoning death and His present and eternal living intercession at God's right hand.

c. The supremacy of the Son. In v. 4, the author clinches the point toward which he has been building. All that has been said about God's revelation in His Son shows how much better is His gospel than the word given by messengers either angelic or human. The superiority of Christ's nature and His mission is seen in the superiority of His name.

Again this thought is paralleled in the writings of Paul. In Phil. 2:9, Paul says that "God also hath highly exalted him, and given him a name which is above every name." This is the name "Lord," *kurios*—the term used in the Greek translation of the Old Testament to translate *Yahweh*, the sacred, personal name of the living and true God. The eternal sonship of Christ comes into view again, since this name is His by inheritance—by right of relationship as well as by gift.

This is the transition truth that leads into the thought which follows. To say that Christ is better than the angels is to say that He eclipses the whole Old Testament revelation. *Better*, the key word of the book, is used 13 times in contrasting Christ with the old order.

The writer meets his readers on their own ground. It was a generally accepted belief that, while Moses had brought the Law to Israel, he had himself received it, not directly from God, but through the mediation of angels (Acts 7:51-53; Gal. 3:19). This then is the first of a series of skillfully made points showing that, while the Old Testament was indeed the authentic word of God, it has now been fulfilled and therefore surpassed by Christ's atoning death and victorious resurrection.

The Person of Christ
Hebrews 1:5—4:16

The Deity and Eternity of the Son

After the Preface (1:1-4), chapter 1 states two major ideas: the superiority of the Son over angels; and the eternity of the Son's nature contrasted with the transient and uncertain nature of angels and of the whole created order.

Hebrews 1:5-14
> 5 For unto which of the angels said he at any time, Thou art my son, this day have I begotten thee? And again, I will be to him a Father, and he shall be to me a Son?
> 6 And again, when he bringeth in the firstbegotten into the world, he saith, And let all the angels of God worship him.
> 7 And of the angels he saith, Who maketh his angels spirits, and his ministers a flame of fire.
> 8 But unto the Son he saith, Thy throne, O God, is for ever and ever: a sceptre of righteousness is the sceptre of thy kingdom.
> 9 Thou hast loved righteousness, and hated iniquity; therefore God, even thy God, hath anointed thee with the oil of gladness above thy fellows.
> 10 And, Thou, Lord, in the beginning hast laid the foundation of the earth; and the heavens are the works of thine hands:

> 11 They shall perish; but thou remainest; and they all shall wax old as doth a garment;
> 12 And as a vesture shalt thou fold them up, and they shall be changed: but thou art the same, and thy years shall not fail.
> 13 But to which of the angels said he at any time, Sit on my right hand, until I make thine enemies thy footstool?
> 14 Are they not all ministering spirits, sent forth to minister for them who shall be heirs of salvation?

At this point, we enter the carefully reasoned and scripturally supported argument of the book. In the 10 verses that make up this section, we have a chain of 7 citations from the Old Testament—5 from the Psalms, 1 from Deuteronomy, and 1 from 2 Samuel. All three major sections of the Hebrew Scriptures are represented and all are treated as equally authoritative: the Law (Deuteronomy), the Prophets (2 Samuel was in "The Former Prophets"), and the Writings (Psalms).

Commentators have noted the difference between the sweeping statements of vv. 1-4, made without scripture citation, and the carefully reasoned and biblically supported arguments throughout the balance of the book. It would seem that the preface (vv. 1-4) is a summary of Christian teaching known to and accepted by the readers and needing no proof. It contains, as William Manson says, "The *presuppositions* of faith, the foundation-truths of the Christian religion. . . . These truths do not need to be demonstrated or explained. They belong to the givenness of the received gospel."

In developing the implications of these received truths, the author takes care to support each step in his argument both logically and biblically. He does this first in regard to the inherent superiority of a Son over angelic servants. A series of contrasts is made between the Son of God and His angelic servants.

1. Angels are never addressed as "Son"; Messiah (Christ) is. Ps. 2:7 and 2 Sam. 7:14 are quoted from the Greek translation of the Old Testament (the Septuagint) to illustrate this point. Both verses occur in contexts recognized by the Jews of that day as referring to the Messiah. The Messiah ("Anointed One") was the divine Figure expected in Old Testament times to come as the Deliverer of God's

people. "Christ" (Greek, *Christos;* used first in Hebrews in 3:6) is the English form of the New Testament Greek term meaning "Messiah."

This day have I begotten thee (5) has been understood in a variety of ways. Some think it refers to the "day" of eternal generation; others to the day of incarnation, the birth of Jesus; others to the day of anointing, when the Voice spoke at Christ's baptism, "Thou art my beloved Son." It is more likely, however, in harmony with Acts 13:33 and Rom. 1:3-4, that the reference is to the day of Christ's resurrection. H. Orton Wiley wrote: "The words 'this day' refer most properly, then, to the day of Resurrection, in which God gave the fullest proof that Jesus was both innocent and righteous. The miraculous power by which He was raised from the dead declares Him to be the Son of God; and His body, which never saw corruption, was raised a spiritual body—the first-born from the dead, and the first fruits of them that sleep."[1]

2. The angels are bidden to worship *the firstbegotten* (6). In His humanity, Jesus was the first man to be truly a son of God. But *the* Son of God, Paul says, is "the firstborn among many brethren" (Rom. 8:29; cf. Heb. 2:11-12). The angels worshipped when Messiah was born (Luke 2:9-14). When He comes again into the world, they will be His retinue (Matt. 16:27; 25:31). To worship anything or anyone other than God is idolatry. Christ properly receives the worship due only to Deity. He therefore is fully divine.

3. The angels are servants of the will of God. The Greek, *angelos,* means "messenger." Here is no depreciation of angels. It is the highest honor a creature can know to do the bidding of the Creator. But the purpose of the writer is to show the greater glory of the Son. The angels are swift as the wind in obedience; they are strong as fire in power; but they cannot be compared in dignity and honor with the strong Son of God.

4. The angels have no thrones; *"But unto the Son he saith, Thy throne, O God, is for ever and ever: a sceptre of righteousness is the sceptre of thy kingdom* (8). Again, in most unmistakeable terms, Christ is addressed as God. An Old

Testament passage, which in its original setting referred to the Lord God of the Old Testament, is here addressed to Jesus with no sense of incongruity whatever. This practice, common to all the major writers of the New Testament, is the strongest possible evidence of their conviction that Jesus Christ was indeed God in human form. In contrast to the limited and temporal service of angels, Christ's is an eternal throne. He rules His kingdom in righteousness. His sovereignty is always right and just.

The basis of Christ's righteous reign is His love for righteousness and His hatred of iniquity (9). Something of the relationship of Father and Son in the Trinity is seen in that, in v. 8, Christ is addressed as "God" and in v. 9 it is said of Him that *thy God, hath anointed thee with the oil of gladness above thy fellows.* Although He was eternally one with the Father, the incarnate Son was the Servant of His Father's will and acknowledged His dependence upon the Father (John 10:30-38). New Testament expressions of the "subordination" of the Son to the Father have sometimes been used to argue against the Christian concept of a triune God. In point of fact, they are an essential part of that truth.

To love righteousness and hate lawlessness are two sides to the same coin. He who truly loves God will hate evil. This, for us as for Jesus, is a sign of the "anointing" God gives.

5. A final contrast between the Son and angels is the eternity of the Son. This is the heart of vv. 10-14. Angels are created beings. The Jews of the first century thought their existence might even be temporary. That is, when they had done their work as servants of those who are heirs of salvation (v. 14), they might cease to exist. While this is not sure, what is sure is that the Son is eternal.

In the beginning (10)—as stated in v. 2—Christ, as the eternal Second Person of the Trinity, *laid the foundation of the earth.* Here, as often in the New Testament, the Old Testament name of God ("Lord") is given to Jesus. The created world is temporal and owes its existence only to the will of its Creator: it *shall perish; but thou remainest* (11).

Like an old garment, it will be folded up and exchanged for something better (11-12). But the Creator Lord remains. He is the same "yesterday, and to day, and for ever" (13:8). Even His enemies will become His footstool (13).

There was tremendous inspiration here for the Christians to whom this book was addressed. The old order of ceremonial righteousness had been changed for something better. But it is the same Lord who administers the new.

There is tremendous inspiration here for us also. We also live in a changing world. The old is passing away. The new is at hand. Yet the same Lord who walked the dusty roads of Judaea and taught by the blue waters of Galilee walks with us through the changing scenes of life.

HEBREWS 2

Our Responsibility to Hear God's Son

Chapter 2 opens with one of the most characteristic features of the entire Book of Hebrews. Alternating with doctrinal teaching are practical application and exhortation. Paul usually followed a different pattern. He dealt first with doctrine, then with ethics; first the "believing side" of the gospel, then the "behaving side." The author of Hebrews alternated teaching and application, the doctrinal and the practical conclusion.

Hebrews 2:1-4

> 1 Therefore we ought to give the more earnest heed to the things which we have heard, lest at any time we should let them slip.
> 2 For if the word spoken by angels was stedfast, and every transgression and disobedience received a just recompence of reward;
> 3 How shall we escape, if we neglect so great salvation; which at the first began to be spoken by the Lord, and was confirmed unto us by them that heard him;
> 4 God also bearing them witness, both with signs and wonders, and with divers miracles, and gifts of the Holy Ghost, according to his own will?

1. *Therefore*—because of the great truths of c. 1—*we ought to give the more earnest heed to the things which we have heard* (1). The thought is that with utmost care we

should "hold our minds to" the truths spoken, not by angels, but by the Son himself.

The practical danger is that we *let them slip*. The imagery in the Greek here concerns water—either leaking almost imperceptibly from a vessel or as a current that carries a vessel beyond its mooring place. William Barclay writes: "For most of us the threat of life is not so much that we should plunge into disaster, but that we should drift into sin. There are few people who deliberately and in a moment turn their backs on God; there are many who day by day drift farther and farther away from Him. There are not many who in one moment of time commit some disastrous sin; there are many who, bit by bit and almost imperceptibly, involve themselves in some situation, and suddenly awake to find that they have ruined life for themselves and broken someone else's heart. We would do well to be continually on the alert against the peril of the drifting tide."

2. *The word spoken by angels* (2) has already been shown to be inferior to the word that comes by the eternal Son of God. Yet even that word *was stedfast*. It could not be broken (John 10:35). *Every transgression*—all sins of commission—*and disobedience*—all sins of omission—do receive just punishment. The logic is simple and inescapable. If those who disregarded the Law, the lesser truth, endangered their immortal souls, *How shall we escape, if we neglect so great salvation?* (3).

Charles Erdman says that this salvation "is shown to be 'great' in at least three particulars: first of all, in its original proclamation; second, in its secure transmission; and third, in its divine attestation. . . . It is not want of evidence that turns one from the Christian faith; nor can it be the discovery that Christianity lacks foundation in historic fact. Apostasy is caused by the failure to face evidence and by indifference to a divinely attested gospel."[2]

Salvation is the great word of the gospel. It includes all God does for us in relation to our total need. It includes both justification and sanctification (2 Thess. 2:13). It is past, present, and future: we have been saved (Eph. 2:8);

we are being saved (1 Cor. 1:18, Greek); and we shall be saved (Rom. 13:11; Heb. 9:28; 1 Pet. 1:5). Salvation is "free, full, and final."

Nor is it necessary to reject this great salvation defiantly in order to lose its value. The warning is against neglect—a term that implies the intention of doing something about it later, but failing to take care of the obligation now. Neglect can destroy anything we cherish: home, family, church, occupation, our souls themselves.

3. News of this great salvation does not come from angels. It *first began to be spoken by the Lord* (3). All His divine authority lies behind the gospel He preached and then committed to faithful men to pass along. It *was confirmed unto us by them that heard him*. Jesus spoke of those who would believe through the word of His apostles (John 17:20). He said, "He that heareth you heareth me" (Luke 10:16). The inspired words of the apostles are thus the very words of the divine Lord himself.

God confirmed the apostolic witness by signs, wonder-inspiring works, mighty acts of power, and gifts of the Holy Spirit. The climactic evidence lies in the presence of the Holy Spirit. Johannes Schneider writes: "God is not only a God of the Word, but also a God of power. From Him proceed the word of salvation *and* the deed of salvation. Finally, there is the impartation of the Spirit. God is Spirit. And He attests the truth and efficaciousness of His being by giving to His own the power of His Spirit. The proportion of spiritual power which God imparts to the individual lies within His power. But one thing is certain: where God is at work, there He gives the Word of salvation, the wonder-working power of the Holy Spirit. The Church of Christ lives of these gifts to this present day. In times of revival as in times of persecution the manifestations of God corroborating the proclaimed Word become particularly visible."[3]

While the natural man seeks "a sign," something spectacular or dramatic, the spiritual man sees the transforming power of the gospel in human life as the greatest of all the wonderful works of God. Even bodies that are healed will return to the dust from which they came. But souls healed of the disease of sin will live forever. When skeptical friends asked a new convert if he really believed that Christ changed water into wine, he said, "Why not? In my life He changed booze into food and clothes and a home for my family!"

The Humanity of the Redeemer

Hebrews 1 expounds the deity of Jesus. Chapter 2, after the introductory exhortation of vv. 1-4, turns to the humanity of Christ. It is worthy of note that those very books in the New Testament (e.g., Hebrews and John) that put strongest emphasis on the deity of Jesus also most clearly stress His humanity. Wiley calls this portion of c. 2 "The Humanity and Humiliation of Christ."

Hebrews 2:5-9

> 5 For unto the angels hath he not put in subjection the world to come, whereof we speak.
> 6 But one in a certain place testified, saying, What is man, that thou art mindful of him? or the son of man, that thou visitest him?
> 7 Thou madest him a little lower than the angels; thou crownedst him with glory and honour, and didst set him over the works of thy hands:
> 8 Thou hast put all things in subjection under his feet. For in that he put all in subjection under him, he left nothing that is not put under him. But now we see not yet all things put under him.
> 9 But we see Jesus, who was made a little lower than the angels for the suffering of death, crowned with glory and honour; that he by the grace of God should taste death for every man.

Throughout c. 2, the contrast with angels continues. After this, no reference is made to angels. But the immediate problem is, How is it that One so superior to the angels should, in His humanity, be so weak that He could be put to death?

The author moves into his theme with a quotation from Psalm 8. Here is the very essence of the biblical view of man. It combines two contradictory elements: man's dignity, and his humiliation or lowliness. In Francis Thompson's phrase, "Man is kin to clod and cherubim." Blaise Pascal spoke of man as "the glory and scum of the universe."

It is not to angels that God has given sovereignty over *the world to come,* literally, "the age to come"—that is,

His "new order" (v. 5). It was rather to man in Christ. Although made a little lower than the angels, God is *mindful of him* (6) and *visitest him*. To "visit" in biblical language means to express regard or concern for and to act in behalf of. "Thou lookest after him" (Berkeley), and, "Thou art concerned about him" (NASB).

God has crowned His human creation with *glory and honour* (7), and *set him over the works of* (His) *hands*. Man was appointed to "subdue" the earth and "have dominion over it" as God's representative (Gen. 1:27-30).

Thoughtless men have blamed the ecological crisis of the late twentieth century on what they call the Judeo-Christian view of nature. They have completely misunderstood the meaning of the biblical text. To subdue and have dominion over the works of God's hands as His representative is a far cry from the exploitation and greed that strips nature of its resources and is fast turning the world into a garbage dump. Environmental pollution is not the result of man's obedience to his commission from God. It is the result of his sinful rebellion against his Creator.

Yet the author is keenly aware of the contrast of man's temporal condition with God's ideal. All things, without exception, were to be *put under him* (8). But this is not what we see. The real is in sorry contrast with the ideal. Sin has marred and broken the purpose of God for His earthly order.

What mankind has failed to achieve, Jesus has triumphantly accomplished. We see a shattered and broken humanity. But we see something else. *We see Jesus, who was made a little lower than the angels for the suffering of death, crowned with glory and honour; that he by the grace of God should taste death for every man* (9).

This is the first use of our Lord's human name in the Book of Hebrews. *Jesus* is the English form of the Old Testament *Joshua* and means "The Lord is Salvation" or "The Lord our Salvation." It is fitting that it should be used in connection with "so great salvation" (v. 2).

The parallel with Psalm 8 is worked out. Jesus, as human, was made a little lower than angels. He is *crowned with glory and honour*. The traditional version is a bit misleading here. Jesus was not crowned with glory and honor in order to suffer death but "because He suffered death" (Williams). It would seem to the natural mind to be a strange glory. It is "the glory of the Cross."

"Taste death" is a literal translation of the Greek. But "tasting" does not have here the modern connotation of superficial action. It means to experience to the full (cf. Mark 9:1; Matt. 16:28; Luke 9:27; John 8:52 for parallels). Yet it carries the suggestion that, while fully experienced, death was not the final word. The Resurrection shattered death's power. Life has the last word, not death.

Christ's death was an expression of the grace of God. Christians never look upon the Cross merely as the end result of historical events. The Cross revealed God's love and grace as it could never be made known in any other way (Rom. 5:8). It is a fatal flaw to think of Calvary in such a way as to set Jesus against the Father. Christ is not a Refuge from the Father's wrath but the way to His mercy. What was accomplished on the Cross was the Father's will making possible the reconciliation of sinful men to God.

Christ died *for every man*. This is an unqualified denial of every sort of "limited atonement": either that Christ died for only a chosen few; or that, while He died for all, God's efficacious call is given only to a preselected group. He died *for* all in both meanings of the term *for:* on on behalf of, and instead of. This was, as Richard S. Taylor has noted, "substitutionary in an ethical rather than a legal sense." Christ's death is effective for all who through obedient faith receive Him as their Lord and Saviour.

Christ's Identification with His People

Now the author pens a paragraph which follows the preceding as both explanation and consequence. The incongruity of a divine Messiah suffering death is explained. Its purpose and method are set forth. In spite of the paradox involved—that the sovereign God of the universe should accomplish the redemption of His erring creatures through the sufferings of their Founder-Leader—*it became him* (10) as eminently fitting. E. C. Wickham writes: "The writer is justifying what Jewish prejudices of his readers stumbled at . . . a true incarnation. . . . It was in the fitness of things. . . . It was what God's nature demanded."

Hebrews 2:10-13

> 10 For it became him, for whom are all things, and by whom are all things, in bringing many sons unto glory, to make the captain of their salvation perfect through sufferings.
> 11 For both he that sanctifieth and they who are sanctified are all of one: for which cause he is not ashamed to call them brethren,
> 12 Saying, I will declare thy name unto my brethren, in the midst of the church will I sing praise unto thee.
> 13 And again, I will put my trust in him. And again, Behold I and the children which God hath given me.

1. Christ is *the captain of* our *salvation.* The word translated *captain* is *archegos.* "Author," "Princely Leader," and "Pioneer" have all been suggested as English equivalents. None of them entirely fit. William Barclay recalls a helpful illustration: "Suppose a ship was on the rocks, and suppose the only way to rescue was for someone to swim ashore with a line, in order that, once the line was secured, others might follow. The one who was first to swim ashore would be the *archegos* of the safety of the others. That is what the writer to the Hebrews means when he says that Jesus is the *archegos* of our salvation. Jesus was the pioneer who blazed the trail to God for us to follow."[4] Alexander Purdy writes, "Jesus is the completely adequate and completely victorious leader of salvation."

The Pioneer of our salvation, made perfect through sufferings, sanctifies His people. He is one with those *who are sanctified. He is not ashamed to call them brethren* (11). The verb "to sanctify" is found in Hebrews more often than in any other New Testament book. One-fourth of all its New Testament uses are in this book.

As Wiley points out, sanctification has both an objective and a subjective use. Objectively, it refers to the work which Christ has done for us in making atonement for sin. It is His finished work.

Subjectively, sanctification, according to Wiley, is "that which Christ works *in* us by His Holy Spirit. It is not enough to say that Christ has provided an atonement *for* us; we need Christ *in* us as much as we need His atoning work *for* us. It is not alone what Christ did on the Cross that saves us; it is what He does *in* us by virtue of what He did *for* us on the Cross. Christ not only expiates our sins; He dwells within us through the Holy Spirit; and it is His personal presence within that sanctifies us in the deeper meaning of the word *hagiazein* ("to sanctify"). Here the word *hagios* or 'holy' signifies not only the act of purifying or cleansing, but the indwelling presence of Christ in His cleansed temple; and it is this Presence within that sanctifies and makes us His possession."

All of one sounds unfinished. Translators and commentators have supplied what they believe to be the proper finishing phrase: "one family," "one stock," "one origin," "one nature," and "one Father." All are appropriate in some measure. The last is probably best.

2. Three quotations from the Old Testament are put together in vv. 12-13 expressing the identification of Christ with humanity. Jesus identifies himself with His people in their worship of the Father—a quotation from Ps. 22:22. This verse identifies the Church of the New Testament with the "congregation" of the Old Testament. Jesus also sets the example in His filial trust—a quotation from 2 Sam. 22:3 and Isa. 8:17. His disciples are the younger brothers God has given Him—a quotation from Isa. 8:18.

The Reasons for the Incarnation

Hebrews 2:14-18

> 14 Forasmuch then as the children are partakers of flesh and blood, he also himself likewise took part of the same; that through death he might destroy him that had the power of death, that is, the devil;
> 15 And deliver them who through fear of death were all their lifetime subject to bondage.
> 16 For verily he took not on him the nature of angels; but he took on him the seed of Abraham.
> 17 Wherefore in all things it behoved him to be made like unto his brethren, that he might be a merciful and faithful high priest in things pertaining to God, to make reconciliation for the sins of the people.
> 18 For in that he himself hath suffered being tempted, he is able to succour them that are tempted.

Two reasons are now offered for Christ's identification with humanity:

1. The first is to deliver His own from the *fear of death* (14-15). Because Christ's death was followed by His resur-

rection, He showed that death does not have the final word in human existence. He destroyed *him that had the power of death, that is, the devil* (14). He did this *through His own death:* "Christ turned Satan's own weapon against himself" (Wiley).

This is the *Christus Victor* motif in the New Testament, as Gustaf Aulen called it. Christ delivers us because He overcame our enemy. By His cross, "having drawn the sting of all the powers ranged against us, he exposed them, shattered, empty and defeated, in his final glorious triumphant act!" (Col. 2:15, Phillips).

William Neil writes: "The conviction of the Church was that in principle Satan had been defeated. Evil still flourished in the world and would fight for the mastery until the final victory of Christ, when he would reign supreme. The Church was summoned to battle for Christ against the power of the Devil until the end. But victory was assured since Christ had by his Resurrection wrested the power of death from Satan's hands. The death of the body, epitomizing all the pain and suffering of mankind, ruthless and relentless, irrational and hideous, and more than death the terror of the unknown beyond, was the thralldom from which Christ had delivered men. The empty tomb was the symbol of Satan's downfall."[5]

2. The second reason for the Incarnation was that Christ *might be a merciful and faithful high priest in things pertaining to God* (16-18). The idea of Jesus as our great High Priest will be emphasized much more later. It is introduced here in order to show that Christ's earthly nature was not that of angels but of Abraham.

Two functions of the priest are mentioned, to be enlarged on later:

a. The priest offers the sacrifice that makes *reconciliation for the sins of the people.* The word translated *reconciliation* is the term used in the Greek translation of the Old Testament to describe the mercy seat, on which the blood of atonement was sprinkled. It means, as W. E. Vine has written, that God "has so dealt with sin that He can show mercy to the believing sinner in the removal of his guilt and the remission of his sins.... Never is God said to be reconciled, a fact itself indicative that the enmity exists on man's part alone, and that it is man who needs to be reconciled to God, and not God to man.... The expiatory work of the Cross is therefore the means whereby the barrier which sin interposes between God and man is broken down. By the giving up of His sinless life sacrificially, Christ annuls the power of sin to separate between God and the believer."[6]

b. The priest represents the people before the throne of God. To do this, he must share their feelings. Christ can help those who are tempted because He was himself tempted. Johannes Schneider writes concerning the priestly sympathy of Christ: "Mercy one can learn only in the fellowship of the poor and needy. Jesus came to those who were in need of mercy. He did not only proclaim a new doctrine, but He also took upon Himself the painful destiny of us human beings. He stood among His people with a priestly heart."

HEBREWS 3

The Builder and the House

Another step in the argument of the book is introduced at this point. Just as Christ was shown to be superior to angels, He is also found to be superior to Moses, giver of the Law; and to Joshua, who led the nation in its conquest of Canaan. Again doctrine and exhortation alternate. Truth and action must go hand in hand.

Hebrews 3:1-6

1 Wherefore, holy brethren, partakers of the heavenly calling, consider the Apostle and High Priest of our profession, Christ Jesus;
2 Who was faithful to him that appointed him, as also Moses was faithful in all his house.
3 For this man was counted worthy of more glory than Moses, inasmuch as he who hath builded the house hath more honour than the house.
4 For every house is builded by some man; but he that built all things is God.
5 And Moses verily was faithful in all his house, as a servant, for a testimony of those things which were to be spoken after;

6 But Christ as a son over his own house; whose house are we, if we hold fast the confidence and the rejoicing of the hope firm unto the end.

1. For the first time, the readers are directly addressed. They are called *holy brethren* (1). They are *partakers of* (sharers or partners in) *the heavenly calling.* F. F. Bruce says, "Two common New Testament designations of Christians are joined together in the phrase 'holy brethren,' while the insistence on the heavenly character of their calling marks them out as citizens of a realm not circumscribed by the conditions of earthly life."

To *consider* is to fix one's attention on. The word used does not mean merely to notice or look at a thing. One can do this without really seeing it at all. The term means, as William Barclay writes, "to fix the attention on something in such a way that the inner meaning of the thing, the lesson that the thing is designed to teach, may be learned. In Luke 12:24 Jesus uses the same word when He says: '*Consider* the ravens.' He does not merely mean, '*Look* at the ravens.' He means, 'Look at the ravens and *understand and learn* the lesson that God is seeking to teach you through them.' If we are ever to learn Christian truth, a lack-lustre, disinterested, detached glance is never enough; there must be a concentrated gaze in which we gird up the loins of the mind in a determined effort to see its meaning for us."[7]

Our careful consideration is to be given to *the Apostle and High Priest of our profession, Christ Jesus.* Here only in the New Testament is Jesus called an Apostle. An apostle was God's representative among men, just as the priest was man's representative in the presence of God. Jesus both represents God to us and represents us to God.

2. The builder is better than the household and its servants (2-6). Although Moses was faithful in the discharge of his responsibilities, he was part of the household and not the one who founded or established the household. Moses was a servant in the household of God; Christ is *a son over his own house* (6), both as one in nature with its Founder-God and His Heir of all things.

The household is the Church—*whose house are we.*

The condition is clearly stated: *If we hold fast . . . unto the end.* There is total security for the people of God. But it is not "unconditional security." It is conditioned on continued faithfulness, walking in obedient faith. As F. F. Bruce said, "The conditional sentences of this epistle are worthy of special attention. Nowhere in the New Testament more than here do we find such repeated insistence on the fact that continuance in the Christian life is the test of reality. The doctrine of the final perseverance of the saints has as its corollary the salutary teaching that the saints are the people who persevere to the end."[8]

Warning Against Disobedience

The reference to Moses brings to mind the rebellion of the people in the wilderness against both Moses and the God he represented. There is danger that Christians may fall into the same sin. Again the author leaves argument for exhortation. Since Jesus is so supremely great, His people must be the more careful to give Him complete obedience.

Hebrews 3:7-19

> 7 Wherefore (as the Holy Ghost saith, To day if ye will hear his voice,
> 8 Harden not your hearts, as in the provocation, in the day of temptation in the wilderness:
> 9 When your fathers tempted me, proved me, and saw my works forty years.
> 10 Wherefore I was grieved with that generation, and said, They do alway err in their heart; and they have not known my ways.
> 11 So I sware in my wrath, They shall not enter into my rest.)
> 12 Take heed, brethren, lest there be in any of you an evil heart of unbelief, in departing from the living God.
> 13 But exhort one another daily, while it is called To day; lest any of you be hardened through the deceitfulness of sin.
> 14 For we are made partakers of Christ, if we hold the beginning of our confidence stedfast unto the end;
> 15 While it is said, To day if ye will hear his voice, harden not your hearts, as in the provocation.
> 16 For some, when they had heard, did provoke: howbeit not all that came out of Egypt by Moses.
> 17 But with whom was he grieved forty years? was it not with them that had sinned, whose carcases fell in the wilderness?
> 18 And to whom sware he that they should not enter into his rest, but to them that believed not?
> 19 So we see that they could not enter in because of unbelief.

1. The writer turns again to the Old Testament, to Ps. 95:7-11. The thought of these verses controls the rest of chapter 3 and all of chapter 4. Chapter 3 draws out the

warnings given in the psalm. Chapter 4 majors on the promise implied in the psalm.

This reference to the history of Israel is another evidence that early Christians saw in the salvation they had through Christ a new Exodus, bringing them out of the bondage of sin into a Promised Land of spiritual victory and rest. Luke spoke of the crucifixion of Jesus as His "exodus" (Luke 9:31, Greek). Paul referred to it as our Passover (1 Cor. 5:7). The Last Supper was the institution of a "new covenant." Christian baptism is compared with crossing the Red Sea (1 Cor. 10:2). Jesus was a new Moses giving a new law from a new mount and creating a new Israel in the fellowship of His followers.

The emphasis of the warning is upon two elements in Ps. 95:7-8: "To day" and "harden not your hearts." H. Orton Wiley commented, "Satan's word is 'tomorrow,' and delay always hardens the heart. Here the word 'to day' speaks of the eternity of God. To Him there is no past or future, but all His blessedness is gathered up into one eternal 'now.' So every believer who would avail himself of the riches of God's grace must respond to this 'now' with a present trust. Mr. Wesley once said, 'Hereby know we whether we are seeking by works or by faith; if by works, there is always something to be done first; but if by faith, why not now?'"

The author's application of the psalm to his readers is made in vv. 12-13. Like the old Israel in the wilderness, the new Israel is in danger of missing its full heritage through disobedience and unbelief. The result is the loss of the rest promised (v. 11) and ultimately *departing from the living God* (12). The term "rest" is *katapausin*—a term that suggests settling down in a permanent relationship. It is the opposite of *anapausin,* which means "rest by a cessation of labor and may be only temporary" (Wiley).

2. Wiley points out that "evil" in the phrase *an evil heart of unbelief* suggests that it is "but another name for that odious thing which St. Paul calls 'the law of sin which is in my members' and 'the carnal mind' which is enmity to God. It is, as Mr. Wesley calls it, 'a bent to sinning,' for it tends to issue in actual sins."

While it is called To day suggests that a time might be near when "today" would no longer be applicable. The time for hearing God's voice would be past. The heart would *be hardened through the deceitfulness of sin.* The actual expression in the Greek is "the deceitfulness of *the* sin," of that "evil heart of unbelief."

3. Verse 14 expresses again the condition for final salvation. It states the need for each child of God to "walk in the light, as he is in the light" (1 John 1:7). The fate of unbelieving Israelites in the wilderness (vv. 15-17) is an eloquent description of the results of unbelief and disobedience. W. H. Griffith-Thomas quotes lines that express this truth:

> *They came to the gates of Canaan,*
> *But they never entered in!*
> *They came to the very threshold,*
> *But they perished in their sin.*
>
> *On the morrow they would have entered,*
> *But God had shut the gate;*
> *They wept, they rashly ventured,*
> *But alas! it was too late.*
>
> *And so we are ever coming*
> *To the place where two ways part;*
> *One leads to the land of promise,*
> *And one to a hardened heart.*

Up to this point, the author has been emphasizing the warning expressed in Psalm 95. The moral, as E. C. Wickham says, is, "Do not treat your own greater Moses" as the forefathers had treated the first Moses. But there is a note of promise within the words of warning. It is to this the writer now turns.

HEBREWS 4

Promise of a Greater Rest

F. B. Meyer gives an eloquent description of the transition in chapter 4 from warning to promise:

"The contrast between the third and fourth chapters of this epistle is very marked. The former is like a drear November day, when all the landscape is drenched by sweeping rain, and the rotting leaves fall in showers to find a grave upon the damp and muddy soil. The latter is like a still clear day in midsummer, when nature revels in reposeful bliss beneath the unstinted caresses of the sun. There is as much difference between them as between the seventh and eighth chapters of the epistle to the Romans.

"But each chapter represents an experience of the inner Christian life. Perhaps the majority of Christians live and die in the third chapter to their infinite loss. Comparatively few pass over into the fourth. Yet why, reader, should you not pass the boundary line today, and leave behind for ever the bitter unsatisfactory experiences which have become the normal rule of your existence? Come up out of the wilderness, in which you have wandered so long. Your sojourn there has been due, not to any desire on the part of God, or to any arbitrary appointment of His, or to any natural disability of your temperament; but to certain grave failures on your part, in the regimen of the inner life."[9]

Hebrews 4:1-10

1 Let us therefore fear, lest, a promise being left us of entering into his rest, any of you should seem to come short of it.
2 For unto us was the gospel preached, as well as unto them: but the word preached did not profit them, not being mixed with faith in them that heard it.
3 For we which have believed do enter into rest, as he said, As I have sworn in my wrath; if they shall enter into my rest: although the works were finished from the foundation of the world.
4 For he spake in a certain place of the seventh day on this wise, And God did rest the seventh day from all his works.
5 And in this place again, If they shall enter into my rest.
6 Seeing therefore it remaineth that some must enter therein, and they to whom it was first preached entered not in because of unbelief:
7 Again, he limiteth a certain day, saying in David, To day, after so long a time; as it is said, To day if ye will hear his voice, harden not your hearts.
8 For if Jesus had given them rest, then would he not afterward have spoken of another day.
9 There remaineth therefore a rest to the people of God.
10 For he that is entered into his rest, he also hath ceased from his own works, as God did from his.

The logic of the passage is clear and unmistakable. If God's promises in the Old Testament had been fulfilled by

Joshua, then there would have been no further word as is found in the psalm. Schneider comments: "Since the fulfillment of the divine promise is still forth-coming, and since the fulfillment is bound to faith, it is the Church of faith, that is, the New Testament redemptive community, which is the heir of the promise. Because the Christians have believed in the word of proclamation, it is to them that the word concerning entering into God's rest belongs."[10]

There are those who have understood the rest in Hebrews 4 to refer to heaven. Others have said it was salvation by faith instead of by works. Neither of these suggestions is very promising. The Christians to whom the author writes are told that this is a possession to take hold of in this present life, and it is to those already converted that the exhortation is given to enter into rest. Rather, this is a second rest, distinctively for the people of God, and providing a foretaste or earnest of the final rest of heaven.

Thomas Hewitt writes: "The rest of Canaan is a type of consecration rest, that is, of the rest which comes from a surrender of the mind, will and heart to God's power and influence which enables the believer to conquer sin." Joshua in the Old Testament led the people in a geographical conquest of Canaan. Our greater Joshua—recalling that *Jesus* is the English form of *Joshua*—the Captain of our salvation, brings us into our spiritual inheritance.

The author makes it clear that the promise of God has not failed. The failure is that of the people. The gospel itself is of no avail unless it is received in obedient faith. Not the hearers, but the doers, of the truth are those who receive the promised blessing. We must never forget that *apeitheia,* translated "unbelief" in v. 6, also means disobedience.

The rest that is promised is therefore a rest for the people of God; it is a rest of faith; it is entering a state compared to God's own rest. Gone are the ceaseless strivings for perfection in human endeavor. Gone are the struggles with a self against itself, the double-mindedness of a carnal heart. This is not the rest of inactivity; it is the rest of equilibrium.

F. B. Meyer also writes: "We are not summoned to the heavy slumber which follows over-taxing toil, nor to inaction or indolence; but to the rest which is possible amid swift activity and strenuous work; to perfect equilibrium between the outgoings and the incomings of the life; to a contented heart; to peace that passeth all understanding; to the repose of the will in the will of God; and to the calm of the depths of the nature which are undisturbed by the hurricanes which sweep the surface, and urge forward the mighty waves."[11]

It is the rest of the overflowing life. W. R. Adell wrote some lines he entitled "Overture":

*God would not have us **overwork** or **overstrain**,*
  Our giant task and puny power He doth know—
*But **overcomers** be, His power obtain,*
  *And by His gracious Spirit **overflow**.*

Bishop H. C. G. Moule wrote:

My Saviour, Thou hast offered rest.
  Oh! grant it then to me:
The rest of ceasing from myself
  To find my all in Thee.

O Lord, I seek a holy rest,
  A victory over sin;
I seek that Thou alone should'st reign
  O'er all without, within.

In Thy strong hand I lay me down;
  So shall the work be done.
For who can work so wondrously
  As the Almighty One?

The Searching Word of God

In a paragraph opening with his last and climaxing reference to the second rest, the author turns to the motivation that comes through the searching and powerful Word of God. We are to be diligent, eager, to enter this rest of faith. As Ebrard put it, "Let us beware therefore, lest we neglect the second more excellent and more powerful call of grace, and lest we also in our turn, become an example of warning to others."

Hebrews 4:11-13
> 11 Let us labour therefore to enter into that rest, lest any man fall after the same example of unbelief.
> 12 For the word of God is quick, and powerful, and sharper than any twoedged sword, piercing even to the dividing asunder of soul and spirit, and of the joints and marrow, and is a discerner of the thoughts and intents of the heart.
> 13 Neither is there any creature that is not manifest in his sight: but all things are naked and opened unto the eyes of him with whom we have to do.

Johannes Schneider offers a list of the characteristics of the Word here stated: [12]

1. The Word of God is living. *Quick* in the KJV does not mean fast but alive. It is both the Word of the "living God" and a Word which is the Source of life.

2. The Word of God is *powerful.* Schneider says that it is "a power laden with highest energy. . . . Judgment and forgiveness of sins, the death of the old man and the resurrection of the new, the transformation of the world and the establishment of God's Lordship on earth: these are the goals towards which the energy of the divine Word is aiming."

3. The Word of God is a separating power. "It severs the most established relationships. Like a sharp, two-edged sword that penetrates into the depths of the body bringing about sharp separations between the individual parts of the organism, so the Word of God penetrates into the depths of man's being and uncovers the most secret connections. The confusing strains in man's innermost being are laid bare and separated so that clarity and order emerge. . . . We get inside knowledge about ourselves. It belongs to the most painful experiences of men that they do not know themselves. For that reason they do not understand one another. One can only then understand oneself if one allows God's Word to tell us who one is. God alone knows us in such a way as we really are. And when He gives us clarity about ourselves—and He does that

through His Word—only then do we know who we are and what we are."

4. The Word of God is "a judge of our plans and secret thoughts." We hide the depths of our being from others. But the Word judges the "very thoughts and motives of a man's heart" (Phillips).

5. The Word of God "describes the situation of the creature before God." There is a transition from the Word to God himself. "Everything lies bare and completely exposed before the eyes of Him" (Weymouth) to whom we are responsible.

The Support of Our Great High Priest

Hebrews 4:14-16

> 14 Seeing then that we have a great high priest, that is passed into the heavens, Jesus the Son of God, let us hold fast our profession.
> 15 For we have not an high priest which cannot be touched with the feeling of our infirmities; but was in all points tempted like as we are, yet without sin.
> 16 Let us therefore come boldly unto the throne of grace, that we may obtain mercy, and find grace to help in time of need.

This paragraph summarizes the conclusions to be drawn from what has been said, and prepares the way for what is to come. Wiley entitles this "The Transitional Paragraph."

The tone of the preceding passage has been awesome. We are told of our openness and nakedness before the infinite God, to whom we are accountable. But immediately our author tells us of our great High Priest, Jesus, the Son of God. J. C. Macaulay comments: "That is the end of fear. From here on our vocabulary stresses new words. Sympathy, confidence, grace, mercy, help—these give a new tone to the passage, and become the big words in our experience."

Three points are made concerning our High Priest:

1. The supremacy of our High Priest. He is *a great high priest*. He has *passed into the heavens,* exalted at the right hand of the Father himself. He is *Jesus*—spotless humanity; and *the Son of God*—undimmed deity. Both aspects of our Lord's nature are important. The human

side is as essential to His high priesthood as His deity.

2. The sympathy and compassion of our High Priest. As Alexander Purdy writes, "Hardly a sentence in Hebrews is packed so full of meaning as vs. 15." Christ could be the perfect High Priest only if He experienced the trials and testings of those men He represents before the throne of God. He can truly feel for us in our weakness, for He himself was tempted in all points *as we are, yet without sin* —or literally, "apart from sin." No kind of temptation that comes to us, except those that arise from our previous sinning, was strange to Jesus.

Some have felt that the sinlessness of Jesus weakens the thought here. The very opposite is the case. As William Temple says, "This is not even a paradox to one who has seriously considered what is involved in the temptation felt by a man of high character to act contrary to his character: he is attracted by the wrong course; he has to keep a hold on himself; he knows he is making a real choice; yet (being himself) he could not yield. The effort needed to overcome the temptation is a real effort, but it is also a necessary effort because his character, being such as it is, must so react to the situation."[13]

That Jesus did not yield to temptation increases rather than diminishes its force upon Him. A temptation to which a bad man yields readily may be torture to the good man who resists it.

One who gives in to temptation has not felt its full power. He has broken before the full weight was placed upon him. Only one who did not yield could experience the full force of the tempter's power.

1 Cor. 10:13 at least suggests that the strength of temptations permitted to come to us are in direct relation to our ability to withstand them. If this be the case, then, as Leon Morris suggested, "Christ's temptations must have been of an intensity inconceivable to us."

William Barclay uses the analogy of pain: "There is a degree of pain which the human frame can stand—and then when that degree is reached a person faints and loses consciousness; he has reached his limit. There are agonies of pain he does not know, because there came collapse. It is so with temptation. We collapse before temptation; but Jesus went to our stage of temptation and far beyond it and still did not collapse. It is true to say that He was tempted in all things as we are; but it is also true to say that never was man tempted as He was."[14]

3. The sufficiency of our High Priest's help. Because of our High Priest's sympathy, we can come with confidence to His throne. It is a *throne of grace*. There we *obtain mercy*—a reference to forgiveness for the past—and *grace to help in time of need*—a reference to the future.

Here are our two great needs. We need *mercy*—forgiveness, the putting away of the sins of the past. We also need *grace to help*—"Help to walk through the valleys; and to walk on the high places, where the mountain goat can hardly stand. Help to suffer, to be still, to wait, to overcome, to make green one tiny spot of garden ground in God's great tillage. Help to live and to die" (Meyer). The throne to which we are invited now is not the great white throne of judgment and condemnation. It is the rainbow-circled *throne of grace*.

HEBREWS 5

The Priesthood of Christ
Hebrews 5:1—7:28

The Qualifications of the High Priest

Our author has now come to the place where he can begin to work out the doctrine which is his distinctive contribution to Christian thought, the high priesthood of Jesus.

The priesthood had previously been mentioned. But the emphasis had been on the identity of the person of Jesus as High Priest. The emphasis now shifts to His role and work as our High Priest.

Hebrews 5:1-4

> 1 For every high priest taken from among men is ordained for men in things pertaining to God, that he may offer both gifts and sacrifices for sins:
> 2 Who can have compassion on the ignorant, and on them that are out of the way; for that he himself also is compassed with infirmity.
> 3 And by reason hereof he ought, as for the people, so also for himself, to offer for sins.
> 4 And no man taketh this honour unto himself, but he that is called of God, as was Aaron.

Wiley lists six requirements for the high priestly office as here indicated:

1. The high priest was a man, of the same nature as those he represented.

2. The high priest was ordained or appointed as a representative man. He stood in the place of those who themselves could not or would not stand before God.

3. The high priest made two kinds of sacrificial offerings: *gifts* (the thank offerings of the Old Testament) and *sacrifices for sin* (the sin offerings of the Old Testament).

4. The high priest must be understanding in his attitude toward the ignorant and the sinful.

5. The high priest in the Jewish ritual must make an offering for himself as well as for the sins of the people.

6. The high priest is called or appointed by God. He does not take this office and this honor by his own choice or desire.

All six qualifications may be summarized in two: The high priest must be a man, since he represents man before God; and he is a man called or appointed by God.

The Special Qualifications of Jesus

The author has now reached the point toward which he has been moving. Jesus is supremely qualified to be our great High Priest.

Hebrews 5:5-10

> 5 So also Christ glorified not himself to be made an high priest; but he that said unto him, Thou art my Son, to day have I begotten thee.
> 6 As he saith also in another place, Thou art a priest for ever after the order of Melchisedec.
> 7 Who in the days of his flesh, when he had offered up prayers and supplications with strong crying and tears unto him that was able to save him from death, and was heard in that he feared;

> 8 Though he were a Son, yet learned he obedience by the things which he suffered;
> 9 And being made perfect, he became the author of eternal salvation unto all them that obey him;
> 10 Called of God an high priest after the order of Melchisedec.

Five special qualifications are here listed:

1. Jesus was specially called by God. Again a verse from the Psalms, cited earlier in 1:5, is given in evidence. In 1:5, the emphasis was upon "I"—God said, "I [have] begotten thee." Here, the emphasis is upon "to day." Jesus was the Son of God in His humanity in a way totally unique among men. Since He glorified not himself, His glory was the glory of the Father—"Father, the hour is come; glorify thy Son, that thy Son also may glorify thee" (John 17:1).

2. Jesus was made a Priest *after the order of Melchisedec*. That is, His was a priesthood of a different kind than the Levitical priesthood. *Order* is from a word that means "quality, kind, rank, or position." Psalm 110, from which these words were quoted, was universally believed to refer to the Messiah. It is the passage from the Old Testament most often quoted in the New, and always in reference to Jesus as the Messiah.

The idea of the Melchisedec priesthood is worked out in detail in c. 7. The application to Jesus is superbly fitting.

3. Jesus was mighty in prayer—the most important aspect of the high priest's daily ministry. *In the days of his flesh,* He went through the struggles and pressures we must endure. This is probably a reference to the prayer in Gethsemane. The words of Ella Wheeler Wilcox express this:

> *All those who journey, soon or late,*
> *Must pass within the Garden's gate;*
> *Must kneel alone in darkness there,*
> *And battle with some fierce despair.*
> *God pity those who cannot say:*
> *"Not mine, but Thine," who only pray:*
> *"Let this cup pass," and cannot see*
> *The purpose in Gethsemane.*

In what sense was Jesus *heard* in His Gethsemane prayer? It was not in the sense that He was saved from dying. It was in the sense that He was saved "out of death" (literal) by the Resurrection.

This is the way God often delivers us today. We are not kept from going into the fiery furnace (cf. Daniel 3). We go into the flames (Isa. 43:2), not to perish, but with His sustaining presence.

4. Jesus *learned . . . obedience* through suffering. Our author does not mean that the Son was disobedient and had to be brought to obedience by suffering. Rather, as William Neil says, "What Jesus learned by bitter experience was that true obedience entails suffering. There is no escaping the penalties of the service of God." In order therefore to be perfect man, the Pattern of true sonship, Jesus had to experience what such sonship involves. He had to pay the price in pain of body and anguish of mind, but having touched the depths of human sorrow He is able to lead His brethren to God. The glorious and searching truth is that He did all this for us and for our salvation.

5. Jesus therefore is *the author of eternal salvation unto all them that obey him.* It is characteristic of our author that he puts the qualification "them that obey him" in the present tense. It is not "those who obeyed Him once and have since lapsed back into disobedience." It is "those who are obeying Him," whose Christian walk is a life of obedient faith.

The Immaturity of the People

Doctrine is again set aside for exhortation. The author feels keenly the difficulty of making his thought clear to his readers. There are two barriers in the way: (1) the immaturity of the people (5:11-14); (2) failure to go on to perfection (6:1-8).

Hebrews 5:11-14

> 11 Of whom we have many things to say, and hard to be uttered, seeing ye are dull of hearing.
> 12 For when for the time ye ought to be teachers, ye have need that one teach you again which be the first principles of the oracles of God;

> and are become such as have need of milk, and not of strong meat.
> 13 For every one that useth milk is unskilful in the word of righteousness: for he is a babe.
> 14 But strong meat belongeth to them that are of full age, even those who by reason of use have their senses exercised to discern both good and evil.

Although they would appear to have been Christians for some time, the author senses that his readers have not grown in grace and knowledge as they should have. His subject is most exalted. His readers are *dull of hearing*—"so slow to grasp spiritual truth" (Phillips). The problem is not one of limited intelligence. It is dullness that comes from indifference and inattention. One may have a Ph.D. in nuclear physics and have no more comprehension of spiritual truth than a child.

These Christians had been converted long enough to have been teachers of others. Instead, they needed to learn again *the first principles of the oracles of God.* Barclay notes: "He is face to face with the problem of the Christian who refuses to grow up." *The oracles of God* usually means the Old Testament. Until the people had at least mastered the rudiments or beginnings of God's revelation they were scarcely in a position to appreciate the full truth of the new age in which they lived.

Like children, they still needed milk. They were not able to digest solid food. The result was that they could not clearly distinguish between good and evil.

Here an important truth is given. Certainly there is more to holy living than the grasp of sound doctrine. Yet the quality of life is affected by failure clearly to apprehend truth. It is with good reason that Peter joined growth in grace with growth in the knowledge of our Lord Jesus Christ (2 Pet. 3:18).

E. F. Scott comments: "Religion is something different from mere strenuous thinking on the great religious questions, yet it remains true that faith and knowledge are inseparable, and that both grow stronger as they react on one another. More often than we know, the failure of a religion as a moral power is due to no other cause than intellectual sloth."[15]

HEBREWS 6

Failure to Go On to Perfection

Related to but really deeper than simple immaturity, the author senses a failure on the part of his followers to *go on unto*—literally, "be borne on to"—*perfection*. The result is the danger of outright apostasy—falling away from the faith of Christ entirely.

Hebrews 6:1-8
> 1 Therefore leaving the principles of the doctrine of Christ, let us go on unto perfection; not laying again the foundation of repentance from dead works, and of faith toward God,
> 2 Of the doctrine of baptisms, and of laying on of hands, and of resurrection of the dead, and of eternal judgment.
> 3 And this will we do, if God permit.
> 4 For it is impossible for those who were once enlightened, and have tasted of the heavenly gift, and were made partakers of the Holy Ghost,
> 5 And have tasted the good word of God, and the powers of the world to come,
> 6 If they shall fall away, to renew them again unto repentance; seeing they crucify to themselves the Son of God afresh, and put him to an open shame.
> 7 For the earth which drinketh in the rain that cometh oft upon it, and bringeth forth herbs meet for them by whom it is dressed, receiveth blessing from God:
> 8 But that which beareth thorns and briers is rejected, and is nigh unto cursing; whose end is to be burned.

Some have understood *perfection* here to be no more than the maturity of 5:14. The use of a passive verb suggests that more is in mind. Perfection in the Bible is not the static, changeless absolute of Greek philosophy. It is being true to type. It means, as R. Gregor Smith says: "to be whole or sound or true . . . wholly turned, with the whole will and being, to God, as he is turned to us. This is a response of obedience and of effort carried out *in faith*. It is a call to purify our heart and to will one thing. . . . Our obedience in faith is not the beginning of some vague progress on a shadowy moral way, but is the acceptance of grace, which is always whole, complete, perfect; and in the strength of this encounter our life is lived. 'Perfection' is something belonging to God and coming to us by our contact with God, not as a possession but as a gift."[16]

Referring to 10:14 ("By a single offering he has perfected for all time those who are sanctified," RSV), Oscar

Cullmann says, "*teleioun* (to make perfect) is almost a synonym for *hagiazein* (to sanctify)." In the fullest sense, this is a call to Christian holiness.

Leaving the principles of the doctrine of Christ does not mean discarding them. It means leaving them as a child leaves the *a-b-c*s to go on to reading, or leaves the multiplication table to go on to arithmetic and algebra.

The principles of *repentance from dead works, and of faith toward God; . . . of baptisms, and of laying on of hands;* of the *resurrection* and *eternal judgment* are to be mastered and thoroughly understood. But we cannot stop at this stage. We must go beyond. *This will we do, if God permit* is better translated, "Yes and, with God's help, we will" (TCNT). It is not God's permission we need but His help through His Spirit.

Continued failure to *go on unto perfection* results in the danger of apostasy. Preachers of "eternal security" have explained away these verses in two ways. They have sometimes said that those enlightened, tasting the heavenly gift, partakers of the Holy Spirit, tasting the goodness of God's Word, and the powers of the world to come, are yet not really Christians. They have never really been born again. Yet every statement in vv. 4-5 is paralleled elsewhere in the New Testament in terms that leave little doubt of the genuineness of the experience so described.

Others have said that the "if" of v. 6 shows that this is a purely hypothetical case which could not actually happen. K. S. Wuest says that this is a "straw man"—to which F. F. Bruce aptly replies, "Biblical writers . . . are not given to the setting up of men of straw." The danger is real, not imaginary.

Do these verses take hope from the backslider? By no means. H. Orton Wiley has pointed out that the original Greek uses present participles that may be translated "while" or "during the time" rather than "since" such persons *crucify . . . the Son of God afresh*. This is given in the ASV margin, "It is impossible to renew them again unto repentance; the while they crucify to themselves the Son of God afresh, and put him to an open shame."

There is also the idea that what is discussed here and

in 10:26-29 is not backsliding but a total and final apostasy that renounces the whole of the Christian faith and returns to the shelter of the Old Testament ceremonial law—or in the case of Gentiles, to their pagan idol worship. Christ is the only means of salvation. Those who forsake Him, therefore, forsake their only hope of eternal life.

The backslider may yet return in repentance and be forgiven (Luke 15:11-24; 1 John 2:1-2). Unless he does so return, he is "lost" and "dead" (Luke 15:24). If he persists in his backsliding, year after year, there is the danger that he will so destroy his faith that he finally becomes an apostate. He no longer believes that Christ lives and can and will save. When this point is reached, he has become like the field that bears only thorns and briers, *whose end is to be burned* (8).

Things That Accompany Salvation

The thought of 6:4-8 was solemn and fearful. But the author has a true pastor's heart. He never stops with the message of judgment. He passes on to the word of consolation and promise. He is convinced that these to whom he writes are not apostate. He would lead them on into the deep things of God.

Hebrews 6:9-20

9 But, beloved, we are persuaded better things of you, and things that accompany salvation, though we thus speak.
10 For God is not unrighteousness to forget your work and labour of love, which ye have shewed toward his name, in that ye have ministered to the saints, and do minister.
11 And we desire that every one of you do shew the same diligence to the full assurance of hope unto the end:
12 That ye be not slothful, but followers of them who through faith and patience inherit the promises.
13 For when God made promise to Abraham, because he could swear by no greater, he sware by himself,
14 Saying, Surely blessing I will bless thee, and multiplying I will multiply thee.
15 And so, after he had patiently endured, he obtained the promise.
16 For men verily swear by the greater: and an oath for confirmation is to them an end of all strife.
17 Wherein God, willing more abundantly to shew unto the heirs of promise the immutability of his counsel, confirmed it by an oath:
18 That by two immutable things, in which it was impossible for God to lie, we might have a strong consolation, who have fled for refuge to lay hold upon the hope set before us:
19 Which hope we have as an anchor of the soul, both sure and stedfast, and which entereth into that within the vail;

20 Whither the forerunner is for us entered, even Jesus, made an high priest for ever after the order of Melchisedec.

Even in their spiritual infancy the author recognizes *things that accompany salvation* (9), though he has sounded a clear warning. Three characteristics are named as "things that have to do with salvation" (Norlie):

1. A *work and labour of love.* The thought is not that they will be saved from their lethargy as a reward for good works. It is rather that God is dependable. There is no need for concern about the help He will give. They have served in the past, and are to continue to do so.

2. *Full assurance of hope.* This is hope in full measure. Hope is an essential ingredient in human life. Reflecting on his experiences in a Nazi concentration camp, psychiatrist Viktor Frankl has written: "The prisoner who had lost faith in the future—his future—was doomed. With his loss of belief in the future, he lost his spiritual hold; he let himself decline and become subject to mental and physical decay."

3. *Faith and patience* to *inherit the promises. Patience* here is steadfast endurance. Phillips translates it "sheer patient faith." Here is the familiar combination of love, hope, and faith we see in 1 Cor. 13:13 and 1 Pet. 1:21-22. With faith we need patient endurance. God's timetable is not always the same as ours. We must always remember that His delays are not denials.

Hope returns to control the thought of the remainder of the chapter. Our hope—hence our faith and patience—is based on nothing less than the nature of God himself. God's naked promise should be enough. But that promise has been confirmed by an oath. Since an oath depends on invoking a greater power and there is none greater than God, God's oath is based on His own steadfast being.

Abraham was a prime example of the faith and patience that substantiate the Christian hope. Abraham waited 24 years for evidence of the fulfillment of God's promise, *Blessing I will bless thee, and multiplying I will multiply thee.* But the promise did not fail.

Zacharias, father of John the Baptist, spoke of the

scope of this promise in Luke 1:73-75, "The oath which he sware to our father Abraham, that he would grant unto us, that we being delivered out of the hand of our enemies might serve him without fear, in holiness and righteousness before him, all the days of our life."

This hope is an anchor "sure and steadfast" (RSV). That anchor reaches *within the veil.* Some commentators see an abrupt change of figure here from the vessel securely anchored, to the priest entering through the veil that separates the holy place from the outer court, or the holy of holies from the holy place. Wiley, however, has made an interesting suggestion. Instead of a change of figures, there is a blending of figures. The *anchoria* in ancient times was the name given to a strong rock inside the harbor entrance to which a vessel might attach its cable. When the tide was too low to permit the ship to enter the harbor, sailors would launch a small boat, carry the anchor across the bar, and secure it to the *anchoria.* Then as the tide rose, the seamen would draw in the anchor chain and pull the ship across the bar into the harbor.

This is exactly what Jesus has done. He has carried our anchor into the harbor and fastened it to the rock. This He has done because, as our great High Priest, He has entered through the veil into the very presence of God, there to represent us before the throne.

HEBREWS 7

Melchisedec, the Type of Christ

The author is now ready to make the first of a series of telling points to show the superiority of the gospel of Christ over the ceremonial cult of the Old Testament. He starts first with a comparison of the priesthood of Christ with that of Aaron, who represented the entire line of priests ministering before the altar in Tabernacle and Temple from Moses' time to the destruction of the Temple by Titus in A.D. 70.

The entire argument as it relates to the priesthood of

Jesus hinges on an understanding of the priesthood of Melchisedec ("Melchizedek" in its Old Testament spelling). Melchisedec has already been mentioned three times (5:6, 10; 6:20), but each time more or less incidentally. Now the author is ready to drive home the point.

Melchisedec is spoken of in three books in the Bible: Gen. 14:18-20, the historical event; Ps. 110:4, in reference to the Messiah; and here in Hebrews, where the doctrinal conclusion is drawn. Just as the author had done in cc. 3—4 in relation to Israel and Canaan, so now here he combines an item of Old Testament history with a quotation from the Psalms to establish a Christian doctrine.

Hebrews 7:1-10

> 1 For this Melchisedec, king of Salem, priest of the most high God, who met Abraham returning from the slaughter of the kings, and blessed him;
> 2 To whom also Abraham gave a tenth part of all; first being by interpretation King of righteousness, and after that also King of Salem, which is, King of peace;
> 3 Without father, without mother, without descent, having neither beginning of days, nor end of life; but made like unto the Son of God; abideth a priest continually.
> 4 Now consider how great this man was, unto whom even the patriarch Abraham gave the tenth of the spoils.
> 5 And verily they that are of the sons of Levi, who receive the office of the priesthood, have a commandment to take tithes of the people according to the law, that is, of their brethren, though they come out of the loins of Abraham:
> 6 But he whose descent is not counted from them received tithes of Abraham, and blessed him that had the promises.
> 7 And without all contradiction the less is blessed of the better.
> 8 And here men that die receive tithes; but there he receiveth them, of whom it is witnessed that he liveth.
> 9 And as I may so say, Levi also, who receiveth tithes, payed tithes in Abraham.
> 10 For he was yet in the loins of his father, when Melchisedec met him.

It is well to remember that the writer's interest is not in Melchisedec. It is in Christ. Melchisedec is introduced only to serve one purpose: "to prove the existence of another order of priesthood, older, superior, and so superseding both the Levitical priesthood and the law which rests on it" (Alexander Purdy).

1. In summary, the priesthood of Christ is illustrated by that of Melchisedec in the following ways:

   a. Melchisedec was a priest in his own right, by direct

appointment of God and not by virtue of descent from a priestly ancestor in the past. Jesus was not a member of the tribe of Levi, as were the priests of the Temple. He was a Descendant of Judah. His priesthood was by God's immediate purpose, not by human ancestry.

b. Melchisedec represents an eternal priesthood, without substitute or succession. This is what is meant by the statement that he was *without father, without mother* (3). It is not that Melchisedec was a superhuman heavenly or angelic being. It is rather that his ancestry had nothing to do with his priesthood.

c. He offered Abraham bread and wine, the same symbols Christ offered His disciples at the Last Supper. No animal sacrifices are mentioned in his priestly ministry.

d. He combined both priestly and kingly offices. This was not true of the Jewish priesthood. Levi was the priestly tribe, and Judah was the kingly tribe.

e. His priesthood was a priesthood of righteousness and peace, not one of ceremonial ritual. This is stated in the meaning of Melchisedec's name and place of residence. *Melek* is the Hebrew term for "king." *Tsedek* means "righteousness." Melchisedec means "king of righteousness." But he is described as "king of Salem," the place later known as Jerusalem, "city of peace." *Salem* comes from the familiar Hebrew *shalom,* meaning "peace." Righteousness and peace are precisely the Old Testament descriptions of Messiah's reign.

2. The author is careful to say that it was Melchisedec who was *made like unto the Son of God* (3), not that Jesus was like Melchisedec. Much of his reasoning is based on what the Scriptures do *not* say concerning this ancient figure. To the author, "the silences of the Scriptures were as much due to divine inspiration as were its statements" (F. F. Bruce). Melchisedec is viewed as a divine mystery breaking into time. He is thereby typical of Christ.

3. The significance of tithing is mentioned several times in these verses (2, 4, 5, 6, 8, 9). Some argue against tithing

as a matter of Christian stewardship because it is part of "the law," which they presume was done away by Christ. If this be said in the interest of showing that Christian stewardship requires more than one-tenth of the "increase," the point may be helpful. Usually, however, it seems designed to put a ceiling on giving rather than a floor beneath it. In point of fact, the argument is based on a historical fallacy. Hundreds of years before the Sinai law was given, tithing was recognized by Abraham and by Jacob as a principle of religious devotion (cf. Gen. 14:20; 28:22).

Another point comes out here. The author regards tithing as a symbol of submission. It becomes an important link in his chain of reasoning. Priests of the line of Aaron receive tithes from the people. But Aaron's ancestor Abraham paid tithes to Melchisedec. Melchisedec is said in Ps. 110:4 to be a prototype of Christ. Christ is therefore superior to the priests of the line of Aaron and entitled to receive tithes, instead, of them. In the old dispensation, *men* who *die receive tithes;* in the new dispensation, He receives tithes *of whom it is witnessed that he* lives forever (8).

4. The author does not intend us to take the relationship of Levi to Abraham in the sense of the theologian's "federal headship," in which the action of an ancestor would be taken literally as the responsible action of his descendants. *As I may so say* (9) is like Paul's expression, "I speak after the manner of men" (Rom. 3:5; 6:19; 1 Cor. 9:8; etc.). The relationship is a logical one, seen as an analogy. The Levites' authority came through Abraham. It was therefore subject to the authority of Christ, the Fulfillment, as Abraham was subject to Melchisedec, the type.

Changing Priesthoods Imply Changing Law

The balance of this chapter and the next three are devoted to showing that a new priesthood demands a new law, a new covenant, and a new sacrifice. Melchisedec now drops out of sight except for an incidental mention in vv. 15, 17, and 21. Christ comes into full focus as representing a totally new and different order of priesthood.

Hebrews 7:11-14
> 11 If therefore perfection were by the Levitical priesthood, (for under it the people received the law,) what further need was there that another priest should rise after the order of Melchisedec, and not be called after the order of Aaron?
> 12 For the priesthood being changed, there is made of necessity a change also of the law.
> 13 For he of whom these things are spoken pertaineth to another tribe, of which no man gave attendance at the altar.
> 14 For it is evident that our Lord sprang out of Juda; of which tribe Moses spake nothing concerning priesthood.

The promise of a new priesthood (Ps. 110:4) is taken by the author to indicate that the Levitical priesthood was inadequate. It could not bring perfection, the wholeness and soundness of human experience and life demanded in both the Old Testament (Gen. 17:1) and the New (Matt. 5:48). If the priesthood changes, the law must also change, since the priesthood was set up under the provisions of the ceremonial law.

This change is sweeping and fundamental, as we shall see in vv. 18-19. The first indication of such a change is the fact that Christ was not of the tribe of Levi, as were the Jewish priests. He was of the tribe of Judah, which had no connection with the old priestly order.

The Total Superiority of the New Priesthood

In a series of forceful statements, the author now proceeds to show how far the priesthood of Christ surpasses the Levitical priesthood.

Hebrews 7:15-28
> 15 And it is yet far more evident: for that after the similitude of Melchisedec there ariseth another priest,
> 16 Who is made, not after the law of a carnal commandment, but after the power of an endless life.
> 17 For he testifieth, Thou art a priest for ever after the order of Melchisedec.
> 18 For there is verily a disannulling of the commandment going before for the weakness and unprofitableness thereof.
> 19 For the law made nothing perfect, but the bringing in of a better hope did; by the which we draw nigh unto God.
> 20 And inasmuch as not without an oath he was made priest:
> 21 (For those priests were made without an oath; but this with an oath by him that said unto him, The Lord sware and will not repent, Thou art a priest for ever after the order of Melchisedec:)
> 22 By so much was Jesus made a surety of a better testament.
> 23 And they truly were many priests, because they were not suffered to continue by reason of death:

> 24 But this man, because he continueth ever, hath an unchangeable priesthood.
> 25 Wherefore he is able also to save them to the uttermost that come unto God by him, seeing he ever liveth to make intercession for them.
> 26 For such an high priest became us, who is holy, harmless, undefiled, separate from sinners, and made higher than the heavens;
> 27 Who needeth not daily, as those high priests, to offer up sacrifice, first for his own sins, and then for the people's: for this he did once, when he offered up himself.
> 28 For the law maketh men high priests which have infirmity; but the word of the oath, which was since the law, maketh the Son, who is consecrated for evermore.

1. Christ's priesthood is eternal and unchanging, 15-17, 23-25. It is not constituted *after the law of a carnal commandment,* that is, "not according to a legal requirement concerning bodily descent" (RSV). It is based rather on *the power of an endless life.* It is spiritual rather than legal, eternal rather than temporal, abiding rather than changing.

This great thought is clinched in vv. 23-25. Christ, like Melchisedec, has a priesthood without end. Death ended the priestly ministry of Aaron and all who followed him. Christ's priesthood is *unchangeable*—permanent, inviolable.

Because His priesthood is permanent, Christ *is able also to save . . . to the uttermost* all who *come unto God by him* (25). The phrase *to the uttermost* is understood by some to refer to duration—eternally, for all time. Others take it to mean completeness—fully, without flaw or defect. The balance of logic, together with a parallel use in Luke 13:11, seems to favor completeness more than simple duration. J. B. Phillips translates it, "This means that he can save fully and completely those who approach God through him." However, the two ideas are by no means contradictory. A. M. Hills combines them in the phrase "clear to the end of every possible need of the soul." The *Amplified New Testament* gives "completely, perfectly, finally and for all time and eternity."

Christ *ever* lives *to make intercession* for those He saves. F. F. Bruce remarks that the Lord's high-priestly prayer in John 17 "will help us considerably to understand what is intended here when our Lord is described as making intercession for those who come to God through him."

Jesus prayed, "Sanctify them through thy truth: thy word is truth. . . . Neither pray I for these alone, but for them also which shall believe on me through their word" (vv. 17, 20).

2. Christ's priesthood makes perfection possible, 18-19. The problem of the old order was its *weakness and unprofitableness.* Paul explains the source of that weakness in Rom. 8:3-4: "For what the law could not do, in that it was weak through the flesh, God sending his own Son in the likeness of sinful flesh, and for sin, condemned sin in the flesh: that the righteousness of the law might be fulfilled in us, who walk not after the flesh, but after the Spirit."

Because the commandment has shown that neither it nor the priesthood it established could bring the perfection God requires (vv. 11, 19), it is "disannulled." This word means "cancelled, set aside, abrogated." Barclay says, "The whole paraphernalia of the sacrificial and ceremonial law is wiped out in the priesthood of Jesus."

The bringing in of the *better hope* has done what the Law could not do. It has made possible the soundness, the wholeness, the integrity of Christian character described elsewhere as "holiness" and sometimes called "Christian perfection." It has "doomed sin in the flesh" (Rom. 8:3, literal). It makes possible the righteousness which was the unreachable goal of the ceremonial law.

3. Christ's priesthood is established on God's very oath, 20-22. The old order was established by simple decree. It was continued simply by being handed down from father to son. Contrary to this, the priesthood of Christ was established, as Ps. 110:4 proves, on a divine oath—the most sacred and inviolable affirmation possible.

As a consequence of this sacred oath, Jesus has become *the surety of a better covenant* (22, RSV). The covenant is mentioned here for the first time. It will be discussed at length in cc. 8 and 10. Here it is mentioned to show that Jesus himself is the Guarantor of the new relationship to God into which He brings His people under the new covenant.

> *My hope is built on nothing less*
> *Than Jesus' blood and righteousness;*
> *I dare not trust the sweetest frame,*
> *But wholly lean on Jesus' name.*
> *On Christ, the solid Rock, I stand;*
> *All other ground is sinking sand.*
> —EDWARD MOTE

4. Christ's priesthood is validated by His supreme character (26). The sad but universally acknowledged fact was that many of the high priests in later Judaism were very corrupt men. The high priesthood, which carried tremendous political as well as religious authority, was literally sold to and bought by the highest bidder. Any hereditary order is liable to become degenerate, and the Jewish priesthood was no exception.

In total contrast to such corruption, Jesus is the kind of High Priest we need. He *is holy, harmless, undefiled, separate from sinners.* He not only intercedes for us; He is our great Example in life. "Jesus, then, is the High Priest that meets our needs. He is holy; he has no fault or sin in him; he has been set apart from sinful men and raised above the heavens" (TEV).

We are not to think that Jesus' separation from sinners was isolation. He lived in constant touch with human need. He did not isolate himself and His disciples to form a little enclave of holiness in a suffering world. He is not the Author of the "ghetto mentality" that afflicts so many of His professed followers in our day. He was known as the Friend of publicans and sinners, and He did not get that reputation by holding them off at arm's length. His separation was as ours should be—"insulation," not isolation.

5. Christ's priesthood relates to an infinitely better sacrifice, 27-28. The thought of Christ's sacrifice will also be considered at length in succeeding chapters. Here it is mentioned to show that Christ's great, once-for-all sacrifice of himself surpasses by infinite degree the daily sacrifices of those who must offer for their own sins before they could make an offering for the sins of the people.

The law made priests of weak and sinful men. The divine oath has made Him Priest who is the eternal Son. Because He had no sins of His own, He could offer the all-sufficient sacrifice for the sins of the whole world. For the Offerer becomes the Offering in a way no human being could ever come near.

HEBREWS 8

The Ministry of Christ
Hebrews 8:1—10:39

Christ Ministers in a Better Tabernacle

Chapter 8 introduces a new major division in the author's thought. He has been stressing *who Christ is* in relation to angels, to Moses, to Joshua, and to the Levitical priests. Now he turns to talk of *what Christ does* on our behalf as our great High Priest. Chapter 8, the shortest in the book, serves as an introduction to the material that follows down to 10:18.

Hebrews 8:1-5
> 1 Now of the things which we have spoken this is the sum: We have such an high priest, who is set on the right hand of the throne of the Majesty in the heavens;
> 2 A minister of the sanctuary, and of the true tabernacle, which the Lord pitched, and not man.
> 3 For every high priest is ordained to offer gifts and sacrifices: wherefore it is of necessity that this man have somewhat also to offer.
> 4 For if he were on earth, he should not be a priest, seeing that there are priests that offer gifts according to the law:
> 5 Who serve unto the example and shadow of heavenly things, as Moses was admonished of God when he was about to make the tabernacle: for, See, saith he, that thou make all things according to the pattern shewed to thee in the mount.

William Manson's translation of vv. 1-2 gives the key to the thought here: "And now to crown the argument, the High Priest whom we have is one who has taken His seat at the right hand of the throne of Majesty in heaven, a minister in the Sanctuary or true Tabernacle which the Lord, not man, has fixed." V. 1 stresses Christ's kingly exaltation. V. 2 moves on to His priestly ministry.

The Tabernacle which served as the center of Israel's worship for 500 years, and the Temple which followed its floor plan and arrangement, are but a *shadow* (5) of the heavenly reality. Christ's ministry is not in the earthly Tabernacle. Jesus could never have been a priest under the Old Testament law. What Jesus does is infinitely beyond what transpired in the earthly Tabernacle. There, gifts and sacrifices are offered continually. Christ's sacrifice was offered but once—a truth indicated by the use of an aorist verb in speaking of what He offered.

Christ Ministers Under a Better Covenant

Hebrews 8:6-13

> 6 But now hath he obtained a more excellent ministry, by how much also he is the mediator of a better covenant, which was established upon better promises.
> 7 For if that first covenant had been faultless, then should no place have been sought for the second.
> 8 For finding fault with them, he saith, Behold, the days come, saith the Lord, when I will make a new covenant with the house of Israel and with the house of Judah:
> 9 Not according to the covenant that I made with their fathers in the day when I took them by the hand to lead them out of the land of Egypt; because they continued not in my covenant, and I regarded them not, saith the Lord.
> 10 For this is the covenant that I will make with the house of Israel after those days, saith the Lord; I will put my laws into their mind, and write them in their hearts: and I will be to them a God, and they shall be to me a people:
> 11 And they shall not teach every man his neighbour, and every man his brother, saying, Know the Lord: for all shall know me, from the least to the greatest.
> 12 For I will be merciful to their unrighteousness, and their sins and their iniquities will I remember no more.
> 13 In that he saith, A new covenant, he hath made the first old. Now that which decayeth and waxeth old is ready to vanish away.

The changing priesthood in the true tabernacle implies the giving of a new and better covenant. Under this new covenant, Jesus *is the mediator* (6). Chapter 7:22 had spoken of Jesus as the Guarantee of the new covenant. He is its Guarantee because He stands between God and man as the One Tyndale described as the "At-One-Maker." A mediator conserves "the interest of both parties for whom He acts" (F. F. Bruce).

1. *Covenant* now becomes a major term in Hebrews. It has been used only once incidentally up to this point. From

here on, it is found no less than 16 times. No term is more important in understanding the message of the Bible than this one. It gives the titles to the two major divisions of the entire Bible. The "Old Testament" is the old covenant; the "New Testament" is the new covenant.

In its biblical usage, a covenant is never an agreement between equals. It is God who offers a relationship with himself, and who states the terms on which that relationship may exist.

The covenant Christ offers is better than the old because, unlike the old, it is faultless. It is a *new covenant* (8). The Greek language has two words for *new*. One of them *(neos)* means new only in point of time. In other respects, what is *neos* is just like what went before it. The other term for new is *kainos*. It means not only new in time but new in quality. It means new and different. The new covenant is a *kainos* covenant—new in point of time and different in quality.

It is *established upon better promises*. They are better not in that they are more dependable. They are better in what they provide.

2. In setting out the fact and value of the new covenant, the author quotes the promise of Jer. 31:31-34, part of which he quotes again in 10:16-17. His whole discussion yields six points of contrast between the old and the new as H. Orton Wiley lists them:

a. The old covenant was not faultless; the new covenant is perfect.

b. The old covenant was national and dealt with men in the aggregate; the new covenant is individual, resting on the promise made to Abraham and his seed as individuals.

c. The old covenant had reference chiefly to material things. It was based on secular promises as related, for example, to possession of and prosperity in the land of Palestine. The new covenant is spiritual, affecting the minds and hearts of those under its influence.

d. The old covenant set up a rule or standard of life

but could give no power or disposition to obey; the new covenant writes the law of God within, and creates a disposition to obedience.

e. The old covenant could not take away sins in spite of its continual offerings; in Christ the promise is fulfilled, *I will be merciful to their unrighteousness, and their sins and their iniquities will I remember no more.*

f. The old covenant was limited to the sons of Abraham after the flesh; the new covenant is universal in scope. It takes in people of all nations and so fulfills God's ancient promise to Abraham, "In thee shall all families [nations] of the earth be blessed" (Gen. 12:3).

3. Johannes Schneider summarizes three characteristics of the new covenant:

a. It rests on the inwardness of the law. "In the Old Covenant God's demand approached men from the outside. In the end-time, however, the Law of God is to be written upon men's hearts. It is to become their inward possession, indissolubly joined to their very being. Thus real obedience develops. For only an obedience which, affirmed by the heart and rendered through man's free and voluntary resolve, guarantees the realization of the God-willed order."

b. It is marked by an immediate knowledge of God. "In the redemptive order of the end of time men will have a personal religious experience, a personal assurance of salvation, and a personal knowledge of God."

c. It will result in the forgiveness of sins. "God will reveal the whole riches of His grace. He will blot out of His memory the sins of men and thus put His relation to them upon a new foundation."

HEBREWS 9

The Heavenly Sanctuary

All has been moving toward the truth now to be stated. The Cross stands at the heart of the Book of Hebrews.

Everything centers in the fact that the Saviour-Priest is himself the perfect Sacrifice. His sacrifice makes the blood of animals both unnecessary and ineffective.

Hebrews 9:1-14

> 1 Then verily the first covenant had also ordinances of divine service, and a worldly sanctuary.
> 2 For there was a tabernacle made; the first, wherein was the candlestick, and the table, and the shewbread; which is called the sanctuary.
> 3 And after the second vail, the tabernacle which is called the Holiest of all;
> 4 Which had the golden censer, and the ark of the covenant overlaid round about with gold, wherein was the golden pot that had manna, and Aaron's rod that budded, and the tables of the covenant;
> 5 And over it the cherubims of glory shadowing the mercyseat; of which we cannot now speak particularly.
> 6 Now when these things were thus ordained, the priests went always into the first tabernacle, accomplishing the service of God.
> 7 But into the second went the high priest alone once every year, not without blood, which he offered for himself, and for the errors of the people:
> 8 The Holy Ghost this signifying, that the way into the holiest of all was not yet made manifest, while as the first tabernacle was yet standing:
> 9 Which was a figure for the time then present, in which were offered both gifts and sacrifices, that could not make him that did the service perfect, as pertaining to the conscience;
> 10 Which stood only in meats and drinks, and divers washings, and carnal ordinances, imposed on them until the time of reformation.
> 11 But Christ being come an high priest of good things to come, by a greater and more perfect tabernacle, not made with hands, that is to say, not of this building;
> 12 Neither by the blood of goats and calves, but by his own blood he entered in once into the holy place, having obtained eternal redemption for us.
> 13 For if the blood of bulls and of goats, and the ashes of an heifer sprinkling the unclean, sanctifieth to the purifying of the flesh:
> 14 How much more shall the blood of Christ, who through the eternal Spirit offered himself without spot to God, purge your conscience from dead works to serve the living God?

The comparison begun in 8:1-5 is now completed. It is worked out in skillful detail. Alexander Purdy illustrates the contrast between the earthly ritual and the heavenly reality in a series of four particulars arranged in tabular form:[17]

	The Earthly Ritual	*The Heavenly Reality*
The place	vv. 1-5	v. 11
The action and approach to God	vv. 6-7	v. 12a
The offering	v. 7	v. 12b

	The Earthly Ritual	The Heavenly Reality
An estimate of the value	vv. 8-10	vv. 12c-14

1. Having prepared the way by showing from the Scriptures that the Tabernacle and Temple were copies of a heavenly sanctuary (8:5; Exod. 25:40) and that a new covenant was promised even while the old was in effect (8:6-13; Jer. 31:31-34), the author now moves to his full position. The entire Levitical system has been superseded. He begins by conceding a full measure of dignity and beauty to the Mosaic ritual. But he points out that it was typical of what was to come and therefore temporary.

Attention is focused chiefly on the holy of holies (*the Holiest of all,* v. 3). This was set off from the holy place by *the second veil,* the veil torn from top to bottom at the death of Jesus (Matt. 27:50-51). Within the holy of holies was the ark of the covenant. Originally the ark held the pot of manna, Aaron's rod, and the two tables on which were inscribed the Ten Commandments. The lid of the ark was the most sacred altar of Judaism, the mercy seat—overshadowed by carved figures of the cherubim.

2. While the ordinary priests came and went from the outer sanctuary, the holy place, only the high priest went into the holy of holies. This was on the Day of Atonement described in Leviticus 16, still observed as *Yom Kippur* by the Jews. The high priest entered the holy of holies with the blood of the atonement sacrifice to cover his own sins and the sins of the people. The meaning of all this was that *the way into the holiest of all* had not as yet been opened (8).

Wiley suggests a symbolism in terms of Christian experience involved in the second veil and access to the holy of holies. He remarks that the worshiper in the holy place "realizes that there is something 'deeper down and further back' to use Fletcher's strong expression, that prevents him from entering the holy of holies, where dwells the Shekinah of God's presence. This something is 'the second veil of sin conditions,' the inbred sin that remains even in the regenerate, and must be cleansed by the blood of Jesus before one can enter through the veil into the presence of God."[18]

The author reminds his readers that the Tabernacle and its ritual was *a figure for the time then present* (9). It was a symbol or type pointing beyond itself to a spiritual reality yet to come. Its sacrifices and ceremonies could not satisfy the conscience—man's inner experience of God's true demands. "Fleshly ordinances and outward washings can never reach the depths of the conscience or satisfy the hearts of men. The cry of the soul is far deeper and more intense; it is the cry for a clean heart and a right spirit" (Wiley).

3. The contrast is now drawn between the old and the new, the earthly ritual and the heavenly reality. In successive steps the supremacy of the atonement wrought by Christ is proved:

a. His offering was made in the heavenly shrine of which the earthly Tabernacle and Temple were but shadowy copies.

b. His offering was not the blood of animal victims. It was His own "precious blood . . . as of a lamb without blemish and without spot" (1 Pet. 1:19).

c. He entered the heavenly sanctuary once. His was an unrepeatable offering, eternally valid.

d. "The very nature of eternity is in the redemption He procures" (Manson).

While the sacrifice and death of Christ had been mentioned a number of times earlier in Hebrews, here for the first time His blood is said to open the holy of holies (9:11-14), to seal the new covenant (9:15-22), and to be borne into the heavens (9:23 ff.). The word *blood* is used 12 times in this one chapter.

B. F. Westcott summarizes the ways in which Jesus' sacrifice differs from the sacrifices of the Old Testament: (1) It was voluntary, not forced. (2) It was spontaneous, the result of His love, not of following the regulations of the law. (3) It was rational in the sense that Jesus knew fully what He was doing and why. (4) It was moral, not mechanical—a sacrifice made *through the eternal Spirit* (14).

4. The climactic contrast of vv. 13-14 can never be surpassed. It is made clear that to sanctify is to purify or purge. If the blood of animal sacrifices could sanctify the ritually unclean person in the Old Testament, purifying his physical body, *how much more shall the blood of Christ, who through the eternal Spirit offered himself without spot to God, purge your conscience from dead works to serve the living God?*

Johannes Schneider writes: "The blood of Christ cleanses our conscience. It takes from us the consciousness of guilt. Our sins no longer accuse us before God. The torture of conscience is ended. The blood of Christ looses us from dead works and liberates us unto a new worship of God. The new worship of God consists in this that we adore God and do living works in obedience towards His commandment. We no longer torture ourselves with a cult service that has lost its meaning. The worship of the Church of Christ is a worship of prayer and love."[19]

> *Not all the blood of beasts*
>   *On Jewish altars slain*
> *Could give the guilty conscience peace,*
>   *Or wash away the stain:*
> *But Christ, the heavenly Lamb,*
>   *Takes all our sins away,*
> *A Sacrifice of nobler name*
>   *And richer blood than they.*

Christ's Blood Seals the New Covenant

Hebrews 9:15-22

15 And for this cause he is the mediator of the new testament, that by means of death, for the redemption of the transgressions that were under the first testament, they which are called might receive the promise of eternal inheritance.

16 For where a testament is, there must also of necessity be the death of the testator.

17 For a testament is of force after men are dead: otherwise it is of no strength at all while the testator liveth.

18 Whereupon neither the first testament was dedicated without blood.

19 For when Moses had spoken every precept to all the people according to the law, he took the blood of calves and of goats, with wa-

> ter, and scarlet wool, and hyssop, and sprinkled both the book, and all the people,
> 20 Saying, This is the blood of the testament which God hath enjoined unto you.
> 21 Moreover he sprinkled with blood both the tabernacle, and all the vessels of the ministry.
> 22 And almost all things are by the law purged with blood; and without shedding of blood is no remission.

The author now returns to the idea of the new covenant. He is concerned to show how the death of Christ was necessary to establish the new covenant, just as the blood of sacrificial offerings had been necessary under the old covenant.

1. In part, the reason for this approach is given by E. C. Wickham: "The writer is seeking (as he seeks throughout the Epistle) to meet the feelings of readers who shrink from associating the Messiah, Who comes to renew and perfect the Covenant between God and His people, with the death of the Cross. He says, in effect, Think of the Covenant as, what it is indeed, a *Testament* rather than a Covenant proper—as an arrangement made in advance for securing to God's children a desired inheritance. Such a 'testament' does not take effect unless the testator himself die."[20]

The reasoning here rests upon the fact that the Greek term for *covenant (diatheke)* has a twofold meaning. It means "covenant" in the Old Testament sense—an arrangement God makes with His people. But it also means a "testament" in the sense of "last will and testament."

Very skillfully our author employs both meanings to express the full range of truth. As a covenant, the compact made through Christ is *new.* "New *testament*" in v. 15 is the same term in the Greek as "better *covenant*" in 8:6 and "new *covenant*" in 8:13.

The covenant, therefore, is also a testament. This means that *the death of the testator* (16) must occur before the covenant-testament becomes effective. Until the testator dies, the will may be changed at any time. After the testator dies, the will can no longer be altered. It is forever fixed.

2. Actually, the same principle was illustrated when the old covenant was put into effect. It *was dedicated* with

blood (18). The death of the sacrificial animal was understood to represent the death of the contracting parties in the sense that they put themselves beyond the power of revoking their agreement—just as if they were dead. When Moses sprinkled the blood of animal sacrifices upon "the book of the covenant," it was with the words, "Behold the blood of the covenant" (Exod. 24:8). Our author changes the wording slightly: "This is the blood of the testament" —probably an echo of the words Jesus used at the Last Supper (Mark 14:24).

V. 22 expresses the principle of atonement by blood alone: *Without shedding of blood is no remission*—"Sins are forgiven only if blood is poured out" (TEV). The context is a reference to the atonement sacrifices of the Old Testament. God had told Moses, "The life of the flesh is in the blood: and I have given it to you upon the altar to make an atonement for your souls: for it is the blood that maketh an atonement for the soul" (Lev. 17:11).

Forgiveness is never cheap. It has been correctly said that for God to create the world was easy. He had but to say, "Let there be—," and there was. But to redeem a rebellious race created in His own image was infinitely difficult. It cost the blood, the sweat, and the tears of Gethsemane. It cost the agony of God's only begotten Son in lifeblood poured forth at Calvary.

In an eloquent passage, William Barclay writes: *"Forgiveness is a costly thing. Human forgiveness* is costly. A son or a daughter may go wrong; a father or a mother may forgive; but that forgiveness has brought tears; it has brought whiteness to the hair, lines to the face, a cutting anguish and then a long dull ache to the heart. It did not cost nothing. There was the price of a broken heart to pay. *Divine forgiveness* is costly. God is love, but God is *holiness*. God, least of all, can break the great moral laws on which the universe is built. Sin must have its punishment or the very structure of life disintegrates. And God alone can pay the terrible price that is necessary before men can be forgiven. Forgiveness is never a case of saying: 'It's all right; it doesn't matter.' Forgiveness is the most costly thing in the world. Without the shedding of heart's blood there can be no remission and forgiveness of sins. There is nothing which brings a man to his senses with such arresting violence as to see the effect of his sin on someone who loves him in this world, or on the God who loves him for ever, and to say to himself: 'It cost *that* to forgive *my* sin.' Where there is forgiveness someone must be crucified on a cross."[21]

Christ's Atonement Is Spiritual and Eternal

Hebrews 9:23-28

> 23 It was therefore necessary that the patterns of things in the heavens should be purified with these; but the heavenly things themselves with better sacrifices than these.
> 24 For Christ is not entered into the holy places made with hands, which are the figures of the true; but into heaven itself, now to appear in the presence of God for us:
> 25 Nor yet that he should offer himself often, as the high priest entereth into the holy place every year with blood of others;
> 26 For then must he often have suffered since the foundation of the world: but now once in the end of the world hath he appeared to put away sin by the sacrifice of himself.
> 27 And as it is appointed unto men once to die, but after this the judgment:
> 28 So Christ was once offered to bear the sins of many; and unto them that look for him shall he appear the second time without sin unto salvation.

What is meant by stating that *the heavenly things themselves,* after which the earthly Tabernacle was copied, needed to be cleansed? Various theories have been offered. The most probable suggestion is that we do not cease to need the atonement when we are first forgiven and cleansed here on earth. We shall need its merits forever. We shall never cease to be "sinners saved by grace." E. C. Wickham comments, "Heaven without the sense of atonement would not be heaven—would be no place of untroubled memory. It could not welcome the sin-stained."

There are three great appearances of Christ mentioned here:

1. Jesus *has appeared* (past tense)—*to put away sin by the sacrifice of himself* (26). This was a Sacrifice whose "once-for-all" character is illustrated by human death and judg-

ment: "The death of a person is an event which happens once and cannot be repeated" (Schneider). Christ's sacrifice can never and need never be made again. It is effective for all men everywhere through all time.

The appearance of Christ in history to die once for our sins is *incarnation*—God's *provision* for our complete and eternal salvation.

2. Jesus *is now appearing* (present tense)—*in the presence of God for us* (24). This is His ministry as our great High Priest at the right hand of the throne of God.

The appearance of Christ in heaven to be our Advocate with the Father (1 John 2:2) is *intercession*—His divine *priesthood*.

3. Jesus *will appear* (future)—*the second time without sin unto salvation* to those who *look for him* (28). This thought completes the analogy begun in v. 27 with reference to a man's death. He dies only once. His dying can never be repeated. But he still must appear before the judgment bar of God. So Christ died once for our sins—and He will appear again, not then as a Sin Offering, but to bring final salvation to those who are ready for His appearing.

The appearance of Christ in the clouds as King of Kings is *intervention*—His *parousia* or *presence* when He comes again.

H. Orton Wiley points out the complete parallel in c. 9 with the atonement ritual in Leviticus 16. The high priest laid aside his beautiful vestments and donned the simple, white robe of an ordinary priest to offer the sacrifice and carry the blood into the holy of holies. But when he had completed the ritual, he put off the blood-stained robe he had worn. He resumed the splendid high-priestly apparel and appeared at the gate of the Tabernacle or Temple to bless the waiting congregation. "So also Christ, after He had made the one offering for sin and entered once into the holiest of all, will come again, not now in His humiliation, but in His garments of glory and beauty, transformed into brightness above that of the sun shining in his strength."

HEBREWS 10

Repeated Sacrifices Show Their Inadequacy

The author now writes a great resume of what he has been saying. Along with this, as his style is, he makes a significant advance in thought.

Hebrews 10:1-4

> 1 For the law having a shadow of good things to come, and not the very image of the things, can never with those sacrifices which they offered year by year continually make the comers thereunto perfect.
> 2 For then would they not have ceased to be offered? because that the worshippers once purged should have had no more conscience of sins.
> 3 But in those sacrifices there is a remembrance again made of sins every year.
> 4 For it is not possible that the blood of bulls and of goats should take away sins.

The very fact that the ceremonial law required continual sacrifices is an evidence of the fact that the sacrifices were unable to do what needed to be done. If they could have cleansed the conscience by breaking the power of sin, they would automatically have ceased.

The reasoning here rests on the truth that a real purifying of the heart delivers from sin. Christianity is not, as some have assumed, perpetual forgiveness for perpetual sinning. F. F. Bruce wrote: "The implication of our author's argument is that the true inward cleansing is permanently effective and therefore unrepeatable. When he speaks of the worshippers as 'having been once cleansed' he means 'once for all,' and emphasizes this by his choice of the perfect tense."

Rather than putting away man's sin as the sacrifice of Christ has (9:26), the annual cycle of sin offerings in the Old Testament kept the reality of sin's hold on human life continually in mind. Whether intended or not, there is a contrast between the "remembrance of sins" involved in the annual Jewish Day of Atonement and the "remembrance of me" of which Jesus spoke when He instituted the Lord's Supper. Instead of remembering his sins, the Christian is able to remember his Saviour with eternal gratitude.

Christ's Supreme Sacrifice

Hebrews 10:5-10

> 5 Wherefore when he cometh into the world, he saith, Sacrifice and offering thou wouldest not, but a body hast thou prepared me:
> 6 In burnt offerings and sacrifices for sin thou hast had no pleasure.
> 7 Then said I, Lo, I come (in the volume of the book it is written of me,) to do thy will, O God.
> 8 Above when he said, Sacrifice and offering and burnt offerings and offering for sin thou wouldest not, neither hadst pleasure therein; which are offered by the law;
> 9 Then said he, Lo, I come to do thy will, O God. He taketh away the first, that he may establish the second.
> 10 By the which will we are sanctified through the offering of the body of Jesus Christ once for all.

The author turns to the Psalms for another key text. The quotation is from Ps. 40:6-8. Its thought again is that the Old Testament itself recognizes the inadequacy of animal sacrifices. The Old Testament prophets themselves repeatedly pointed out that ritual without righteousness was an offense to God. What made the sacrifice effective in any measure was the love, loyalty, and sincere desire for a right relationship with God it expressed.

In the words *a body hast thou prepared me,* H. Orton Wiley sees an allusion to the virgin birth of Jesus. Our Lord was truly human. All characteristics normal to man (except, of course, the stain of inbred sin) were Christ's legacy from Mary. But God was, in a totally unique way, His Father. Dr. Wiley writes: "He was the eternal Son of the Father, the preincarnate *Logos* become flesh; He received His entire humanity from the Virgin Mary, who through the power of the Holy Spirit was given power to conceive—and thus two natures, the divine and the human, were forever conjoined in one Person, the God-Man. This prepared body, representing as it does the whole of humanity, made possible His expiatory sacrifice to the holiness of God." [22]

Our author points out that the Old Testament itself had said, "Burnt offering and sin offering hast thou not required" (Ps. 40:6), or as the Greek translation had put it, *In burnt offerings and sacrifices for sin thou hast had no pleasure* (6). Even in Old Testament times, ritual and ceremony could never take the place of a yielded will. The thought here is that if the moral obedience of one in Old

Testament times was better than the requirements of the ritual, how much more does the complete submission of the eternal Son of God to the Father's will surpass the Mosaic sacrifices!

By Christ's sacrificial obedience, He took *away the first* covenant in order *that he may establish the second* or new covenant (9). The supreme act of obedience by Jesus to the Father's will both satisfies the requirements of God's eternal law and sanctifies the believer: *By the which will we are sanctified through the offering of the body of Jesus Christ once for all* (10). As Peter Forsyth incisively put it, "The Cross that satisfies God sanctifies us."

It is of more than passing interest to note that the very Sacrifice that provides forgiveness for us also procures our cleansing. All the classical theories of the atonement are concerned with the way the death of Jesus makes possible our justification. But the New Testament makes it clear that the death of Jesus is the basis not only of our justification but of our sanctification as well (Rom. 6:6; Eph. 5:25-27; Heb. 13:12; 1 John 1:7).

Christ's Finished Work

Hebrews 10:11-18

> 11 And every priest standeth daily ministering and offering oftentimes the same sacrifices, which can never take away sins:
> 12 But this man, after he had offered one sacrifice for sins for ever, sat down on the right hand of God;
> 13 From henceforth expecting till his enemies be made his footstool.
> 14 For by one offering he hath perfected for ever them that are sanctified.
> 15 Whereof the Holy Ghost also is a witness to us: for after that he had said before,
> 16 This is the covenant that I will make with them after those days, saith the Lord, I will put my laws into their hearts, and in their minds will I write them;
> 17 And their sins and iniquities will I remember no more.
> 18 Now where remission of these is, there is no more offering for sin.

1. Our author speaks of the completed work of Christ by contrasting His posture with that of the priests in the Temple. The priest stands daily at the altar making the same offerings and sacrifices. This fact in itself proves that such sacrifices cannot deal with the deep problem of sin in human nature (11; cf. v. 2). In contrast to the standing priest is the seated Saviour. He has *offered* His

one sacrifice . . . for ever (12). Now He is seated *on the right hand of God* in His mediatorial ministry as our great High Priest.

There is reference again to Psalm 110, this time to v. 1. The Melchisedec type priest sits at God's right hand until *his enemies be made his footstool* (13). When His own are gathered home and His enemies forever banished, Christ's priestly ministry will have fulfilled its purpose. New Testament writers lived with the final triumph ever in view.

2. Christ's finished offering *hath perfected for ever them that are sanctified* (14), literally, "By one offering He has perfected in perpetuity those being sanctified." Thomas Hewitt points out that these words do not necessarily suggest sanctification as a process but mean "those who from age to age receive sanctification," right down to the present time.

This verse is of special interest because it relates perfection and sanctification. "Has perfected" is in the perfect tense, a use that means "has perfected and continues to keep perfect." Since the time of John Wesley, "perfection" has been a stumbling block to many. We must always remember, "perfection" needs with it "guardian adjectives Christian or Evangelical," as W. B. Pope expressed it.

The inwardness of sanctification is stated in another reference to Jer. 31:33 (cf. 8:8-12). In c. 8, the reference was made to drive home the idea that the Old Testament itself had predicted the coming of a new covenant or new testament. Here the point of the reference is that the new covenant works inwardly, writing God's laws in the hearts and minds of His people.

3. *The Holy Ghost* as *a witness to us* (v. 15) shows the nature of biblical inspiration as New Testament writers viewed it. It is an inspiration, not of words as such, but of the truth those words convey. This is what theologians call "dynamic" rather than mechanical verbal inspiration. In the very place where the author of Hebrews quotes most freely and without regard to verbal identity, in that very

place he most explicitly characterizes the truth as the witness of the Holy Spirit.

The KJV is incomplete in vv. 15-17. It should read, *After that he had said before* . . . he then added, *And their sins and iniquities will I remember no more.*

That the Holy Spirit is *a witness to us* means more than simply saying, "The Holy Spirit said." The Spirit witnesses in two ways. He witnesses objectively to the truth of the gospel in His inspired Word. He also witnesses subjectively to us in writing the divine law on our hearts as well as assuring us of the forgiveness of sins. Paul makes a special point of the subjective witness of the Spirit (Rom. 8:15-17; 1 Cor. 2:12). John also relates the presence of the Holy Spirit to Christian assurance (1 John 3:24; 4:13).

4. The author's great argument has come to an end. He has shown the infinite superiority of Christ's person, of His priesthood, and of His sacrifice. He will still use terms drawn from the reasoning that has been completed. But now he turns from instruction to exhortation.

E. C. Wickham has written: "Here the strictly argumentative portion of the Epistle ends. The argument has been coloured by the purpose of exhortation; and so the hortatory portion which follows will add points (as the hortatory passages hitherto have done) to the argument. But the tone will become at once more urgent and more tender, and the practical risks and duties which went along with the spiritual conditions which we have been considering will come more fully into view."[23]

Acting on the Promises
Hebrews 10:19-25

19 Having therefore, brethren, boldness to enter into the holiest by the blood of Jesus,
20 By a new and living way, which he hath consecrated for us, through the vail, that is to say, his flesh;
21 And having an high priest over the house of God;
22 Let us draw near with a true heart in full assurance of faith, having our hearts sprinkled from an evil conscience, and our bodies washed with pure water.
23 Let us hold fast the profession of our faith without wavering; (for he is faithful that promised;)

24 And let us consider one another to provoke unto love and to good works:
25 Not forsaking the assembling of ourselves together, as the manner of some is; but exhorting one another: and so much the more, as ye see the day approaching.

1. In the manner that is typical to him, the writer now gathers into one great sentence both the conclusions to which he has brought his readers and the exhortation he wishes to lay upon them. The death, resurrection, and living mediation of Christ give us *boldness to enter into the holiest by the blood of Jesus* (19).

The term translated *boldness (parresia)* is a favorite expression with the author. He uses it in 3:6; 4:16; and 10:35 as well as here. It means "in confidence, with cheerful courage, without fear."

The holiest is a reference to the holy of holies, the most sacred spot in the Temple, where the presence and glory of God were most distinctively manifest. Wiley wrote: "It is a place of spiritual purity with Christ, our great High Priest, where we live and work in the presence of God, our Father. It is the fullness of the Spirit, the promise of the Father, and the gift of the risen and glorified Christ. It is a life within the veil, where burns the Shekinah of God's presence over the mercy seat, illuminating the mind, satisfying the heart, and shedding its radiance throughout all the wide expanses of man's being."[24]

2. The way into the holiest is *by a new and living way* (20). It is *new* because it sets aside the atonement ritual of the Old Testament. It is *living* because it has been provided for us by the living Christ in contrast to the dead sacrifices of the Jewish altar. It is *through the veil,* identified here as the flesh of the Redeemer—torn on the Cross just as the veil in the Temple was rent from top to bottom at the moment of Jesus' death (Matt. 27:51).

The veil both separates and unites. It stands between the spiritual aspirations of man and the realized presence of God. When torn, it opens the way. E. C. Wickham comments: "'Such a veil,' says the writer in this place, 'was Christ's human nature in its physical, mortal aspect.' In it He came near to man: and then He rent it, passed through it into heaven. And His people's hearts could go with Him, could from thenceforth have in Him perpetual access to the Father."

There are three exhortations here, the familiar combination of faith, hope, and love such as Paul makes in 1 Cor. 13:13:

a. Let us draw near with a true heart in full assurance of faith (22). The *heart* in biblical use includes the whole of the inner life as the body stands for the whole of the outer life. Together they constitute the whole man. Our hearts are to be *sprinkled from an evil conscience, and our bodies washed with pure water.* There are not two ceremonies or processes here. These are symbolic ways of describing total cleansing.

Our access to the holiest depends upon two factors. The first is the objective rending of the veil, the body of Christ—our Lord's atoning death on the Cross. The second is the cleansing described here. It had already taken place. This is the subjective aspect, the inner work of the Holy Spirit in the believer's heart. In view of the sacrifice of the Cross and the sanctification of the Christian heart, we are privileged to draw near with hearts that are *true*—that is, real, genuine.

Robert Slocum told of his struggles to find faith in God. He dueled often with his doubts. But he began to realize something of the depravity of his own nature. "Then," he said, "the important question became not whether I thought *God* was real, but whether God thought *I* was real." In times when so many are phony, it is all the more important that God's people come to Him with hearts that are genuine and real.

b. Let us hold fast the profession of our faith (Gr., *elpidos,* "hope") *without wavering* (23). *Profession* or "confession" of faith always means public espousal. This was apparently the point at which the Hebrews were being tempted. They had made a public profession of Christ. But the threat of persecution made it all too easy to draw back under the umbrella of their Jewishness, where —at least until the outbreak of the Jewish War in A.D. 66— they would have the protection of the Roman Government.

    c. *Let us consider one another* to encourage each other in the loving fellowship of the Church (24). Individual and personal Christianity always involves incorporated and public Christianity. "The Bible knows nothing of solitary religion," said John Wesley. The Church is described in the New Testament as the body, the building, the bride, and the brotherhood of Christ.

    To provoke in this context is "to incite, to stimulate, to arouse." Literally it is, "To the end of sharpening the edge of love." This is part of the value of the public worship described as *the assembling of ourselves together* (25). Evidently some even in the writer's day were neglectful of the church, even as some are today.

    To the excuse, "I can worship God anywhere—at the beach, in the mountains, on the golf course," Norman Snaith returns the appropriate answer in his volume *Hymns of the Temple:* "The man who does not worship God at a particular place and at a particular time, ceases in the end to worship God anywhere. He who would be conscious of the Presence of God, must deliberately make use of the associations of hallowed places and hallowed times, in order that, not only that place and time, but every place and time may become doorways for the invasion of the Holy Spirit."[25]

    Our need for the church assumes special urgency—*so much the more, as ye see the day approaching.* More than 1,900 years have passed since these words were penned. We are just that much closer to *the day* than were the author and his original readers.

    It is important to remember that New Testament writers speak of what is absolutely certain as that which is near at hand. They can even speak of that of which they are completely sure as if it had already occurred (Mark 11:24; Rom. 8:30). Their insistence that the day of the Lord is at hand is as much logical certainty as it is chronological proximity. We live 19 centuries closer to the end than did the writers of the New Testament. Thus we need to hear Jesus' admonition, "Therefore be ye also ready: for in such an hour as ye think not the Son of man cometh" (Matt. 24:44).

The Hopelessness of Apostasy from Christ

Hebrews 10:26-31

> 26 For if we sin wilfully after that we have received the knowledge of the truth, there remaineth no more sacrifice for sins,
> 27 But a certain fearful looking for of judgment and fiery indignation, which shall devour the adversaries.
> 28 He that despised Moses' law died without mercy under two or three witnesses:
> 29 Of how much sorer punishment, suppose ye, shall he be thought worthy, who hath trodden under foot the Son of God, and hath counted the blood of the covenant, wherewith he was sanctified, an unholy thing, and hath done despite unto the Spirit of grace?
> 30 For we know him that hath said, Vengeance belongeth unto me, I will recompense, saith the Lord. And again, The Lord shall judge his people.
> 31 It is a fearful thing to fall into the hands of the living God.

Words of exhortation are followed by words of warning. These verses are parallel to those we read in 6:4-8. They have been similarly misunderstood. They are not written to take hope from the backslider. They are written to warn the complacent and the self-assured.

1. Mention of the day of the Lord has brought to mind the judgment which attends His coming. Charles Erdman writes: "There are two phases of the return of Christ. One is associated with hope, the other with wrath. The first secures deliverance and blessedness for the followers of Christ. The second brings judgment upon his enemies. The author has made reference to the former phase to encourage his readers in faithful attendance upon the meetings for common worship. He uses the punitive phase to give solemn sanction to his warning against willful sin."

Not only is the thought parallel to 6:4-8; the grammatical construction is similar. V. 26 literally reads, "Sinning willfully . . . there remains no sacrifice for sins," or, "While one is sinning willfully," or, "During the time that one is sinning willfully." H. Orton Wiley comments that this is "a present participle which means, not a single sin alone, but a continuous practice of sin. These words therefore can only mean deliberate and determined sinning, committed with willful intention, and marking a constant decision against light and truth." Erdman says, "The sinful course here described is deliberate, presumptuous, insistent. It is equivalent to a denial of Christ and to the abandonment of Christianity. It denotes actual and avowed apostasy."

The whole point is that Calvary is God's only remedy for sin. To deliberately reject the only remedy is to doom oneself to die of the disease. It should be said, solemnly but urgently, that this principle applies whether one has previously known Christ or not.

2. Again the Old Testament provides an illustration. Deut. 17:2-6 pronounced sentence of physical death upon the Israelite who was convicted of rejecting the law of Moses. How much more terrible, then, the fate of one who rejects not only the messenger, but the Message Sender; not the servant, but the Son (28-29)!

Persistent willful sinning treads under unholy feet the Son of God. It treats "with scorn and insult the highest and best of all beings . . . the only begotten Son of God" (Erdman). It counts the sanctifying *blood of the covenant* as *unholy* (Gr., *koinon*, "common, profane"). It does insult and wanton outrage to *the Spirit of grace* (29). This comes very close to the blasphemy against the Holy Spirit about which Jesus warned (Matt. 12:31-32).

While these words do not take hope from the backslider, they do strip him of any delusion created by a theory of unconditional eternal security. So long as he lives in sin, the sacrifice of Christ does not avail for him. But he may turn from sin to the Saviour. When he does, though his "sins be as scarlet, they shall be white as snow" (Isa. 1:18). 1 John 1:9—2:2 gives further assurance.

3. *The Lord shall judge his people* (30) reminds us that special privilege means special responsibility. It is a dreadful thing deliberately to provoke the wrath of *the living God* (31). *The hands of the living God* suggests opposite thoughts. The persistent sinner risks falling into hands of judgment. The Christian is happy to place his life in the hands of the living God (Ezra 7:9; 8:18; Isa. 62:3; John 10:28-29). For the sinner, *it is a fearful thing to fall into the hands of the living God.* For the Christian, as Robert Louis Stevenson once said, "It is a thousand times worse to fall out of His hands."

Past Loyalty Yields Future Hope

Hebrews 10:32-39

> 32 But call to remembrance the former days, in which, after ye were illuminated, ye endured a great fight of afflictions;
> 33 Partly, whilst ye were made a gazingstock both by reproaches and afflictions; and partly, whilst ye became companions of them that were so used.
> 34 For ye had compassion of me in my bonds, and took joyfully the spoiling of your goods, knowing in yourselves that ye have in heaven a better and an enduring substance.
> 35 Cast not away therefore your confidence, which hath great recompence of reward.
> 36 For ye have need of patience, that, after ye have done the will of God, ye might receive the promise.
>
> 37 For yet a little while, and he that shall come will come, and will not tarry.
> 38 Now the just shall live by faith: but if any man draw back, my soul shall have no pleasure in him.
> 39 But we are not of them who draw back unto perdition; but of them that believe to the saving of the soul.

We have here the same sequence of warning and encouragement as in 6:4-20. The warning is given because the danger is real. But the Hebrews have not yielded to their temptations. They have full right to take heart and press on. They can do this because they have already overcome fierce persecution (32-33). "Through many dangers, toils, and snares" they have already come. It has been grace that brought them thus far. They can be confident that grace will lead them on.

That these Christians had come so far and suffered so much was but more reason why they should go on. The old saint said, "I've gone past the 'go-back' corner." They must *cast not away therefore* their *confidence, which hath great recompence of reward* (35). To receive the promise they must do *the will of God* and have *patience*—literally, "steadfastness, endurance" (36). The time is short. They will not have long to wait (37). In the meantime, *the just* are to *live by faith* and not *draw back* (38).

Vv. 37-38 are virtually a quotation from Hab. 2:3-4. The writer now draws the conclusion in terms of himself and his readers: *We are not of them who draw back unto perdition; but of them that believe to the saving of the soul* (39). Here the issue is clear: on to perfection (6:1) or *back unto perdition*. The Christian life, said T. M. Anderson, is like riding a bicycle—you've got to either go on or get off.

F. B. Meyer sets in perspective the last part of 39: "Here, as so often, the salvation of the soul is viewed as a process. True we are, in a sense, saved when first we turn to the cross, and trust the Crucified. But it is only as we keep in the current that streams from the cross, only as we remain in abiding fellowship with the Saviour, only as we submit ourselves habitually to the gracious influences of the Divine Spirit, that salvation pervades and heals our whole being. The soul may be said to be *gained* (R.V., *marg.*), *i.e.* restored to its original type as conceived in the mind of God, before He built the dust of the earth into man, and breathed into him the breath of life, and he became a living soul."[26]

HEBREWS 11

The Life in Christ
Hebrews 11:1—13:19

Hebrews 11 has rightly been called "one of the great chapters of the entire Bible" (Wiley). E. C. Wickham titles it, "The History and Glory of Faith." Alexander Purdy describes it as "a rhetorical masterpiece." Yet it is more than a summary of the triumphs of faith in the past. It is "an outline of the redemptive purpose of God, advancing through the age of promise until at last in Jesus, Faith's 'pioneer and perfecter,' the age of fulfilment is inaugurated" (F. F. Bruce).

William Neil reminds us of the timeliness of Hebrews 11 for our day. "It was written to men who had lost the keen edge of their former conviction. Their religious life had gone stale. In addition to that their world had become a dangerous place. The forces arrayed against them appeared to be overwhelming. Wherever they looked there seemed to be no break in the clouds. To summon them to witness for Christ in the world was to invite them to face even more hazards. It was an adventure into the unknown with no guarantee of a safe return. How much wiser to stay secure among the old familiar ways and to hold fast to the beliefs and practices that had stood the test of time!"[27]

The Definition of Faith

Hebrews 11:1-3

> 1 Now faith is the substance of things hoped for, the evidence of things not seen.
> 2 For by it the elders obtained a good report.
> 3 Through faith we understand that the worlds were framed by the word of God, so that things which are seen were not made of things which do appear.

1. There is some question whether this is a definition or a description. Perhaps it is some of both. "And what is faith? Faith gives substance to our hopes, and makes us certain of realities we do not see" (1, NEB). *Substance (hypostasis)* means "assurance, confidence, ground," or "firmly grounded confidence." *Evidence (elegchos)* is "conviction, demonstration, putting to actual proof"; literally, "a title-deed as to property."

Faith has to do with a reality that is not accessible to our senses and which lies beyond the grasp of reason. It is the subjective certainty that holds to the reality of what cannot be demonstrated or seen with the natural eye. In the context of this chapter, it is almost the equivalent of "faithfulness." It is faith as leading to faithfulness with which the writer is concerned. In Kirsopp Lake's terms, "Faith is not belief in spite of evidence; it is life in scorn of consequence." T. S. Eliot writes, "The greatest proof of Christianity for others is not how far a man can logically analyze his reasons for believing, but how far in practice he will stake his life on his belief."

The object of faith is that which has been revealed by God. The underlying idea is that faith is man's response to God's revelation. "It is implied that this confidence and this conviction are based on revelations which God has made. In fact, any real definition of faith must include the idea of a divine revelation. Otherwise what is called faith may be mere credulity or conjecture" (Erdman).

"Faith," says Andrew Murray, "is the unceasing

reaching out heavenward of that spiritual sense to which things future and unseen reveal themselves as near and present, as living and powerful. Faith must in the spiritual life be as natural, as unceasing, as our breathing. . . . an unceasing intercourse with the unseen world around us."[28] Faith concerns both the present unseen reality and the promised future.

2. Verse 2 may be paraphrased, "It is faith in this sense, faith that involves venture on the unseen, that has made your history so memorable." Each illustration that follows points to the fact that what we believe is not something we tip our hats to. It is what we meet with a response— the response of obedience. Faith accepts as true what God has said and then acts on it.

3. Creation itself is the first illustration of faith's grasp. It is *through faith we understand* ("perceive, apprehend" in a form of knowledge not derived from the senses) *that the worlds were framed by the word of God, so that things which are seen were not made of things which do appear* (3). The visible creation testifies to its invisible Creator.

In passing, one might note that modern physics has come to the same conclusion our author reached centuries ago. The "matter" that seems so solid—that we see—is composed of units not visible in themselves. Electrons, positrons, and neutrons are not only invisible to the most sophisticated microscopes but are thought to be in actuality charges of electrical or some other form of energy.

Examples of Faith: Abel to Noah

Hebrews 11:4-7

> 4 By faith Abel offered unto God a more excellent sacrifice than Cain, by which he obtained witness that he was righteous, God testifying of his gifts: and by it he being dead yet speaketh.
> 5 By faith Enoch was translated that he should not see death; and was not found, because God had translated him: for before his translation he had this testimony, that he pleased God.
> 6 But without faith it is impossible to please him: for he that cometh to God must believe that he is, and that he is a rewarder of them that diligently seek him.
> 7 By faith Noah, being warned of God of things not seen as yet, moved with fear, prepared an ark to the saving of his house; by the which he condemned the world, and became heir of the righteousness which is by faith.

The examples of faith that follow are chosen to show its many aspects. Faith does not always show itself in the performance of the spectacular. It often finds expression in suffering and patient endurance through difficult days. A great triumvirate is named here: Abel, the worship of faith; Enoch, the walk of faith; and Noah, the work of faith. All are alike in that each pioneered some new and before unseen aspect of man's relationship with God.

1. Abel, the worship of faith (4). Abel's sacrifice of a lamb from his flock came to symbolize for biblical writers the true approach to God in worship as contrasted with Cain's offering of the product of his fields. "The way of Cain" (Jude 11) stands for a bloodless, humanistic religion. The acceptance of Abel's sacrifice "testified" that God was pleased with it as foreshadowing the offering of the Lamb whose atoning death would take away the sin of the world (John 1:29). Though Abel was killed by his brother, he still speaks through the reality of which his sacrifice was a type.

2. Enoch, the walk of faith (5-6). Gen. 5:22-24 affirms that "Enoch walked with God." This is an expression of perfect fellowship. One homespun exegete explained that Enoch walked with God so far one day that the Lord said to him, "Enoch, we are nearer My home than we are yours. Come on home with Me tonight!"

The term rendered *translated* literally means "to transfer to another place" or "to put over into another position." The KJV uses "carry," "change," and "turn" in other places as its English equivalent.

What it was about Enoch that *pleased God* is explained: *Without faith it is impossible to please him* (6). The faith that pleases God must go beyond bare faith in His existence—*that he is.* It must include the conviction *that he is a rewarder of* those who *seek him* earnestly and sincerely. The original makes it clear that the reward is given to those who seek God for himself, not for His gifts.

3. Noah, the work of faith (7). Noah is a striking example of one who believed the warning of a coming catastrophe

the like of which had never been seen. Nothing like the Flood had ever been experienced by men. It was in a very real sense the sort of thing *not seen as yet*.

Noah was said to have been *moved with* (by) *fear;* literally, "being devout," that is, guided by reverent awe for God and His word. The New Testament has another word it often uses for fear: *phobos,* from whence comes the English "phobia." This includes all kinds of human fears. But the writer here used the term *eulabeomai,* which means "to act with holy or godly reverence." Noah's obedience both condemned an unbelieving world and resulted in the saving of his own household.

All three of the illustrations in these verses describe the triumph of faith over death. Abel's faith points to the fact that death is the gateway to eternal life—he yet speaks. Enoch's faith points to the triumph of life over death—he does not experience death. Noah's faith saved others from death by the work it did for them. Through his faith, Noah becomes an *heir of the righteousness which is by faith,* a phrase Paul used with great effect in Rom. 4:5, 13.

Abraham, the Obedience of Faith

As would be expected, special attention is given to the story of Abraham, "the father of the faithful." In a special way, Abraham represents the man who accepts what he cannot understand. William Barclay aptly comments: "Into life for everyone at some time there comes something for which there seems to be no reason, something which passes comprehension and something which defies explanation. It is then that a man is faced with life's hardest battle—the battle to accept when he cannot understand. At such a time there is only one thing to do—to submit, to accept, to obey; and to do so without resentment and without rebellion, saying: 'God, Thou art love! I build my faith on that.'"[29]

Hebrews 11:8-12
> 8 By faith Abraham, when he was called to go out into a place which he should after receive for an inheritance, obeyed; and he went out, not knowing whither he went.
> 9 By faith he sojourned in the land of promise, as in a strange coun-

> try, dwelling in tabernacles with Isaac and Jacob, the heirs with him of the same promise:
> 10 For he looked for a city which hath foundations, whose builder and maker is God.
> 11 Through faith also Sara herself received strength to conceive seed, and was delivered of a child when she was past age, because she judged him faithful who had promised.
> 12 Therefore sprang there even of one, and him as good as dead, so many as the stars of the sky in multitude, and as the sand which is by the sea shore innumerable.

Three examples of Abraham's faith are listed at this point. A fourth is given in v. 17.

1. Abraham *obeyed* God (8). The Greek literally says, "While he was being called." He went out *not knowing whither* (where) *he went,* but in complete confidence in the One with whom he went. This is the venture of faith. The land became his only when he had moved into it before it was his.

2. Abraham *sojourned in the land of promise* (9-10). The word translated *sojourned* means to dwell as a stranger. Williams translates the verse, "By faith he made his temporary home in the land that God had promised him." The thought is reinforced by the fact that Abraham, as well as his son and grandson after him, lived in tents. This is taken to show the pilgrim character of man's life. Abraham's ultimate goal was the *city which hath foundations, whose builder and maker is God* (10).

The author makes much of this point in the parenthetical verses that follow (13-16). Robert Cargill tells of a missionary couple returning with broken health to retire in the States after a lifetime of service in Africa.[30] By chance, they sailed on the same boat that brought Colonel (later President) Teddy Roosevelt home from an African safari.

When the vessel sailed into New York harbor, a brass band and a thousand people turned out to welcome the big game hunter home again. There was no one to meet the missionaries.

The man and his wife carried their worn luggage ashore and found a room in a cheap hotel. Then something of the frustration of it all boiled up in the missionary's heart. He turned to his wife and said, "It isn't fair!

Here we spend our lives in Africa serving God and no one cares, while this tin-horn politician comes home to a brass band and a crowd of people to welcome him!"

His wife said, "Dear, I'm going out for a while. I think you'd better talk to the Lord about that!"

The missionary said he dropped to his knees and began to pray: "Lord, You know we have given our lives for You in Africa, and when we get home . . ."

That was as far as he got. The Lord seemed to say, "But, Son, you aren't home yet!"

Not New York but the New Jerusalem is the Christian's home. Not a harbor at the mouth of the Hudson River but heaven with the river of life is the destination of faith.

3. Abraham obtained the promised son and heir in the face of impossibilities (11-12). Sarah's faith is mentioned with Abraham's in the birth of Isaac. Both father and mother were long past the age of parenthood. There was no human possibility that they would ever have a child of their own. But their faith clung to the promise of God. Faith that brings life out of one *as good as dead* (12) is a hint of the resurrection of Christ, a point Paul makes explicit in Rom. 4:17-25.

Faith and the Pilgrim Life

Hebrews 11:13-16
> 13 These all died in faith, not having received the promises, but having seen them afar off, and were persuaded of them, and embraced them, and confessed that they were strangers and pilgrims on the earth.
> 14 For they that say such things declare plainly that they seek a country.
> 15 And truly, if they had been mindful of that country from whence they came out, they might have had opportunity to have returned.
> 16 But now they desire a better country, that is, an heavenly: wherefore God is not ashamed to be called their God: for he hath prepared for them a city.

Mention of Abraham's many children by physical descent and by faith (v. 12) brings to mind the pilgrim character of man's life on earth. A description of the faith of Abraham is resumed in v. 17 in connection with its most severe test. But the birth of Isaac marked the end of a definite stage in the process of divine revelation. "The son of promise" represents a new stage. The tents in which the patriarchs lived are in fact a confession *that they were strangers and pilgrims on the earth.*

Nairne compares the patriarchs to nomads on their way to a city across a vast desert. They can see its towers dimly in the distance. But they cannot reach it in that day's march. They are cheered and encouraged by the sight. But they pitch their tents once more afar off.

There is a practical point in the psychology of Christian living in v. 15. *If they had been mindful of that country from whence they came out,* "they would have had" (RSV) *opportunity to have returned.* Jesus had clearly made this point. To lay up treasures on earth, to put one's priorities in the things of time and sense, is to imperil the soul. To keep lines to the shore will make the voyage impossible.

General George Washington and his staff discussed what to do with the boats in which the Continental Army had crossed the Potomac. Cautious staff officers argued that the boats be kept should retreat be necessary. The general ordered the boats to be burned. There could be no thought of turning back. Christian security, in the same way, depends on "burning the bridges behind." Retreat becomes impossible and victory that much more certain.

Faith's Supreme Test

Hebrews 11:17-19

> 17 By faith Abraham, when he was tried, offered up Isaac: and he that had received the promises offered up his only begotten son,
> 18 Of whom it was said, That in Isaac shall thy seed be called:
> 19 Accounting that God was able to raise him up, even from the dead; from whence also he received him in a figure.

After a brief comment on man's pilgrim nature, a fourth and climaxing example of Abraham's faith is given. This was his willingness to offer Isaac as a sacrifice, knowing that it was through Isaac God's promise was to be fulfilled. *Only begotten* means specially or uniquely loved, since Abraham had begotten Ishmael and six sons by Keturah (Gen. 25:1). The supreme test of Abraham's faith was not obeying a call to go out into another country. It was obeying a command that seemed to surrender the only tangible pledge of God's promise.

Although God stopped the sacrifice when Abraham's perfect obedience became evident, the patriarch had indeed *offered up his only begotten son* on the altar of his own heart. In the back of the author's mind is the sacrifice of God's only begotten Son—a sacrifice brought to complete fulfillment.

A hint is given here that Abraham had resolved in his own mind the paradox of a command to slay the son through whom the promise was to be fulfilled. He was confident that God would raise Isaac from the dead. Isaac's birth itself had been a miracle of life out of death. Having sacrificed his son on the altar of his own heart, Abraham indeed received him again from the dead.

Charles R. Erdman writes: "Here faith won its supreme victory. Faith believed that the blessing would come, even though Isaac should be slain. Yet how could this be? Only by having Isaac raised from the dead. Thus faith . . . [discovered] the truth of the resurrection, 'accounting that God is able to raise up, even from the dead.' It was 'from the dead,' figuratively speaking, that Abraham did receive back his son. Isaac had been given up by his father. In all reality his life had been offered, when by an act of God he was rescued, and raised up, and restored.

"So faith ever reconciles the love of God with the mysterious providences of God. To solve the problem it introduces the factors of resurrection and immortality. It rests confident that in the light of eternity we shall understand the riddles of time."[31]

Faith's Farsightedness

Hebrews 11:20-22

> 20 By faith Isaac blessed Jacob and Esau concerning things to come.
> 21 By faith Jacob, when he was a dying, blessed both the sons of Joseph; and worshipped, leaning upon the top of his staff.
> 22 By faith Joseph, when he died, made mention of the departing of the children of Israel; and gave commandment concerning his bones.

Faith looks to the future. This is the lesson our author sees in the stories of Isaac, Jacob, and Joseph. These examples span the time from Abraham to the Exodus, from the promise to the first steps in its fulfillment. In spite of delay and discouragement, faith looks ahead. In Isaac, Jacob, and Joseph, faith "overcame darkness, distance, and death." They represent the vision of faith.

Moses, the Choice of Faith

The writer now comes to another epoch in Old Testament history, the Exodus. The Exodus is another great manifestation of faith, not in patience and endurance in hope, but for "active resistance, choice, enterprise" (Wickham). Moses is brought to the front, as Abraham had been. Around him are grouped lesser figures, just as about Abraham had been grouped the patriarchs.

Hebrews 11:23-28

> 23 By faith Moses, when he was born, was hid three months of his parents, because they saw he was a proper child; and they were not afraid of the king's commandment.
> 24 By faith Moses, when he was come to years, refused to be called the son of Pharaoh's daughter;
> 25 Choosing rather to suffer affliction with the people of God, than to enjoy the pleasures of sin for a season;
> 26 Esteeming the reproach of Christ greater riches than the treasures in Egypt: for he had respect unto the recompence of the reward.
> 27 By faith he forsook Egypt, not fearing the wrath of the king: for he endured, as seeing him who is invisible.
> 28 Through faith he kept the passover, and the sprinkling of blood, lest he that destroyed the firstborn should touch them.

Five instances of faith are seen in the career of Moses. Four are given in this paragraph, and one in the paragraph following. Running through all five illustrations is the idea of allegiance to an invisible King before whom earthly monarchs are helpless. As Alexander Purdy has written: "This comes to expression in one of the most memorable verses of the New Testament, for he endured as seeing him who is invisible (v. 27), which is again a statement of the author's understanding of faith."

1. The faith of Moses' parents (23). The unusual charm of the baby Moses inspired faith that through him God's promise would be fulfilled. Deliverance from Egypt had been foretold (Gen. 15:13). Bondage was to end after 400 years. The time had come. Amram and Jochebed, the devout parents of the infant Moses, believed God so firmly that *they were not afraid of the king's commandment*—a

brutal decree ordering the death of all male Israelite babies.

2. Moses' own faith was first seen in his refusal *to be called the son of Pharaoh's daughter* (24-26). "As an infant Moses had stimulated faith; as a man he was impelled by it" (Erdman). Someone remarked that in fact what Moses did was "to pass up the chance to become a mummy in Egypt." Yet it was a heroic choice. It involved surrender of *the pleasures of sin* that last but a little while, and suffering *affliction with the people of God.* Moses compared the best the world had to offer—*the pleasures of sin*—with the worst that could happen to a child of God—to *suffer affliction.* He decided he would rather have God's worst than the devil's best.

What Moses suffered was *the reproach of Christ.* Like the suffering of the Saviour, it was suffering endured through obedient faith and in service to the people of God. Reproach has always been the portion of God's true saints. No one can "go up the down escalator" without experiencing the pressures and tensions brought against him by an ungodly society.

Yet reproach brings reward. Jesus had already said this, for the word translated "revile" in Matt. 5:11 is the same term here translated *reproach:* "Blessed are ye when men shall revile [reproach] you . . . for great is your reward in heaven" (v. 12).

3. *By faith* Moses *forsook Egypt* (27). Scholars have puzzled over exactly which incident is here in mind. It is possible that it was Moses' first visit to his brethren in Goshen, which seems to have been the occasion when he refused to be adopted as the son of Pharaoh's daughter. It may have been his flight into Midian, although this is less likely since that flight was motivated explicitly by fear of the king. It could have been the final departure of Moses and the Israelites from Egypt at the Exodus. It is possible that the author has in mind the whole relationship of Moses to Egypt, telescoped into one phrase—a psychological more than a geographic act.

Just as faith enables us to understand that the visible

world was made by the invisible Creator, so faith enabled Moses to endure through all his dealings with Pharaoh and the Egyptians *as seeing him who is invisible.* The invisible Christ has inspired visible results in the service of His people all down through the centuries. Christians "march to the beat of a different drummer"—inspired by a "heavenly vision" (Acts 26:19).

4. By faith, Moses and the Israelites *kept the passover* (28). The Jewish Passover has great meaning for Christians. Jesus instituted the Lord's Supper in connection with a Passover Feast. "Christ our passover is sacrificed for us," said St. Paul (1 Cor. 5:7). The sprinkling of the blood of the Passover lamb foreshadowed the sprinkling of the blood of Jesus. It is by this Blood that we are saved from the destroyer, as the firstborn of the Israelites were saved from death at the hand of the angel of judgment.

Faith That Conquers All Odds

Hebrews 11:29-31

> 29 By faith they passed through the Red sea as by dry land: which the Egyptians assaying to do were drowned.
> 30 By faith the walls of Jericho fell down, after they were compassed about seven days.
> 31 By faith the harlot Rahab perished not with them that believed not, when she had received the spies with peace.

A fifth example of Moses' faith is the passage through the Red Sea. In connection with this deliverance the term "salvation" is first used in a specific way in the Scriptures (Exod. 14:13). So central was the Exodus in the faith of the Old Testament that recital of the event became Israel's confession of faith. God was identified for His people as "the Lord that brought thee out of the land of Egypt with a mighty arm and an outstretched hand."

The period of the conquest of Canaan is summarized only by reference to the fall of Jericho and the salvation of Rahab. The strongest fortifications fall before faith; those deepest in sin are redeemed by it. "Rahab was a classic example of what faith can do with the most unpromising material" (Purdy).

Rahab believed contrary to all the evidence. Barclay comments: "There seemed not one chance in a million that the children of Israel could capture Jericho. These nomads from the desert had no artillery and no siege-engines. It must have seemed fantastically improbable that they could ever break the walls of Jericho and storm the city. Yet Rahab believed—and staked her whole future on that belief—that God would make the impossible possible."[32]

The Contrast in Faith's Consequences

Hebrews 11:32-38

> 32 And what shall I more say? for the time would fail me to tell of Gedeon, and of Barak, and of Samson, and of Jephthae; of David also, and Samuel, and of the prophets:
> 33 Who through faith subdued kingdoms, wrought righteousness, obtained promises, stopped the mouths of lions,
> 34 Quenched the violence of fire, escaped the edge of the sword, out of weakness were made strong, waxed valiant in fight, turned to flight the armies of the aliens.
> 35 Women received their dead raised to life again: and others were tortured, not accepting deliverance; that they might obtain a better resurrection:
> 36 And others had trial of cruel mockings and scourgings, yea, moreover of bonds and imprisonment:
> 37 They were stoned, they were sawn asunder, were tempted, were slain with the sword: they wandered about in sheepskins and goatskins; being destitute, afflicted, tormented;
> 38 (Of whom the world was not worthy:) they wandered in deserts, and in mountains, and in dens and caves of the earth.

These verses cover the whole of the national period in Israel's history. H. Orton Wiley summarizes the examples of faith here under two heads: the faith of achievement, and the faith of endurance.

1. The faith of achievement (32-35*a*). Three classes of leaders are mentioned—judges, kings, and prophets. Bishop Westcott saw in these verses three sets of triplets:

a. The first triplet summarizes the broad results believers obtained. These included: (1) material victory—they *subdued kingdoms;* (2) moral success in government—they *wrought righteousness* or justice; (3) spiritual reward—they *obtained promises.*

b. The second triplet deals with forms of personal deliverance. Men of faith were delivered from: (1) wild beasts—they *stopped the mouths of lions;* a reference, of course, to Daniel; (2) physical forces—they *quenched the violence of fire,* another reference to the Book of Daniel;

(3) human tyranny—they *escaped the edge of the sword.*

c. The final triplet has to do with the attainment of personal gifts: (1) strength—*out of weakness were made strong;* (2) the exercise of strength—*waxed valiant in fight,* "became mighty in war" (Weymouth); (3) The triumph of strength—*turned to flight the armies of the aliens,* "routed hosts of foreigners" (Moffatt).

The verse division here interrupts the development of the thought. A final triumph of faith was that "women had their dead restored to them" (Goodspeed). Both Elijah (1 Kings 17:22) and Elisha (2 Kings 4:35) were able to restore to life the dead sons of women who had befriended them.

2. Faith in adversity (35*b*-38). There is an abrupt change in the middle of v. 35. It is simply prefaced with the words "and others." "Next to the fighting faith that experiences the wonders of God stands the suffering faith" (Johannes Schneider). It is the same faith. But the circumstances of life are radically different.

In spite of torture, mockery, scourging, imprisonment, stoning, martyrdom by the saw (a fate tradition assigns to Isaiah), bitter testing, and death by the sword, men of old refused to yield their faith. They wandered in destitution; suffering want, oppression, and cruelty. They were exiled in deserts and mountains. They hid in caves and holes in the earth. The writer's comment is, "The world was not worthy of men like this."

All of us would much rather live by the faith that achieves miracles. Yet to many it is given to live by the faith that endures in spite of almost impossible odds. It is not that God loves one class more than the other. Rather, His grace is sufficient whatever the circumstances of life may be.

A farmer painted the words "God is love" on the wind vane on his barn. "Do you mean that God's love is as changeable as the wind?" asked a neighbor.

"No," was the reply, "I mean that 'God is love' no matter which way the wind blows."

Of God's love there can be no reasonable doubt. He has already proved it beyond question in giving His only

Son to be our Saviour. So people of faith can live in the confidence that God works in all things for good to those who love Him and are called according to His purpose (Rom. 8:28; cf. RSV).

A Better Faith for Us

Hebrews 11:39-40

> 39 And these all, having obtained a good report through faith, received not the promise:
> 40 God having provided some better thing for us, that they without us should not be made perfect.

In keeping with his overall purpose, the author moves to what must have seemed a startling conclusion. Whenever he refers to the Old Testament, it is always to move beyond it to the better provision made for the people of God through Christ. The recital of the almost unbelievable faith of Old Testament men is no exception. The faith of the Old Testament was still a forward-looking faith.

H. Orton Wiley points out that we must distinguish between the promises made to men of every age, and *the promise* "which gathers into itself the final and supreme fulfillment of all that has been hoped for through all the ages. This can take place only when Christ comes the second time without sin unto salvation."

The Christian faith is the final faith because "it is faith in the heavenly reality revealed in its full glory in Christ" (Purdy). It can but humble us when we think that our faith rests on the fact of Calvary and Christ's resurrection and should therefore be so much the stronger than the faith of those who lived before the fullness of time in which Jesus came.

HEBREWS 12

The Supreme Example of Faith

Hebrews 12:1-4

> 1 Wherefore seeing we also are compassed about with so great a cloud of witnesses, let us lay aside every weight, and the sin which doth so easily beset us, and let us run with patience the race that is set before us,

> 2 Looking unto Jesus the author and finisher of our faith; who for the joy that was set before him endured the cross, despising the shame, and is set down at the right hand of the throne of God.
> 3 For consider him that endured such contradiction of sinners against himself, lest ye be wearied and faint in your minds.
> 4 Ye have not yet resisted unto blood, striving against sin.

The first four verses of c. 12 actually conclude the thought of the preceding chapter. Here the writer applies the point toward which he had been moving. The *wherefore* that opens the chapter is the most emphatic way of indicating a necessary conclusion. An old rule for Bible interpretation is:

> *Whenever you find a "wherefore,"*
> *Stop and see what it's there for!*

The example of Old Testament heroes encourages the faith of the Christian. But his supreme Example is the Lord Jesus. Christ is *the author and finisher of our faith.* He is its Beginning and its End. He ran the race before us. Now He sits supreme among those who are witnesses of our performance.

1. The symbolism of these verses is magnificent. The metaphor rests upon the order of events in the Greek marathon races. Those who had run in the earlier races took their places in the amphitheater surrounding the track. They became a *great . . . cloud of witnesses*—not as mere spectators, but as those who had run the race before.

Johannes Schneider writes: "For the believing Church of the New Testament it is a gladdening certainty that it is surrounded by figures who are an effective proof of the power and blessing of persisting faith. . . . Above us stands an innumerable number of men and women who have proven their faith. We are not to admire them, but to give heed always that at all times we share in the power that was at work in them."[33]

It is far more true for us than for Napoleon's soldiers before the silent pyramids in Egypt when the emperor said, "Forty centuries look down on you!"

2. To *lay aside every weight* has been variously interpreted. Athletes prepared for the Olympics by running

with weights in their hands and fastened to their bodies in order to build reserves of strength. When the time for the contest came, they would *lay aside* the weights. The word used in the Greek was one used by medical writers for excess body weight. It was superfluous fat to be taken off by rigorous training and came to be used for any sort of encumbrance. It stands for anything, however innocent in itself, that is a hindrance to spiritual progress.

Above all, the Christian must be rid of *the sin which doth so easily beset* him. This is not just one particular sin. It is *the sin,* a generic term—the very principle of sin itself.

Johannes Schneider writes: "Christians most of all must guard against sin. Sin accosts the runner quickly and easily; it ensnares his feet and tries to trip him up. Sin and faith are mutually exclusive. Sin is the most formidable enemy of faith. Where sin creeps in, the heart grows tired, the senses are blurred. . . . He who gives in to sin loses interest in eternal truths and in the invisible realities. But whoever has entered the arena of faith, of him it is required that he endure and that he permit nothing to deter him from his God-assigned duty, whether it be temptation or tribulations of any sort. Without sanctification one cannot attain to the goal."[34]

3. Above all, the secret of a successful race is keeping one's eyes fixed on the goal. *Looking unto Jesus* is literally "Looking away to Jesus" from our own troubles and all that would distract or discourage. He is the One for whom and toward whom we run. Christ Jesus is not just one more name added to a long list. "He is the Leader in the great army, the Perfect Exemplar of the virtue which, 'in many portions and in many modes,' they have illustrated" (Wickham).

Christ *endured the cross, despising the shame,* strengthened as we are to be by *the joy that was set before him.* Men dread shame more than any other sort of opposition—the sense that they are despised by those around them. Jesus met shame with its own weapon—He despised it.

The shame of the Cross has turned to the glory of the crown. Jesus *is set down at the right hand of the throne of God.* The verb in the original is in the perfect tense. Its meaning is, "He has sat down and is seated now."

However much a child of God now suffers, he can never equal what Christ has already endured for him. We protect ourselves against gradually becoming weary and faint in our souls by comparing our own situation with what Jesus bore for us.

4. The best Greek text of v. 3 suggests that the opposition of sinners was directed not only against Christ but against the sinners themselves. This was a consistent note in the Old Testament (Num. 16:38; 1 Kings 2:23; Prov. 22:2; Hab. 2:10). It had become a proverbial phrase. The wicked are their own worst enemies. Persecution is worse for the persecutors than for the persecuted. As Walt Kelly's opossum character in the comic strip "Pogo" said, "We have met the enemy and he is us!"

The emphasis in vv. 3-4 is the tremendous cost of the Christian faith. It cost the lives of saints and martyrs. More, it cost the life of the Son of God. Such a faith is not to be lightly discarded. Barclay wrote: "A tradition like that is not something that a man can let down. A heritage like that is not something that he can hand down tarnished and decadent and belittled. These two verses make the demand that comes to every Christian: 'Show yourself worthy of the sacrifice that men and God have made for you.'"

The Discipline of Our Faith

Hebrews 12:5-13

> 5 And ye have forgotten the exhortation which speaketh unto you as unto children, My son, despise not thou the chastening of the Lord, nor faint when thou art rebuked of him:
> 6 For whom the Lord loveth he chasteneth, and scourgeth every son whom he receiveth.
> 7 If ye endure chastening, God dealeth with you as with sons; for what son is he whom the father chasteneth not?
> 8 But if ye be without chastisement, whereof all are partakers, then are ye bastards, and not sons.
> 9 Furthermore we have had fathers of our flesh which corrected us, and we gave them reverence: shall we not much rather be in subjection unto the Father of spirits, and live?

10 For they verily for a few days chastened us after their own pleasure; but he for our profit, that we might be partakers of his holiness.
11 Now no chastening for the present seemeth to be joyous, but grievous: nevertheless afterward it yieldeth the peaceable fruit of righteousness unto them which are exercised thereby.
12 Wherefore lift up the hands which hang down, and the feeble knees;
13 And make straight paths for your feet, lest that which is lame be turned out of the way; but let it rather be healed.

The scene changes. The Olympic stadium with its racecourse gives way to the home with its essential disciplines. The readers are reminded that *the chastening of the Lord* is the essential mark of every child of God and a true evidence of His love. Chastening must neither be taken too lightly nor allowed to become a source of discouragement.

1. *Chastening* is not identical with either punishment or suffering in general. There is no English word that quite conveys the meaning of the original here. The term is *paideia,* from *pais,* "a child." It means the whole process of training a child—including not only correction or punishment for wrongdoing, but also instruction and encouragement. The verb form is used in Titus 2:12, where the grace of God is said to "teach" us—a training that is gracious and firm. It is the whole disciplinary dealing of God with His children.

There is always mystery in the suffering of God's people. That the way of the transgressor should be hard is only what one would expect in a moral universe. That the way of the righteous should so often be difficult is not as easy to understand. God is not the source of all suffering. Nor is pain always punishment and suffering a proof of sin. This is clearly seen in the fact that the suffering of these Christians, their "chastening," is compared with the sufferings of Christ, who was without sin.

The point of it all is that suffering, however meaningless in itself, can be overruled and made to work to good. Schneider comments: "Often it takes a long time before we understand what God wants to say to us in our suffering. But when the mystery of God's dealings with us has been revealed, then it may happen that we need not only resign ourselves to God's will, but that our very sadness is turned into 'joy,' that is to say, we arrive at the full affirmation of the divine educative dealings with us. He who has reached that stage where sorrow is changed into joy has reached inward maturity; he is on his way to the perfection of his being."[35]

Only the wisdom and grace of God can change affliction to a process of "child training" which results in good. Andrew Murray has written that if Christianity is to be a success, if Christ is to save completely, there must be a provision to prevent suffering from bringing defeat and to transform it into blessing and help. God has made just such a provision. "First of all He gives His own Son, as the chief of sufferers, to show us how close the relation is between suffering and His love, suffering and the victory over sin, suffering and perfection of character, suffering and glory. . . . He has provided us with One, who can sympathize, who can teach us how to suffer, and who as the Conqueror of sin through suffering, can breathe His own life and strength into us."

2. If the discipline of an earthly father is respected by children now grown, how much more should we respect the infinite wisdom that disciplines us for our certain good that we might become sharers in His own holy character? Discipline, at the time, is not always a happy experience. It may be bitter. But afterward it yields the peace of a righteous life to those who have passed through it.

Holiness is profitable (10). Whatever means must be used to produce in us the *fruit of righteousness* (11) is for our eternal good. In our turn, then, we must "strengthen the weak hands, and make firm the feeble knees" (Isa. 35:3, RSV). In this remarkable passage, vv. 12-14, the sequence of ideas follows exactly Isa. 35:3-8.

After metaphors of the race and the home with its character-building discipline is the metaphor of bodily health, vigor, and sturdy strength—walking a straight path with courage and helpfulness. It is important not only that the Christian pilgrim reach the destination himself. It is important that he help as many others as he can along the way. We must avoid doing anything that would cause others to *be turned out of the way* (13).

The parallel in Isaiah 35 and the verse following makes it clear that this is "The way of holiness." The chief obstacle to holiness in the world today is not the opposition of those outside but the fact that some "holiness" people are not holy people. They talk of perfect love, but are mean, narrow, critical, and judgmental in spirit. They talk of the pomegranates and honey of Canaan, but all they have to show are crab apples and sour grapes. To such these words are fittingly addressed.

Exhortation to Peace and Holiness

The imperatives and privileges of the Christian life are the subject of the final section of the Epistle, 12:14—13:19. The author, first of all, exhorts his readers to pursue peace and holiness.

Hebrews 12:14-17
> 14 Follow peace with all men, and holiness, without which no man shall see the Lord:
> 15 Looking diligently lest any man fail of the grace of God; lest any root of bitterness springing up trouble you, and thereby many be defiled;
> 16 Lest there be any fornicator, or profane person, as Esau, who for one morsel of meat sold his birthright.
> 17 For ye know how that afterward, when he would have inherited the blessing, he was rejected: for he found no place of repentance, though he sought it carefully with tears.

The combination of peace and holiness (Greek, "the sanctification") is probably suggested by the same combination in the Beatitudes: "Blessed are the pure in heart: for they shall see God. Blessed are the peacemakers: for they shall be called the children of God" (Matt. 5:8-9).

1. Both Erdman the Presbyterian and Wiley the Nazarene indicate that peace with all men is to be sought at any cost except that of purity. Erdman writes: "For peace almost anything may be sacrificed, but not purity." Wiley writes: "The word *diokete,* 'follow,' carries with it not only a desire for peace but the willingness to go far to obtain it; and the word *hagiasmon,* 'sanctification,' is an implied warning that we are not to seek peace to the extent of compromising 'the sanctification' without which no man shall see the Lord. Thus Westcott says, 'The Christian seeks peace with all alike, but he seeks holiness also, and this cannot be sacrificed for that.'"[36]

Peace in biblical thought is more than the absence of strife. It is positive well-being. *Shalom,* the Old Testament word, means health and wholeness as well as peace. The New Testament term also means both right relationships between man and God and between man and man. It is the sense of restful well-being that comes from such right relationships. Alexander Purdy noted: "The author has something different in mind from the absence of dissension and quarreling in the brotherhood. He means the quiet security of the dedicated and cleansed life, which will, to be sure, have its social consequences in peaceful human relationships."

Holiness—literally, "the sanctification," *without which no man shall see the Lord*—is, F. F. Bruce writes, "as the words themselves make plain, no optional extra in the Christian life but something which belongs to its essence. It is the pure in heart, and none but they, who shall see God (Matt 5:8)."

Sanctification or *holiness,* it should be remembered, is the great biblical term for the entire working of the Holy Spirit within our hearts whereby we are inwardly renewed and made free from sin. Justification emphasizes the act of divine forgiveness; sanctification signifies what happens within us. Justification, it has been said, is "Christ for us"; sanctification is "Christ in us."

"Although he lives in the world," says Barclay of one who is sanctified, he "must always in one sense be different from the world and separate from the world. His standards are not the world's standards, nor is his conduct the world's conduct. His ideal is different; his reward is different; his aim is different. His aim is, not to stand well with men, but to stand well with God."[37]

2. To *see the Lord* has three possible applications:

   a. It means to see God now in a beatific vision (Matt. 5:8). The man who is pure in heart can see the Lord in the circumstances and conditions of his life. He is sensitive to the workings of God in the world around him. He sees God work in answer to believing prayer.

   b. It means to worship God acceptably. This is the

typical Old Testament usage. To "behold the face of the Lord" is the Old Testament idiom for true worship. To "see" a person's "face" is to be favorably received by him. To "cause one's face to shine upon" another is to bestow blessing or favor upon him.

c. It means to stand unashamed in the presence of the Son of Man at His coming again. This is the emphasis of a similar passage in 1 John 3:2-3, "Beloved, now are we the sons of God, and it doth not yet appear what we shall be: but we know that, when he shall appear, we shall be like him; for we shall see him as he is. And every man that hath this hope in him purifieth himself, even as he is pure."

Three reasons are given for pursuing peace and holiness. Each is introduced with the word *lest*. This negative particle means "in order that it may not be." We are to give careful regard to escape the results of failure at this point.

3. The consequences of failure to follow peace and holiness are:

a. Backsliding—*Lest any man fail of the grace of God* (15), or as it should be translated, "fall back from the grace of God." We have already seen this concern in c. 6. The danger before those who fail to go on to perfection is turning back to "the beggarly elements of the world" (cf. also Gal. 4:9). Holiness does not make backsliding impossible. It does make it highly improbable. Not all unsanctified Christians backslide. But most of those who do backslide are unsanctified.

b. Bitterness—*Lest any root of bitterness springing up trouble you, and thereby many be defiled.* There are two views as to the meaning of these words. One would interpret them sociologically—the bitter root is a disaffected member of the group who defiles the fellowship by his quarrelsome and irritable ways. The other would interpret the statement psychologically. The *root of bitterness* is the inner sin that springs up in the heart of an unsanctified believer. It troubles him; but worse than that, it defiles others.

c. Blindness—*Lest there be any fornicator, or profane person, as Esau* (16-17). That Esau was not called a fornicator in the literal sense of the word seems implied by the context. His sin was not sexual impurity but religious infidelity. It was contempt for what the birthright stood for that led Esau to trade it so easily.

To be *profane* in the biblical sense means to be common, unconsecrated, literally, "open to common tread" as a public thoroughfare would be. It is used as the opposite of *holy*. Wickham writes: "It would mean here 'without the religious sense.' Esau in the story showed this lack in treating so lightly his birthright with its religious import, the priesthood of the family and the mysterious promises." Westcott says the word describes the man whose mind knows nothing higher than the earth. He is one for whom there is nothing sacred. Little wonder that he was disqualified, as the term *rejected* literally means.

Esau is another solemn warning of the fact that there are some choices that cannot be reversed. Once made, they must always stand. There are "seasons of the soul" in which the call to pursue holiness is strong and clear. If this call be persistently rejected, the example of Esau warns that it could be lost.

The Christian's Privilege in Worship

The other side of the matter is now set forth. Those who follow peace and holiness are brought, not to Sinai, but to the spiritual worship of a heavenly Zion.

Hebrews 12:18-24

>18 For ye are not come unto the mount that might be touched, and that burned with fire, nor unto blackness, and darkness, and tempest,
>19 And the sound of a trumpet, and the voice of words; which voice they that heard intreated that the word should not be spoken to them any more:
>20 (For they could not endure that which was commanded, And if so much as a beast touch the mountain, it shall be stoned, or thrust through with a dart:
>21 And so terrible was the sight, that Moses said, I exceedingly fear and quake:)
>22 But ye are come unto mount Sion, and unto the city of the living God, the heavenly Jerusalem, and to an innumerable company of angels,
>23 To the general assembly and church of the firstborn, which are

written in heaven, and to God the Judge of all, and to the spirits of just men made perfect,
24 And to Jesus the mediator of the new covenant, and to the blood of sprinkling, that speaketh better things than that of Abel.

Once again, the religion of the Old Testament is compared with the surpassing glory of the New. William Neil comments: "The gloom and fearfulness of life under the Old Covenant is poetically described in terms of the giving of the Law at Mount Sinai, while the light and liberation that the Gospel brings are represented by a picture of the heavenly Mount Zion."

This introduces the last great warning of the Epistle. Wiley writes: "It is the grand finale to the series of exhortations intended to hold Christians fast to their confession. It is presented in the form of a contrast between the two dispensations, set in sharp relief to better stress the advantages of the gospel era."

There is artistry here. The writer is bringing out the grim and foreboding side of the old covenant. It both invited men to come near and yet kept them at a distance. The picture is drawn in a series of seven contrasts between the old and the new:

1. Mount Sinai was a material mountain; Mount Zion is *the heavenly Jerusalem—the city of the living God.*

2. Mount Sinai *burned with fire*—threatenings; Mount Zion introduces the worshiper *to an innumerable company of angels.*

3. Mount Sinai was shrouded with *blackness*—confusion; Mount Zion is the home of *the general assembly and church of the firstborn*, whose names *are written in heaven.*

4. Mount Sinai was covered with *darkness*—hopelessness; Mount Zion is the abode of *God* the Father, *the Judge of all.*

5. Mount Sinai was torn by a *tempest*—unrest; Mount Zion is the refuge of *the spirits of just men made perfect.*

6. Mount Sinai echoed to *the sound of a trumpet*, a call to come together to hear the Law; Mount Zion provides us with access *to Jesus the mediator of the new covenant.*

7. Mount Sinai resounded to *the voice of words* in the giving of the Law; Mount Zion is opened to us by *the blood of sprinkling, that speaketh better things than that of Abel.* "The sprinkled blood of Abel cried out for revenge; the blood of Jesus for purification, and so for entrance into the presence of God" (Purdy). Abel's death called for vengeance. The blood of Jesus opens the way to reconciliation with the Father.

The Unshakable Kingdom

Hebrews 12:25-29

> 25 See that ye refuse not him that speaketh. For if they escaped not who refused him that spake on earth, much more shall not we escape, if we turn away from him that speaketh from heaven:
> 26 Whose voice then shook the earth: but now he hath promised, saying, Yet once more I shake not the earth only, but also heaven.
> 27 And this word, Yet once more, signifieth the removing of those things that are shaken, as of things that are made, that those things which cannot be shaken may remain.
> 28 Wherefore we receiving a kingdom which cannot be moved, let us have grace, whereby we may serve God acceptably with reverence and godly fear:
> 29 For our God is a consuming fire.

Again the writer sounds a clarion call to faithful adherence to the new way. There is a striking contrast in the Greek of v. 25 that does not come through in English. The word used to describe the speaking of Moses on earth is a word that means "transmitter" or "mouthpiece." The word describing the speaking of Jesus *from heaven* implies the direct speech of God. Jesus was not merely the transmitter of God's words to men; He was the Voice. How much greater, then, the condemnation of those who refuse the Voice of God himself—greater by far than the condemnation of those who refused the transmitted word!

God's message through Moses *shook the earth.* Sinai reeled as in a mighty earthquake. The warning is that not earth only but the heavens as well shall be shaken. Everything that may be shaken will pass away. All that is temporal will be swept away, so that the eternal may remain. As Barclay wrote: "All things may pass away; the world as we know it may be uprooted; life as we experience it may come to an end; but one thing cannot change or end or be shaken—the relationship of the Christian to God.

Even if everything else is shattered into eternal destruction that relationship stands eternally sure."

The passage closes with another solemn exhortation to faithfulness. Again the alternatives are stated. Either we are "grateful and worship God in a way that will please him, with reverence and fear" (28, TEV), or we experience the reality of God's *consuming fire* of judgment. In another sense, these are also words of assurance. We who have received the *kingdom* that *cannot be shaken* may be confident that God's consuming fire will devour all that is transient and temporary in order that the timeless and unchanging may be seen in its full glory.

HEBREWS 13

The Christian's Moral Obligations

The concluding chapter of the Book of Hebrews is more informal in style. It seems almost in the nature of a postscript. "The last chapter presents 'rules for Christian living,' which try to clarify what sanctification means in practical life" (Schneider). The one added thought is the Christian's obligation to follow Jesus "outside the camp" of the old faith.

Hebrews 13:1-6

1 Let brotherly love continue.
2 Be not forgetful to entertain strangers: for thereby some have entertained angels unawares.
3 Remember them that are in bonds, as bound with them; and them which suffer adversity, as being yourselves also in the body.
4 Marriage is honourable in all, and the bed undefiled: but whoremongers and adulterers God will judge.
5 Let your conversation be without covetousness; and be content with such things as ye have: for he hath said, I will never leave thee, nor forsake thee.
6 So that we may boldly say, The Lord is my helper, and I will not fear what man shall do unto me.

While these injunctions are not closely related, they do all concern one temptation: to conceal the Christian profession, to disregard fellow Christians, to deny spiritual leadership, and to draw back from the hardships connected with open allegiance to the Saviour. The general ethical principles in vv. 1-6 are divided roughly into two sections:

1. The conduct of church members toward each other (1-3)

a. The first obligation is *brotherly love* (Greek, *philadelphia*). Barclay writes: "It is a great thing to keep the faith clean; but when the desire to do so makes us censorious, critical, fault-finding, condemning, harsh and unsympathetic, brotherly love is destroyed, and we are left with a situation which is worse than the situation which we tried to avoid. Somehow or other we have to combine the two things—a desperate earnestness in the faith and a kindness to the man who has strayed from it."[38]

b. Hospitality is the second duty of the Christian life. This was a practical matter of great importance in New Testament times. Accommodations for travellers were scarce and crude. Particularly in the Church, hospitality made possible the travels of those engaged in missionary work. *Angels* entertained *unawares* were not necessarily supernatural beings. The term *angel* means "messenger." Among the brethren to whom hospitality is given may well be true messengers of God.

c. The remembrance of prisoners was of particular importance when Christian profession was a prime cause for imprisonment. Humane treatment of prisoners depended pretty much on the care of relatives and friends who brought them food and the necessities of life. The obligation would be felt the more keenly in that those at liberty might themselves be imprisoned for their faith at a later time.

In all that is enjoined here there is the memory of Jesus' own words that men should recognize His disciples by their love one for another. In a world cursed by the alienation of race from race, class from class, and one person from another, one of the greatest contributions Christianity makes is in the area of personal reconciliation. Those who love God must prove their love by devotion one to another.

2. The personal life of the Christian (4-6)

a. The writer exalts marriage and enjoins sexual purity. There may have been a tendency among these Christians to the sort of asceticism that would renounce marriage. Paul speaks of those who were "forbidding to marry" (1 Tim. 4:3). Concern for sexual purity was called for in contacts with the Gentile world.

b. There is a warning against the improper love of money: "Keep your lives free from the love of money, and be satisfied with what you have" (5, TEV). As by Paul in 1 Tim. 6:10f., contentment is named as the safeguard against covetousness. The secret of unbounded happiness is always bounded desire. The basis of Christian contentment is found in the assurance of God: *I will never leave thee, nor forsake thee.* Our response to these promises the author finds in Ps. 118:6, "The Lord is on my side; I will not fear: what can man do unto me?" *Boldly* is literally "with good courage."

Following the Changeless Christ

Hebrews 13:7-16

> 7 Remember them which have the rule over you, who have spoken unto you the word of God: whose faith follow, considering the end of their conversation.
> 8 Jesus Christ the same yesterday, and to day, and for ever.
> 9 Be not carried about with divers and strange doctrines. For it is a good thing that the heart be established with grace; not with meats, which have not profited them that have been occupied therein.
> 10 We have an altar, whereof they have no right to eat which serve the tabernacle.
> 11 For the bodies of those beasts, whose blood is brought into the sanctuary by the high priest for sin, are burned without the camp.
> 12 Wherefore Jesus also, that he might sanctify the people with his own blood, suffered without the gate.
> 13 Let us go forth therefore unto him without the camp, bearing his reproach.
> 14 For here have we no continuing city, but we seek one to come.
> 15 By him therefore let us offer the sacrifice of praise to God continually, that is, the fruit of our lips giving thanks to his name.
> 16 But to do good and to communicate forget not: for with such sacrifices God is well pleased.

1. From social and personal duties, the author moves naturally to the Christian's religious obligations. These center around his willingness to follow—first the human leaders God has sent, but essentially the example of *Jesus Christ the same yesterday, and to day, and for ever* (8).

Later (vv. 17, 25) the writer will speak of leaders still

living. Here, the reference is to those who had pioneered the preaching of the gospel and had gone to their reward (cf. 2:3-4). *The end of their conversation* (lives) means both the results of their preaching—that to which they dedicated themselves—and an indication of their death, usually by martyrdom. To contemplate these leaders in life and death will strengthen the Hebrew Christians to imitate their faith.

There is a natural transition from the thought of the apostles to their Lord, who alone is the same forever. Human leaders come and go. Their lives inspire those who know about them. But even the greatest may be forgotten. Our gaze must rise from them to the One of whom they bore witness. Schneider wrote: "Because He remains the same, the message concerning Him also remains the same; and for this reason the contents of faith cannot be subjected to change. The inviolability of the faith is grounded in the eternity of Christ and the unchangeableness of His being."

Charles Spurgeon was said to have made a motto of the words *and to day*. He placed this on his desk. When asked about it, he explained: "I need a reminder that Christ is abiding and real not only yesterday and forever, but today as well." The Christ of the past and the Christ of prophecy is the Christ of the present. His help is available today. His truth is needed today.

2. The readers are warned against being *carried about with divers* ("all sorts of," Weymouth) *and strange doctrines* (9). Paul, in almost the same language, warns "that we henceforth be no more children, tossed to and fro, and carried about with every wind of doctrine, by the sleight of men, and cunning craftiness, whereby they lie in wait to deceive" (Eph. 4:14).

The sects and cults that proliferate in our day do not usually seek those who have no connection with religious faith. They prey on unstable and ungrounded church members whose faith is more traditional than personal and biblical. It is difficult to find a member of any of the deviant religious movements within Christendom who was not first affiliated with or at least brought up in some branch of historic Christianity.

Our source of protection against error is not only grounding in biblical knowledge; it is to have our hearts *established with grace.* The surest safeguard against error is a personal experience of the grace of God wrought within by the Holy Spirit. The Holy Spirit is "the Spirit of truth" (John 14:17; 15:26; 16:13). He is the "Conservator of orthodoxy" (Daniel Steele).

Our religious life must not find its sole expression in *meats*—a kind of shorthand expression for the whole system of ritual and sacrifices. The history of Israel, if it had done nothing else, had given abundant evidence that the external ritual had *not profited them that have been occupied therein*—"from which those who place dependence upon them have derived no benefit" (Weymouth).

In contrast *we* Christians *have an altar*—"the cross of Christ and the saving benefits of His death." Those are excluded who still trust the rites and ceremonies of ritual religion and reject the Saviour, whom God has sent.

3. Here a new element enters the argument of the book. The writer had earlier proved that the Christian does not need the Jewish sacrifices. Now he makes it clear that the Christian must give them up. "This entire section is a protest against mixing spiritual religion with what is material and sensuous" (Wiley).

Referring again to the prescribed order for the Day of Atonement in the Old Testament, the author notes that, while the blood of the sacrificial animals was sprinkled on the mercy seat, their bodies were burned outside the camp (11). In this same way, *Jesus also, that he might sanctify* God's *people with his own blood, suffered without the gate* (12). Even the location of Golgotha—outside the city wall—expresses a truth.

4. Four facts about the death of Jesus in relation to sanctification are here suggested:

a. The persons. *The people* is the typical biblical phrase for God's people or the people of God. "This is the will of God, even *your* sanctification" (1 Thess. 4:3) were words addressed to Christians.

   b. The purpose. Not only are the people of God "justified by his blood . . . [and] saved from wrath through him" (Rom. 5:9); they are to be sanctified also by *his own blood.* Barclay paraphrases v. 12, "That was why Jesus suffered outside the gate, so that He might make men fit for the presence of God by His own blood."

   c. The price. Not only is forgiveness costly; cleansing is costly, too. Its price was the suffering and death of the Redeemer. Only His blood can cleanse "us from all sin" (1 John 1:7).

   d. The prize. V. 14 concludes the author's call to consecration with another reference to the goal of the Christian pilgrimage. The final reward for Christian faithfulness is not in this world. It is in the city which it *to come*—the heavenly Jerusalem which John saw coming down from God out of heaven (Rev. 21:2 ff.).

5. V. 13 conveys one of the strongest calls to consecration in the New Testament. It parallels Paul's great exhortation in Rom. 12:1-2. Jesus had said, "If any man will come after me, let him deny himself, and take up his cross, and follow me" (Matt. 16:24). As Jesus suffered without the gate, so are we in a spiritual way to *go forth . . . unto him without the camp, bearing his reproach.*

The passion of our Saviour must find its echo in our experience: Gethsemane, consecration—"Not my will, but thine, be done"; Golgotha, the death to sin which is cleansing; and the Garden of the Empty Tomb, commitment to Christ in the risen life of holiness. Our going forth is not to "it" but to Him.

6. The Christian life is to be characterized by *the sacrifice of praise* (15). *The fruit of our lips giving thanks to his name* is an offering always acceptable to our Father. Through Christ, we offer a new kind of gift to God. It is not a sin offering. That was offered for us once for all at Calvary. It is a thank offering. The praise of His people is a pleasant aroma to God.

But full-orbed worship requires more from us than

praise alone. It must be linked with true benevolence—"Do not neglect to do good and to share what you have" (16, RSV).

Even our language hints at the essential connection between worship and service. A visitor in an old-fashioned Quaker meetinghouse grew restless as the worshipers waited in silence for the Spirit to move one of their number to speak.

"When does the service begin?" he asked one seated nearby.

"When the meeting ends," was the answer.

Respect for Leadership

An earlier appeal was made to recall past leaders (v. 7). Now the author appeals for obedience to present leadership.

Hebrews 13:17

> 17 Obey them that have the rule over you, and submit yourselves: for they watch for your souls, as they that must give account, that they may do it with joy, and not with grief: for that is unprofitable for you.

This verse gives a thumbnail description of the ideal ministry—*They watch for your souls, as they that must give account.* From the emphasis here and in v. 24 on present leadership, some have concluded that this particular congregation may have shown a tendency to self-assertion and false independence. As E. H. Hewett has written: "Christians must always retain the liberty wherewith Christ has made them free; but insubordination to the spiritual leaders chosen by God can mar the spiritual welfare and progress of the Church."

Failure at this point results not only in grief for the leader but in danger to the people. *Unprofitable* represents the irony that substitutes a milder term for the one really intended. "Disastrous" is the true meaning here. The sheep that "goes it alone" soon falls prey to the wolves.

Prayer for Leadership

Hebrews 13:18-19

> 18 Pray for us: for we trust we have a good conscience, in all things willing to live honestly.
> 19 But I beseech you the rather to do this, that I may be restored to you the sooner.

The writer requests prayer for himself. He implies in what he says about the *good conscience* that he had lived among them and that he was known to them. His request is for continued prayer: literally, "Be praying" or "Keep on praying." His assurance to them of his integrity is important. It is difficult to pray for one in whom the praying Christian has no confidence. The specific request that he may be able to come back to them the sooner also reminds us that general requests are less significant than mention of specific needs.

A Benediction and Concluding Remarks
Hebrews 13:20-25

A Benediction

Hebrews 13:20-21

> 20 Now the God of peace, that brought again from the dead our Lord Jesus, that great shepherd of the sheep, through the blood of the everlasting covenant,
> 21 Make you perfect in every good work to do his will, working in you that which is wellpleasing in his sight, through Jesus Christ; to whom be glory for ever and ever. Amen.

Having requested prayer for himself, the author now records a prayer of benediction for his people. This is "one of the most beautiful and inclusive benedictions that the Scriptures contain" (Erdman). Each word and phrase is important. Wiley gives a valuable nine-point analysis:

1. *The God of peace*—a phrase Paul often used. God is the Giver of peace, and peace is essential to His nature.

2. *That brought again from the dead our Lord Jesus.* The author has throughout emphasized the exaltation of Jesus to the right hand of God. This is his first specific mention of the Resurrection.

3. *That great shepherd of the sheep.* The shepherd cares for his sheep with utmost love and solicitude.

4. *Through the blood of the everlasting covenant.* The Blood gives us access to God. It also provides us escape from spiritual death. Moses had sprinkled the blood of a temporary covenant on the book and on the people. To us

is given the sprinkling of the Blood of an *everlasting covenant*.

5. *Make you perfect in every good work to do his will.* The term *perfect* here is different from that used in 6:1. Here it means "to fit for a proper function," "to set aright whatever is wrong," "to bring about a harmonious combination of different powers." We are to experience fitness to do God's will in every sort of good work.

6. *Working in you that which is well-pleasing in his sight.* Paul puts together the same ideas: "Work out your own salvation with fear and trembling. For it is God which worketh in you both to will and to do of his good pleasure" (Phil. 2:12-13).

7. *Through Jesus Christ.* Jesus, in this great summary statement at the end of the Epistle, is presented as our Lord, the Risen One, the Shepherd of His Church, the Mediator of our salvation, and the Guarantor of the eternal covenant.

8. *To whom be glory for ever and ever.* The ascription of glory reserved in the Bible for the true God is here freely given to Christ Jesus.

9. *Amen.* This is the great Hebrew term carried over into New Testament Greek and from there into English. In the Old Testament, it is one of the titles of the living God. It means "faithful," "sure," "true." When it is spoken by God, it means, "It is and shall be so." When it is spoken by man, it means, "So let it be."

Concluding Remarks

Hebrews 13:22-25

> 22 And I beseech you, brethren, suffer the word of exhortation: for I have written a letter unto you in few words.
> 23 Know ye that our brother Timothy is set at liberty; with whom, if he come shortly, I will see you.
> 24 Salute all them that have the rule over you, and all the saints. They of Italy salute you.
> 25 Grace be with you all. Amen.

No portion of the letter sounds as much like the Apostle Paul as these concluding words. Compared with the vastness of his subject, the author feels that he has written but a *few words*. The statement made about *our brother Timothy* being *set at liberty* could mean release from any sort of limitation of confinement. The author's identification with Timothy in a desire to visit the church would place him with the group of Christians associated closely with the Apostle Paul.

The words *They of Italy salute you* could mean either those who were *from* Italy or those who were *in* Italy. The form of the final benediction, *Grace be with you all. Amen,* shows that the letter was meant to be read aloud in public worship.

There is always something unseemly about comparing portions of scripture as to relative value. But no part of the New Testament has a clearer message for the Church today than the letter to the Hebrews. The neopaganism of the twentieth century is producing among us conditions remarkably like those that faced this Hebrew Christian congregation in the first century.

William Neil describes it well: "We shall find that when we come to grips with the situation in which the first readers of this letter found themselves, it has remarkable points of contact with our situation to-day. The factors which made it necessary for the Author of Hebrews to write this letter to them are operative in striking fashion again in the twentieth century. Danger from outside the Church and disillusionment within it were their lot as they are ours. The temptation to cling to the well-worn paths of traditional churchmanship and to shrink from the full implications of Christian discipleship is ours as well as theirs. We, like them, need to be reminded of the cost of obedience and the need for courage, but at the same time to be reassured as to the eternal validity of our Christian belief and the reality of our Christian hope."[39]

The Epistle of JAMES

Topical Outline of James

Introduction

Preface, 1:1

Some Basic Aspects of True Religion, 1:2-27
    Faith and Wisdom, 1:2-8
    Poor Man, Rich Man, 1:9-11
    Temptation as Testing, 1:12-15
    Our Response to God's Faithfulness, 1:16-21
    Hearing Is Not Enough, 1:22-25
    True Religion, 1:26-27

Keeping Life Consistent with Faith, 2:1-26
    The Sin of Snobbery, 2:1-13
    The Proof of True Faith, 2:14-26

The Tongue and True Wisdom, 3:1-18
    Controlling the Tongue, 3:1-12
    Wisdom: False and True, 3:13-18

Dangers to Christian Living, 4:1-17
    Sources of Defeat in the Christian Life, 4:1-10
    The Sin of Judging, 4:11-12
    The Uncertain Future, 4:13-17

Patience and Prayer, 5:1-20
    Another Warning to the Rich, 5:1-6
    Patient Endurance, 5:7-12
    Prayer and Healing, 5:13-18
    Reclaiming Those Who Stray, 5:19-20

Introduction

When we want to learn the principles of Christian ethics, we turn to three New Testament sources: the Sermon on the Mount, the closing sections of Paul's Epistles, and the Book of James. James, wrote C. L. Mitten, "is largely a series of exhortations to true Christian holiness of life, that is, to perfect love towards God and man." Mitten sees in John Wesley's doctrine of Christian perfection a parallel to James's use of his favorite adjective, *perfect*.

That is to say, the purpose of James is eminently practical. There is little doctrine in James. The book abounds in imperatives—60 in 108 verses. While James does not discount the "believing side" of the gospel, his chief interest is obviously the "behaving side."

This is profoundly important for modern Christians. One of the unfortunate tendencies in the fundamentalism of the twentieth century is to be long on doctrinal conformity and short on ethical consistency.

Faith and experience in the Christian life are of great importance. Yet faith and experience are of little value unless they lead to a consistent life. When all is said and done, the world around is little concerned with what we believe. It is tremendously concerned with the way we live.

So James has much to say to the Church of the twentieth century, as he had much to say to the Church of the first century. The incidentals of human living are very different now. The essentials have changed not at all.

James Who?

A quick look at the introduction to any standard commentary will reveal some uncertainty as to the identity of the particular James who wrote this New Testament letter.

Five men by the name of James appear in the New Testament. Two of them are only named—James the father of Jude, not Iscariot (Luke 6:16); and James the Less or "the Little" (Mark 15:40).

The other three are better known. They are James the son of Alphaeus, one of the 12 apostles; James the son of Zebedee, brother of John, also one of the Twelve; and James known as "the brother of Jesus."

There is no need to follow the intricacies of the argument about which is the man who simply introduces himself as "James, a servant of God and of the Lord Jesus Christ" (1:1). The most likely choice is the one to whom long tradition has assigned the letter, James the brother of our Lord.

While it is natural to wonder why James did not identify himself as the brother of Jesus, two possible reasons may be given.

One is modesty—reluctance to claim added authority on the basis of family relationship. Paul's insistence on apostolic authority is not comparable, since Paul was an apostle by divine choice and his insistence on recognition of this was as natural as James's reticence concerning family ties.

But there is another possible reason why James did not identify himself more definitely. Perhaps he was so well known it was unnecessary. If, as is likely, our author was the James who was head of the Jerusalem church and spokesman for the Council in Jerusalem (Acts 15:13 ff.), then "James, a servant of God and of the Lord Jesus Christ" would be all the identification necessary.

Most New Testament scholars despair of finding any outline in James. The book has been compared to a chain, each link of which is unrelated to the one before and the one after. Other comparisons have been with beads on a string, or in Edgar Goodspeed's words, "a handful of pearls dropped one by one into the hearer's mind."

While an outline may not be too clear, there is little doubt about the subjects James is concerned with. J. A. Findlay finds five topics prominently treated:
1. Temptation (1:2-8, 12-18)
2. The Rich and the Poor (1:9-11; 2:1-13; 4:13-16; 5:1-6)

3. Faith and Works (1:19-25, 27; 2:14-26; 3:13-18; 4:1-10, 17)
4. The Use and Abuse of the Tongue (1:26; 3:1-12; 4:11-17; 5:12)
5. Patience and Prayer (5:7-11, 13-20)

James on Temptation

James offers a practical explanation of the nature and effects of temptation. Nowhere else in scripture are these themes so fully developed.

Any treatment of Christian conduct must give attention to the challenges temptation brings to personal integrity. Temptation is inevitable in this life. In fact, the most dangerous of temptations is to be conscious of none.

But temptation is not without value. It is the testing of commitment, the purging of purpose. "Consider it pure joy, my brothers, whenever you face trials of many kinds, because you know that the testing of your faith develops perseverance" (1:2-3, NIV). Untested faith is unsure faith. Unsure faith is liable to collapse in crisis. Temptation builds faith in those who resist.

Temptation concerns issues of right and wrong that relate to righteousness and sin. But temptation is not sin. Only "after desire has conceived, it gives birth to sin" (1:15, NIV). Clearheaded thinking on these points is important for Christians young and old.

The Rich and the Poor

Christianity was not without wealthy disciples from the first. One has but to think of Joseph of Arimathaea and Barnabas, as well as prosperous merchants Aquila and Priscilla. Yet James recognizes clearly the other side of the coin. The majority of Christ's followers then, as now, were numbered among the poor.

James does not object to wealth on principle. Nor does Jesus or Paul. The problems of wealth are practical, and they are two-pronged. The wealthy tend to trust their riches. And the wealthy tend to use the power of their wealth to take advantage of those who are poor.

James gives particular point to God's concern for the disadvantaged. This concern is evident in both the Old Testament and the New. Affluence, popular opinion to the contrary, is no particular evidence of divine favor.

Faith and Works

His teachings about faith and works have brought much misunderstanding and not a little criticism to James. Martin Luther, for example, will be remembered as having described the Epistle of James as "a right strawy Epistle with no tang of the Gospel about it."

Underlying Luther's doubts about James was the apparent contradiction between James's emphasis on works and Paul's doctrine of justification by faith. It had been Paul's teaching about righteousness by faith that had been Luther's emancipation from the formal ritualism if his early life.

Some have supposed that James was a "Judaizer," deliberately attacking Paul's teaching about salvation by grace through faith apart from works. But James (accepting the brother of our Lord as the author of the Epistle) was a staunch supporter of Paul and Barnabas at the Council at Jerusalem (Acts 15).

What James attacks is not Paul's doctrine at all. As one New Testament scholar wrote, "James simply demands, in a direct untheological way, that faith shall not be distorted into a substitute for work."

James insists that faith shall have results. It must be applied to the whole range of life's experiences and relationships. It is "faith in action" versus a cloistered faith with which James is concerned.

What James complains about are those who talk about their faith but do not show it. While some may use the term *faith* to describe mental assent to truth without a vital apprehension of its meaning, James underlines the uniform insistence of the New Testament that a person's faith is shown, not by what he says, but by what he does.

Archibald Hunter asks and answers the crucial question: "Is James, then, at odds with Paul on this issue of faith and works? On the surface, Yes; at bottom, No. For by faith and works they mean different things. The faith on which James comes down like a hammer is mere lip-service to a creed—not the utter trust in a living Person which is the nerve of Christianity according to St. Paul. Moreover, by 'works' Paul means 'works of law'; James, the lovely deeds of practical religion. . . . There is no essential contradiction between them. For James would have agreed with Paul that 'faith works through love,' and Paul would have agreed with James that 'faith without works is dead'; and both would have agreed that 'the first thing to do with faith is to live by it.'"[1]

The Use and Abuse of the Tongue

No treatment of Christian ethics can be complete that does not consider the power and problems of communication. Human speech is one prime evidence of "the image of God" in humanity. It is fraught with great possibilities and with great peril.

In his treatment of the use and abuse of the tongue, James reminds us most of the Old Testament Book of Proverbs, from which indeed he appears to quote (3:2—Prov. 21:23; 3:6—Prov. 16:27). As incongruous to James as faith without works is a mouth from which "proceedeth blessing and cursing" (3:10 ff.).

Patience and Prayer

Our author's concern with the practical aspects of Christian living leads to a twin emphasis on endurance and on prayer.

No Christian virtue has value unless its practice is maintained. James is an undying foe of the "off again, on again" sort of religious life with which many seem content. He also sees that God's best answers come not to the act but to the attitude of prayer, patiently enduring despite apparent refusals. James would have us learn that God's delays are not denials. The "patience of Job" and the example of "the prophets, who have spoken in the name of the Lord" (5:10-11) should be our inspiration.

JAMES 1

Preface
James 1:1

James 1:1

> 1 James, a servant of God and of the Lord Jesus Christ, to the twelve tribes which are scattered abroad, greeting.

The writing opens in typical letter style. The name and title of the author stand first, much as they might appear on a letterhead in modern correspondence. James identifies himself simply as *a servant of God and of the Lord Jesus Christ. Servant* was a favorite title with Paul (Rom. 1:1; Gal. 1:10; Phil. 1:1; Titus 1:1). Peter also uses it (2 Pet. 1:1). It was the common word for *slave.* It meant one who was the absolute property of another, all of whose time and strength belonged to his master.

But *servant* was also a title used in the Old Testament for the true prophets of God. It was a demanding thing to be the servant of the Lord. But it was also a high honor. Nothing greater could be given to man than to be a servant of the living God.

That James recognized equal allegiance both to God and to the Lord Jesus Christ is clear recognition of the deity of Jesus. The title *Lord* was the term used to translate the sacred name of the true God in the Greek translation of the Old Testament. That the New Testament writers universally applied it to Jesus is the surest possible evidence of their complete faith in the deity of Christ.

In New Testament times, the Jewish people were divided into two major groups. There were the Palestinian Jews. These people were chiefly farmers, fishermen, and shepherds. Their language was Aramaic. The other group was known as the *diaspora* or "the Dispersion" from a Greek verb meaning "to scatter abroad." The Jews of the Dispersion were chiefly traders and professional men. In the west, their language was Greek. In the east, it was largely Aramaic and Syriac. This letter is addressed to the Jews of the Dispersion—*the twelve tribes which are scattered abroad.*

Greeting is from *chairein*. This form of salutation is used thousands of times in papyrus letters of the first century, but in the New Testament only by James. That it occurs in the letter from the church in Jerusalem (Acts 15:23), of which James was the probable author, as well as in Jas. 1:1 is a strong reason for believing that the writer of the Epistle was James the brother of Jesus and ruling elder of the Palestinian church.

Some Basic Aspects of True Religion
James 1:2-27

As already noted, the Epistle of James is lacking in a logically coherent outline of contents. The same themes tend to recur, and transitions are often abrupt. But c. 1 deals in the main with some of the basic aspects of a godly life.

Faith and Wisdom

James 1:2-8

> 2 My brethren, count it all joy when ye fall into divers temptations;
> 3 Knowing this, that the trying of your faith worketh patience.
> 4 But let patience have her perfect work, that ye may be perfect and entire, wanting nothing.
> 5 If any of you lack wisdom, let him ask of God, that giveth to all men liberally, and upbraideth not; and it shall be given him.
> 6 But let him ask in faith, nothing wavering. For he that wavereth is like a wave of the sea driven with the wind and tossed.
> 7 For let not that man think that he shall receive any thing of the Lord.
> 8 A double minded man is unstable in all his ways.

The body of the letter begins with a statement designed to startle and intrigue the reader: "Consider yourselves fortunate when all kinds of trials come your way" (2, TEV).

No New Testament writer ever suggests that the Christian life is an easy, serene existence. Jesus himself had spoken of denial of self, leaving fathers and mothers, homelessness, and persecution. Paul told his converts that it was through much tribulation they would enter the Kingdom. Peter spoke of fiery trials. The paradox of it all is that the Cross leads to the Crown. Death issues in life. Weeping turns to joy. Even in the heaviness and trial of faith there is "joy unspeakable and full of glory" (1 Pet. 1:6-9).

1. The word translated *temptations* is *peirasmos*. It is a word with two meanings. It means "temptation" in the ordinary sense of solicitation to evil, as in 1:14. But more often it means "trial" or "testing," the purpose and result of which may be good. Trials are the proving ground of the Christian life.

What is tested is our faith. Untested faith is unsure faith. So there is joy as a result of trials. Jesus warned Peter that Satan had desired to defeat him. "But," said the Lord, "I have prayed for thee, that thy faith fail not" (Luke 22:31-32). Faith is essentially trust in the truthfulness and dependability of God. It is commitment to the person and will of Christ.

The result of successfully coming through the trial of faith is *patience* (3). This is a word that also has two meanings. Passively, it means endurance—holding on though the pressure is severe. Actively, it means persistence, perseverance in good. It is more than grim endurance. It is the capacity to turn obstacles into stepping-stones.

2. The results of thus meeting trials are given as three:

a. The victor is made *perfect* (4). Perfection in a biblical setting is not a static absolute, something that cannot be changed in any way without marring it. Rather it describes what has reached its inherent end or purpose —that which is finished, complete, and true to type. When used of Christian character in the New Testament, as it often is (Matt. 5:48; Heb. 6:1; etc.), it does not mean flawless humanity but a redemptive relationship with a perfect Saviour.

b. The victor is made *entire*. The Greek word here is *holokleros*. It means "sound in every part," "undamaged," "intact," or "free from blemishes." It is the strong word used in 1 Thess. 5:23—"And the very God of peace sanctify you wholly; and I pray God your whole *[holokleros]* spirit and soul and body be preserved blameless unto the coming of our Lord Jesus Christ."

c. The victor is *wanting* (lacking) *nothing*. "The word [lacking] is used of the defeat of an army, of the giving up of a struggle, of the failure to reach a standard that should have been reached" (Barclay). The songwriter summarized this state with the phrase "Every needed grace supplied, every longing satisfied."

3. As though conscious of the note of paradox in his words, James moves on to the assurance that God will supply any lack of wisdom generously and without reproaching us for not having it on our own (5). *Wisdom* is represented throughout the Old Testament as a gift from God. It is more than knowledge. It is the ability to use knowledge well. It is claimed that there are enough Ph.D.s in the average state penitentiary to staff a good-sized college. A highly knowledgeable person may be quite unwise.

But prayer—for wisdom or anything else—must be *in faith* without *wavering* (6). The term for *wavering* is translated "doubting" elsewhere in the New Testament. It comes from a verb that carries the idea of a mind divided against itself. Doubt makes one like a bit of flotsam on the sea, now swept toward the shore, and again carried away. Only those can successfully come to God who believe both "that he is, and that he is a rewarder of them that diligently seek him" (Heb. 11:6).

The *double minded man* (8) is James's term for the "carnal" Christian whom Paul describes (1 Cor. 3:1-3). The word for *double minded* is literally "two-souled." Such a person has the mind of Christ, but he is pulled by the mind of the flesh (Rom. 8:5-8; Gal. 5:17, 24). He is one of those described in Hos. 10:2, "Their heart is divided; now shall they be found faulty." He has never had the prayer of the Psalmist answered in him, "Unite my heart to fear thy name" (86:11). He cannot sing with Charles Wesley, "Now rest, my long-divided heart; fixed on this blissful Center, rest."

The result of double-mindedness is instability. The Greek term here means "unsteady," "fickle," "staggering," "reeling like a drunken man." It describes the "up and down," "in and out," "back and forth" sort of existence characteristic of all too many believers.

The remedy for double-mindedness is given in 4:8, *Purify your hearts, ye double minded.* The "mind of the flesh" stands for the tendencies and dispositions of human nature apart from God. It must be put to death in order that the mind of Christ may rule within. This is an important part of the grace of entire sanctification in the heart of the Christian.

Poor Man, Rich Man

James 1:9-11

> 9 Let the brother of low degree rejoice in that he is exalted:
> 10 But the rich, in that he is made low: because as the flower of the grass he shall pass away.
> 11 For the sun is no sooner risen with a burning heat, but it withereth the grass, and the flower thereof falleth, and the grace of the fashion of it perisheth: so also shall the rich man fade away in his ways.

One of the persistent themes of the letter is now introduced. *The brother of low degree* is "a Christian who doesn't amount to much in this world" (TLB). His lowliness is a matter of social status and limited possessions. But in the sight of God he stands tall.

While Christians have not always lived up to the ideal, Christianity from the beginning has put major emphasis on the worth of human personality. Quite apart from talents, education, possessions, or abilities, each human being is of infinite value because each human being is the object of the infinite love of God.

While proper humility is a Christian grace, self-depreciation is not. He who despises what God loves and has fashioned in His own image is no friend of God. The "poor, weak worm of the dust" psychology has no proper place in a Christian's attitude.

We cannot love others as ourselves (Mark 12:31) unless we love ourselves with proper self-regard. Self-acceptance is not the same as smugness or self-satisfaction. But to be right with God and with our fellowmen we must be right with ourselves. Only as we accept ourselves as God has accepted us can we properly accept others.

Conversely, the rich must be reminded that their

personal worth is not measured by what they possess but by what possesses them. A common question is, "How much is he worth?" The answer expected is a statement of the economic value of the person's belongings. But Christianity insists that the true measure of an individual's worth is not what he has but what he is.

Life is full of reminders of the transient nature of wealth. A severe illness, a stock-market crash, the loss of a job, or a thousand and one other contingencies of life can strip the rich man of his security. At best, he will soon leave it. Human life on this earth is like the quick growth of desert flowers after a rain. As quickly as they spring up, they wither away and are gone.

Temptation as Testing

James 1:12-15

> 12 Blessed is the man that endureth temptation: for when he is tried, he shall receive the crown of life, which the Lord hath promised to them that love him.
> 13 Let no man say when he is tempted, I am tempted of God: for God cannot be tempted with evil, neither tempteth he any man:
> 14 But every man is tempted, when he is drawn away of his own lust, and enticed.
> 15 Then when lust hath conceived, it bringeth forth sin: and sin, when it is finished, bringeth forth death.

The author returns to the theme with which he started. Before, he had argued the joy of testing from the results that follow in Christian character here. Now he moves to the realm of the eternal reward for testing successfully overcome: *He shall receive the crown of life, which the Lord hath promised to them that love him* (12). The crown here means reward—the wreath given the victor in the Olympic contests of ancient Greece.

Testing here takes on the usual meaning of temptation. It is in the arena of moral conflict that the crown of life is won. No one can properly think of God as the source of solicitation to evil. When the KJV reports that "God did tempt Abraham," the meaning is clearly that God put Abraham to the test, not to entice him to evil, but to prove his faith and obedience.

The source of temptation is man's own desire. "But each person is tempted when he is lured and enticed by his own desire. Then desire when it has conceived gives birth to sin; and sin when it is full-grown brings forth death" (14-15, RSV). Desire itself is not sin. It may arise from purely human instincts and needs. The temptations of the pure in heart come through the avenue of desires that are the natural and legitimate part of our humanness. This is the way Jesus was tempted.

It is when the will of the individual yields to desire at the expense of obedience to God's known will that desire conceives and gives birth to sin. The result of sin "full-grown"—that is, accepted again as a principle of action—is spiritual death.

The way to cope with temptation is the way Jesus met the tempter in the wilderness (Matt. 4:1-11; Luke 4:1-13). He was spiritually prepared—anointed by the Spirit of God and fortified by prayer and fasting. He met each suggestion of Satan with the Word of God. But of key importance was the fact that Jesus made an immediate refusal. He did not toy with the temptation. Those who do soon find ways to rationalize and excuse their surrender. The best time to kill snakes is when they are small. Desire, entertained and fondled in imagination, can become almost irresistible.

Temptation is the common lot of all. It comes to *every man.* Indeed, the most dangerous temptation of all is to be conscious of none. But in all our battles with desire we have the assurance that "there hath no temptation taken you but such as is common to man: but God is faithful, who will not suffer you to be tempted above that ye are able; but will with the temptation also make a way to escape, that ye may be able to bear it" (1 Cor. 10:13).

Our Response to God's Faithfulness

James 1:16-21

> 16 Do not err, my beloved brethren.
> 17 Every good gift and every perfect gift is from above, and cometh down from the Father of lights, with whom is no variableness, neither shadow of turning.
> 18 Of his own will begat he us with the word of truth, that we should be a kind of firstfruits of his creatures.
> 19 Wherefore, my beloved brethren, let every man be swift to hear, slow to speak, slow to wrath:

> 20 For the wrath of man worketh not the righteousness of God.
> 21 Wherefore lay apart all filthiness and superfluity of naughtiness, and receive with meekness the engrafted word, which is able to save your souls.

Do not err is better translated, "Do not be deceived." The danger of deception is always with us. Satan is known as the "deceiver" (Rev. 12:9; 20:10). He comes as an angel of light and his agents present themselves as ministers of righteousness (2 Cor. 11:14-15). His purpose is to deceive, if possible, even the elect. The cults that proliferate in our confused age testify to the importance of James's warning.

Especially are we in danger of being deceived about God and His purpose for man. God is the Source of *every good gift and every perfect gift* (17). He is the great Giver. He gives wisdom (1:5) and grace (4:6), as well as gifts that come more indirectly and therefore may not be recognized as gifts. Life, health, prosperity, friends—the list of such gifts is almost endless. Above all, He gives life in the sacrifice of His Son (1:12).

God is the unchanging *Father of lights. Variableness* and *shadow of turning* are translations of two astronomical terms. They deal with the relative motions of the planets, the sun, and the earth, the "shifting shadows" (NIV) caused by the rising and setting of the sun in its various seasons of the year. Moffatt translates the verse, "Who knows no change of rising and setting, who casts no shadow on the earth." This is a vivid way of expressing the absolute dependability of God. His purposes do not change like shadows cast by the moving sun. His promises are always true.

Since God is unchanging, His *will* and His *word* (18) are unchanging. Therein lies our security. Translators differ in their understanding of this verse. Some think it refers to the original creation, when God's will was expressed in the words, "Let there be . . .," and man became the firstfruits or crown of creation. A better and more usual view is that it is the new creation that is in mind here (2 Cor. 5:17). We are born of God through His will that none should perish in sin. And the instrument of our new birth is *the word of truth,* that is, the gospel.

It is difficult to overestimate the redemptive power of *the word of truth*. By its preaching, God is pleased to save those who believe (1 Cor. 1:21). It is the means both of our new birth (1 Pet. 1:23) and of our sanctification (John 17:17). "The word of God is" living "and powerful" (Heb. 4:12).

There is a very practical *wherefore* (19) attached to all this. We must be *swift to hear,* quick to listen. Hearing the word of the Lord always carries with it the idea of obedience to what is heard, a point developed in v. 22. With readiness to hear, we are to be *slow to speak*—more ready to listen to what God says than to intrude our own ideas and opinions.

Human anger must be controlled because it does not produce the kind of life God desires. The man who is angry, even "righteously," has for the moment lost total self-control. He is using only part of his nature. He is reacting at the "gut level" rather than with full self-possession. Righteous indignation has its place in a holy life. But it cannot be allowed to get out of hand, and never may it be held to become a smoldering resentment (Eph. 4:26).

We are to get rid of "all that is sordid, and the malice that hurries to excess" (21, NEB). In contrast, we are "in a humble manner [to] receive that Message which has been implanted in [our] hearts" (TCNT). *Engrafted* is literally "implanted." The metaphor is that of a seed rooting itself in the soil (Matt. 13:21; 15:13). It is when the Word becomes part of our thinking and choosing that it becomes the means of our full and final salvation.

Hearing Is Not Enough

James 1:22-25

> 22 But be ye doers of the word, and not hearers only, deceiving your own selves.
> 23 For if any be a hearer of the word, and not a doer, he is like unto a man beholding his natural face in a glass:
> 24 For he beholdeth himself, and goeth his way, and straightway forgetteth what manner of man he was.
> 25 But whoso looketh into the perfect law of liberty, and continueth therein, he being not a forgetful hearer, but a doer of the work, this man shall be blessed in his deed.

James returns to a thought he had earlier dropped (v. 19). It is not enough to *be a hearer of the word* (23) only. One must hear before he can do; but to hear without doing is to become guilty of self-deception (22). Such a person is like one who sees himself in a mirror—that smudge on his face that should be washed away—but who does nothing to remedy the situation.

Here James expresses one of his most characteristic ideas. Theory without practice, hearing without doing, faith without works is anathema to him. It is only as we continue in *the perfect law of liberty* as doers *of the work* (25) that we are blessed.

Perfect law of liberty is an apt description of the moral law the Christian keeps as the offering of his love to his Lord (John 14:15). It is not a law that limits. It is a law that liberates. It sets us free to live as our own best interests demand. It brings the wisdom of God to bear on the moral problems of our existence. It marks out the danger spots to avoid. We do not break God's law. We break ourselves on the realities it warns us against. The man who jumps from a tenth-floor window does not "break" the law of gravity. He just illustrates it.

True Religion

James 1:26-27

> 26 If any man among you seem to be religious, and bridleth not his tongue, but deceiveth his own heart, this man's religion is vain.
> 27 Pure religion and undefiled before God and the Father is this, To visit the fatherless and widows in their affliction, and to keep himself unspotted from the world.

Religion (threskeia) is a word seldom used in the New Testament. Except in this passage in James, it is always used in the sense of false religion. It stands for piety in its external manifestation. To be "religious" in the Greek sense was to be careful in the externals of divine service.

Here James uses the term *religious* and *religion* in the sense of the proper and necessary outward expression of inner devotion to God. Religion has two sides: one is inner, subjective, pertaining to the heart; the other is outer, objective, seen in the life. To ignore the inner demands of piety is to fall into Pharisaism and legalism. To ignore the outer demands of piety is to become sentimental and unreal.

Like the wings of a flying bird or the legs of a walking man, both inner and outer are necessary. God has "joined" them together, and man must not put them asunder. James stresses the need to bring the life into harmony with the heart. He gives us three signs of such harmony:

1. A controlled tongue. To this theme he will come back in the third chapter for major emphasis. An unbridled tongue betrays a defective heart. The professing Christian who vents his bitterness, critical spirit, and general lovelessness by faultfinding, cynicism, gossiping, and backbiting only exposes his own spiritual need.

2. Care for the distressed. *To visit the fatherless and widows* (27) is to "go to the help of" (NEB) those unable to help themselves. In connection with what immediately follows, James makes it clear that he would have no part of the modern bifurcation of the gospel into "social gospel" and "individual gospel." There are not two gospels. There is only one gospel that works both in individuals and in society to meet human needs of both soul and body. James comes back to this point in 2:15-17 with a devastating illustration of the foolishness of separating the social and personal aspects of the Christian faith.

3. Keeping unspotted from the world. This is the importance of being untarnished, uncontaminated, and unstained by the sinful spirit of the world. James uses the term *world* here in the sense of mankind without God, living by the law of sin and death.

Christians have the obligation to be "in the world" but not "of the world." They are to relate redemptively to those around them but retain an integrity that does not compromise with the world's evil or the world's standards. They are to be insulated from the stain of the world but not isolated from its need. Like their Master, they are to be friends of publicans and sinners and at the same time "holy, harmless, undefiled, separate from sinners" (Heb. 7:26).

# JAMES 2

Keeping Life Consistent with Faith
James 2:1-26

The Sin of Snobbery

James 2:1-13

1 My brethren, have not the faith of our Lord Jesus Christ, the Lord of glory, with respect of persons.
2 For if there come unto your assembly a man with a gold ring, in goodly apparel, and there come in also a poor man in vile raiment;
3 And ye have respect to him that weareth the gay clothing, and say unto him, Sit thou here in a good place; and say to the poor, Stand thou there, or sit here under my footstool:
4 Are ye not then partial in yourselves, and are become judges of evil thoughts?
5 Hearken, my beloved brethren, Hath not God chosen the poor of this world rich in faith, and heirs of the kingdom which he hath promised to them that love him?
6 But ye have despised the poor. Do not rich men oppress you, and draw you before the judgment seats?
7 Do not they blaspheme that worthy name by the which ye are called?
8 If ye fulfil the royal law according to the scripture, Thou shalt love thy neighbour as thyself, ye do well:
9 But if ye have respect to persons, ye commit sin, and are convinced of the law as transgressors.
10 For whosoever shall keep the whole law, and yet offend in one point, he is guilty of all.
11 For he that said, Do not commit adultery, said also, Do not kill. Now if thou commit no adultery, yet if thou kill, thou art become a transgressor of the law.
12 So speak ye, and so do, as they that shall be judged by the law of liberty.
13 For he shall have judgment without mercy, that hath shewed no mercy; and mercy rejoiceth against judgment.

Another high tribute to the person of Jesus opens this chapter. *Our Lord Jesus Christ* is named *the Lord of glory*. In the Greek, it is simply "our Lord Jesus Christ the Glory," an expression reminiscent of Simeon's characterization of Jesus as "the glory of thy people Israel" (Luke 2:32). "Glory" is always identified with the living God in the Old Testament.

James affirms the incongruity of professing the Christian faith while having *respect of persons*. This phrase comes from a Greek word that means "to show favoritism," "to be partial." It is frequently said in the Bible that "God is no respecter of persons" (Acts 10:34; Rom.

2:11; Gal. 2:6; Eph. 6:9; etc.). It is therefore not right that His people should be. There is no place in the Christian life for snobbery. God respects purpose and character, but is unimpressed with status or wealth.

1. An illustration of snobbery (2-4). An immediate illustration comes to James's mind. If a well-dressed and obviously prosperous man comes into the company at the same time as one poorly clad and of lower social status, preference shown to the better-appearing individual is partiality of the sort James is condemning. *Judges of evil thoughts* (4) should be translated "judges whose thoughts are evil"—"prejudiced judges" (TCNT); judging "by false standards" (NEB); "critics with evil motives" (Williams); "making judgments based on evil motives" (TEV).

Honesty compels admission that the sin of snobbery is almost universal in the Church today. One all too evident sign is the flight of the evangelical church from the inner city to middle-class suburbs.

It is only right to recall that Dr. P. F. Bresee, founder of the first congregation known as the Church of the Nazarene, did not leave the church of his early ministry in a direct confrontation over doctrine. He left it because of his expressed desire to preach full salvation to the poor. He felt that his former denomination was too committed to seeking the upper middle class and the wealthy to fulfill its God-appointed task.

This does not mean that the "up-and-out" do not need the Lord as much as the down-and-out. But the "up-and-out" have little difficulty getting the service they desire from the Church as well as from other institutions of society. It is the poor who are neglected.

James shows no hesitation in naming this kind of discrimination *evil.* He uses the strongest term in the Greek language for that which is malignantly evil in influence and effect *(poneros).*

2. Character is independent of possessions (5-7). Having illustrated the truth, James then proceeds to show the reason for it. God accepts *the poor of this world* who are *rich*

in faith (5). There is a contrast in these verses between the poor rich man and the rich poor man. Those with little of this world's goods may still be rich in the favor of God and *heirs of the kingdom*—"heirs of God, and joint-heirs with Christ" (Rom. 8:17). To their shame, the people to whom James wrote had *despised* (6) the very ones God had honored.

On the other hand, these Christians themselves had been oppressed and haled into court by the very class of people to whom they showed favoritism. While some people of wealth in the New Testament were Christians (e.g., Joseph of Arimathaea, Barnabas, Lydia, Aquila and Priscilla, and Philemon), it was still true that "not many mighty, not many noble" (1 Cor. 1:26) had accepted the calling. Instead, the interest of the well-to-do in maintaining the status quo caused many of them to *blaspheme that worthy name* (7) from which "Christian" is derived.

Affluence is never an unmixed blessing. John Wesley long ago commented on the strange fact that the fruits of revival tend to destroy the revival. When men are converted, they leave the sins that wasted their means and become honest and industrious. As a result, they begin to prosper. But when they begin to prosper, their tendency is to trust their prosperity more than God. Thus the fruits of revival consume the revival.

The solution to the paradox, Mr. Wesley said, is for Christians to "earn all they can and save all they can" in order to "give all they can." When a man of God begins to prosper, it is always a question whether the Kingdom will gain a fortune or lose a man. It is always one or the other. Wealth is a blessing only when it is regarded as a stewardship to be administered for the glory of God.

3. The whole law of God must be kept (8-13). *Thou shalt love thy neighbour as thyself* is *the royal law*. Since discrimination and partiality violate this law, they are sinful attitudes. Those who are guilty are condemned by the law itself *as transgressors* (9).

This is no light matter. James argues that to break one commandment of the law is to break it *in toto*. The reason is that the same God who gave one commandment gave all the rest. "There is no little sin," we say, "because there is no little God to sin against."

Bishop William Taylor used to illustrate this truth by comparing the law to a fence with 10 gates. To go out any one of the gates is to be outside the law. The one who goes out the gate of Sabbath desecration is as surely outside as the one who goes out the gate of adultery. The one who goes out the gate of false witness is as surely outside as the one who goes out the gate of murder.

This does not mean that the consequences of one sin are as serious as another in terms of their effects on others. What it means is that to disregard the will of God in any particular brings condemnation and guilt to the soul, whatever the issue may be. The will of God is a golden chain with many links. To break any link is to break the chain.

In consequence, we are to *speak* and to *do* as those who *shall be judged by the law of liberty* (12). In 1:25, James called it "the perfect law of liberty." The argument concludes with the solemn truth that *judgment without mercy* shall be visited on the one who shows *no mercy* (13).

Nowhere in scripture is this final truth more forcefully stated than by Jesus in the parable of the two debtors (Matt. 18:23-35). The king cancelled one debtor's obligation of $10 million. But when the man refused mercy to one who owed him $20.00, the entire debt was reinstated. Jesus said, "So likewise shall my heavenly Father do also unto you, if ye from your hearts forgive not every one his brother their trespasses" (v. 35).

So "mercy triumphs over judgment" (RSV). "Blessed are the merciful: for they shall obtain mercy" (Matt. 5:7). The Christian who knows true mercy will not judge others. He knows that he will himself be judged with the judgment he imposes on others (Matt. 7:1-2; Rom. 2:1). The sound psychological principle behind this is the fact that the faults we see in others are usually the faults we hide in ourselves.

The Proof of True Faith

James 2:14-26

> 14 What doth it profit, my brethren, though a man say he hath faith, and have not works? can faith save him?
> 15 If a brother or sister be naked, and destitute of daily food,
> 16 And one of you say unto them, Depart in peace, be ye warmed and filled; notwithstanding ye give them not those things which are needful to the body; what doth it profit?
> 17 Even so faith, if it hath not works, is dead, being alone.
> 18 Yea, a man may say, Thou hast faith, and I have works: shew me thy faith without thy works, and I will shew thee my faith by my works.
> 19 Thou believest that there is one God; thou doest well: the devils also believe, and tremble.
> 20 But wilt thou know, O vain man, that faith without works is dead?
> 21 Was not Abraham our father justified by works, when he had offered Isaac his son upon the altar?
> 22 Seest thou how faith wrought with his works, and by works was faith made perfect?
> 23 And the scripture was fulfilled which saith, Abraham believed God, and it was imputed unto him for righteousness: and he was called the Friend of God.
> 24 Ye see then how that by works a man is justified, and not by faith only.
> 25 Likewise also was not Rahab the harlot justified by works, when she had received the messengers, and had sent them out another way?
> 26 For as the body without the spirit is dead, so faith without works is dead also.

This passage is the one that has made James a byword to those who regard Christianity as perpetual forgiveness for perpetual sinning. This is his plea for realism in religion.

1. A favorite catchword of Reformation religion was *sole fide,* "by faith alone." The truth James would make clear is that faith is never alone. To claim saving faith without manifesting obedient love is but to deceive oneself.

If recent New Testament study has made one point certain beyond the possibility of reasonable doubt, it is that evangelical faith and obedience are two sides to one coin. True, there is a sort of intellectual assent to the truth of the gospel which is without fruit in a changed life. But this sort of intellectual assent is far from what the New Testament means by faith.

The Greek language has one word for both unbelief and disobedience. "Whoever believes in the Son has eternal life; whoever disobeys the Son will never have life, but God's wrath will remain on him for ever" (John 3:36, TEV). Faith and disobedience are true contradictories.

So far are Paul and James from being at odds on this that in his great letter on justification by faith Paul speaks of "obedience to the faith" or literally "the obedience which faith is" (Rom. 1:5), and uses the phrase "obey the gospel" as equivalent to "believe the gospel."

2. James gives another of his pointed illustrations. If a brother is *destitute* and the Christian expresses a fine sentiment without relieving the need, what is the value? Baron von Hugel is remembered for his definition of a Christian: "A Christian is one who cares."

E. Stanley Jones has said: "Christians were sensitized to human need. That is important, for 'life is sensitivity.' The lowest life is sensitive only to itself. The higher in the scale of existence you come, the wider the range of sensitivity and the deeper the depth. When you come to the highest life ever lived on this planet, the life of Jesus, you find complete sensitivity. ('Inasmuch as ye did it unto one of the least of these, ye did it unto me.') He was hungry in their hunger, bound in their imprisonment, lonely in their being strangers."[2]

James puts it bluntly: *Even so faith, if it hath not works, is dead, being alone* (17). *Works* is James's shorthand word for all a Christian does for Christ and others. It is impossible to demonstrate faith without the works that are its fruit (18). Even demons *believe* in God, and *tremble* in that belief. But they are demons still (19). The *vain man* ("foolish fellow," RSV; "idle boaster," Weymouth) must be told bluntly and finally: *Faith without works is dead* (20).

3. James now turns to two Old Testament illustrations. They are drawn from opposite realms of experience and stand in sharp contrast to each other. Yet both show clearly the need for holding together true faith and loving obedience.

a. The faith of Abraham, 21-24. No name meant more to a Jew than the name of Abraham. Abraham was universally respected as the father of the nation. His willingness to offer his son Isaac was a clear example of the reflex action of works as the fruit of faith, and faith as made perfect by works (21-23).

This two-way relationship between faith and obedience is of great practical importance. Faith leads to obedience. But obedience in turn strengthens faith. "If any man will do his will, he shall know of the doctrine, whether it be of God, or whether I speak of myself," said Jesus (John 7:17). Augustine wrote, "The Word of God belongs to those who obey it." Both understanding and faith depend upon obedience.

There are indeed real intellectual problems in the Christian faith. Yet in many cases, the root of the problem is "not with the Apostles' Creed but with the Ten Commandments." Disobedience creates doubt. Obedience dissolves doubt.

James does not dispute the record of Gen. 15:6 or the application Paul made of the same truth in Rom. 4:1-3: "Abraham believed God, and it was counted unto him for righteousness." He simply points out that a faith lacking in obedience is not faith at all. The only way the scripture can say that Abraham believed God and was counted righteous is that Abraham's faith was both genuine and full. Justification is not by a truncated faith that has no obedience in it. Justification is by a faith that works (24). Paul says this also in Gal. 5:6.

b. The faith of Rahab, 25-26. The second illustration of faith is Rahab, the Canaanite woman who hid Israel's two spies (Joshua 2). Some have thought to soften the meaning of the term *harlot* as applied to Rahab (Josh. 2:1) on the ground that the same term may mean simply "innkeeper." But the word James uses *(porne)* admits of no softening. It means a prostitute, an immoral woman.

The faith of Abraham, the seeking pilgrim from Ur, was the faith that finds truth and righteousness through obedience. The faith of Rahab, the prostitute, was the faith that redeems and lifts the fallen. How complete was that redemption is testified to by Matthew in his genealogy of Jesus (Matt. 1:5-6). A man of the tribe of Judah by the name of Salmon married Rahab. They had a son named Boaz (Ruth 4:21-22; Matt. 2:5). Boaz married Ruth, the Moabitess widow. Their son Obed was the father of Jesse and the grandfather of King David, from whose line of descent came Jesus the Messiah.

James concludes his discussion with an analogy already introduced in vv. 17 and 20: *For as the body without the spirit is dead, so faith without works is dead also* (26). A religion of externals is a ghost, spirit without body. But a subjective faith without loving obedience to the will of God is a corpse. The one is futile. The other is empty. What our day demands, as has every day, is full-orbed faith expressing itself in love and obedience.

JAMES 3

The Tongue and True Wisdom
James 3:1-18

Two main topics are considered in c. 3. They are closely related. In vv. 1-12, James deals with control of the tongue. In vv. 13-18, he contrasts false and true wisdom.

Controlling the Tongue

James 3:1-12

> 1 My brethren, be not many masters, knowing that we shall receive the greater condemnation.
> 2 For in many things we offend all. If any man offend not in word, the same is a perfect man, and able also to bridle the whole body.
> 3 Behold, we put bits in the horses' mouths, that they may obey us; and we turn about their whole body.
> 4 Behold also the ships, which though they be so great, and are driven of fierce winds, yet are they turned about with a very small helm, whithersoever the governor listeth.
> 5 Even so the tongue is a little member, and boasteth great things. Behold, how great a matter a little fire kindleth!
> 6 And the tongue is a fire, a world of iniquity: so is the tongue among our members, that it defileth the whole body, and setteth on fire the course of nature; and it is set on fire of hell.
> 7 For every kind of beasts, and of birds, and of serpents, and of things in the sea, is tamed, and hath been tamed of mankind:
> 8 But the tongue can no man tame; it is an unruly evil, full of deadly poison.
> 9 Therewith bless we God, even the Father; and therewith curse we men, which are made after the similitude of God.
> 10 Out of the same mouth proceedeth blessing and cursing. My brethren, these things ought not so to be.

> 11 Doth a fountain send forth at the same place sweet water and bitter?
> 12 Can the fig tree, my brethren, bear olive berries? either a vine, figs? so can no fountain both yield salt water and fresh.

James opens with a caution against seeking too quickly the office of teacher. *Be not many masters* (1) is translated, "Do not crowd in to be teachers," by Moffatt. The reason is that those who take it upon themselves to teach others will be judged with greater strictness. "In many things we all stumble" (2, ASV).

1. Particularly difficult to avoid is the misuse of the tongue. Speech is one of God's best gifts to man. But, like all other good gifts, it is subject to the grossest misuse. He who can control his tongue can control the rest of his body.

Four illustrations of the key importance of right speech are given:

a. The tongue is like the bit in a horse's mouth (3)—it controls the entire animal.

b. The tongue is like the rudder of a ship (4). Compared to the bulk of the vessel, it is *very small*. Yet it determines the way the ship will go.

c. The tongue is like a spark that kindles a forest fire (5-6). It both mars the life of the individual and inflames his relationships with all others. An evil tongue is a spark from the fires of hell—the "Gehenna" of everlasting flame.

d. The tongue is an untamed animal (7-9). Nearly all animals may be domesticated. But the tongue is like a poisonous serpent. It will not subject itself to the human will.

2. One characteristic of the untamed tongue is its inconsistency. With the tongue we *bless* (literally, "speak well of") *God.* With the tongue we *curse* (literally, "speak evil of") *men,* who are created in God's image (9). *These things ought not so to be* is a characteristic Hebrew understatement (10). We ought to understand it as Phillips translates it: "This is the sort of thing that never ought to happen!" The incongruity is like a fountain or spring giving both sweet and salty water (11) or a tree or vine that bears mixed fruit (12).

James here but echoes and illustrates what Jesus had

stated: "Out of the abundance of the heart the mouth speaketh" (Matt. 12:34). "By thy words thou shalt be justified, and by thy words thou shalt be condemned" (Matt. 12:37). One may fairly say that there are few injunctions in scripture so widely "honored in the breach" as these.

3. James did not enlarge on these truths. There is little doubt, however, that he had at least two things in mind:

a. He was thinking of what is commonly called gossiping. This is spreading surmises injurious to the good names of others. It was said of one person that he had a "very keen sense of rumor"!

Gossip is generally masked. It is easily rationalized. Ken Anderson penned the lines in his volume of humorous but searching verse entitled *Stains on Glass Windows:*

> *I heard it from a trusted source,*
> *So there's no cause to doubt it,*
> *And only tell it now, of course,*
> *So you can pray about it.*

b. He was thinking of what would be called destructive criticism. There is an evaluation of persons and situations that is constructive and necessary. But there is much more criticism than there ought to be that is pointless and detrimental.

Some of this sort of negative criticism is a reflection of the critic's own sense of inferiority or inadequacy. Those who are forever "downing themselves" inwardly will often be heard putting others down.

In some cases, negative criticism is a sort of "substitute security." When a person makes others appear worse, it seems to make him appear better. It is assumed that censure implies superiority. But, as Disraeli once said, it is "much easier to be critical than to be correct."

Criticism is at its worst when covered with a cloak of religious piety. Edward Carnell, who could have offered a great deal of firsthand evidence at this point, was right in his remark that "Christ did not shed His blood so that we might spend our days as spiritual vultures, feeding on the carrion of other people's shortcomings."

In *No Longer Strangers,* Bruce Larson wrote: "How often we Christians have assumed that our job is to underscore other people's problems, sins, and mistakes! When we really believe in the Holy Spirit and the work which God has said He would do in every heart, then we know that our job is not to criticize. It is God who lets people know where they are wrong and where they need to change. . . . Christians are not meant to take the place of the Holy Spirit and become super-detectives, ferreting out people's sins and weaknesses and underscoring them. When we employ this kind of strategy, it is no wonder people fail to discover the grace of God in and through us."[3]

Wisdom: False and True

The chapter closes with a contrast between wisdom that is false and wisdom that is true. The thought is similar to that expressed by Paul in 1 Cor. 1:17-31. It is stated in the fiery phrases characteristic of James.

James 3:13-18

> 13 Who is a wise man and endued with knowledge among you? let him shew out of a good conversation his works with meekness of wisdom.
> 14 But if ye have bitter envying and strife in your hearts, glory not, and lie not against the truth.
> 15 This wisdom descendeth not from above, but is earthly, sensual, devilish.
> 16 For where envying and strife is, there is confusion and every evil work.
> 17 But the wisdom that is from above is first pure, then peaceable, gentle, and easy to be intreated, full of mercy and good fruits, without partiality, and without hypocrisy.
> 18 And the fruit of righteousness is sown in peace of them that make peace.

The test of the wise man is the same as the test of the man of faith. The wise man, worthy of being heard as a teacher, will "prove it by his good life, by his good deeds performed with humility and wisdom" (13, TEV). As it is with faith, not what one says about it but the style and spirit of his life is what measures a man's wisdom.

1. False wisdom is described as to its nature and source, and as to its results (14-16).

a. False wisdom *is earthly, sensual, devilish* (15) in nature. Its source is *not from above.* It is not from God. *Sensual* is the same term Paul used to describe the "natural" or unregenerate man in 1 Cor. 2:14. This is the person devoid of the Spirit of God who cannot understand the things of the Spirit. *Devilish* is *daimoniodes* in the original—literally, "demonlike."

b. The results of false wisdom are envy and selfish ambition in the individual, and evil practices in the group. *Strife* (14,16) is *eritheia*. It means "ambition," "self-seeking," "the manifestation of stubborn self-will." It is properly coupled with envy and jealousy—a desire for what another has even at cost of depriving the other.

False wisdom puts self at the center of life. The Holy Spirit will not tolerate the so-called *self* sins in any Christian: self-pity, self-seeking, self-confidence, self-righteousness, self-aggrandizement. The drive to be always right, always to have one's own way, is not strength but weakness. Samuel Young commented, "The man who works for himself has the worst employer in the world." The only time some people see their god is when they look in a mirror!

False wisdom does not mean stupidity, dullness, lack of intellect, or even ignorance. It is possible, Peter Forsyth said, to be "too clever ever to be very wise." False wisdom is essentially a spiritual and moral problem. Its correction is not education but enlightenment, not graduation from college but grace from God.

2. In contrast with false wisdom is true wisdom (17-18). The contrast is in both its source and its nature, and in its results. In source, true wisdom *is from above*. It comes from God (1:5). It has seven characteristics:

a. It is *pure*. This is first. The term in Greek is *hagne*, from the same root as *hagios*, "holy." It means uncontaminated, free from defilement.

b. It is *peaceable*, literally "irenic," peace-loving, peaceful. The original term implies harmonious relationships, right order prevailing, quietness.

c. It is *gentle*, considerate, forbearing, "equitable, fair, moderate, not insisting on the letter of the law" (W. E. Vine), not contentious.

d. It is *easy to be intreated*, "conciliatory" (Moffatt), "open to reason" (RSV), "willing to yield" (Goodspeed), literally, "ready to obey, compliant."

e. It is *full of mercy and good fruits,* "full of compassion and produces a harvest of good deeds" (TEV).

f. It is *without partiality,* impartial, free from prejudice. This is literally "not judging" (cf. 2:4).

g. It is *without hypocrisy,* without pretense, sincere, not playacting. The word for *hypocrisy* was used originally of actors in a play, then of the masks they wore, and finally of any sort of pretense.

Just as true wisdom contrasts with false wisdom in its source and in its nature, so it contrasts with the false in its results. Instead of *confusion and every evil work* (16), true wisdom results in *the fruit of righteousness* which *is sown in peace* by those who work for *peace* (18). These are the peacemakers of whom Jesus said they should "be called the children of God" (Matt. 5:9).

JAMES 4

Dangers to Christian Living
James 4:1-17

Three subjects are considered in c. 4. All relate to dangers encountered in Christian living.

Sources of Defeat in the Christian Life

James 4:1-10

> 1 From whence come wars and fightings among you? come they not hence, even of your lusts that war in your members?
> 2 Ye lust, and have not: ye kill, and desire to have, and cannot obtain: ye fight and war, yet ye have not, because ye ask not.
> 3 Ye ask, and receive not, because ye ask amiss, that ye may consume it upon your lusts.
> 4 Ye adulterers and adulteresses, know ye not that the friendship of the world is enmity with God? whosoever therefore will be a friend of the world is the enemy of God.
> 5 Do ye think that the scripture saith in vain, The spirit that dwelleth in us lusteth to envy?
> 6 But he giveth more grace. Wherefore he saith, God resisteth the proud, but giveth grace unto the humble.
> 7 Submit yourselves therefore to God. Resist the devil, and he will flee from you.

8 Draw nigh to God, and he will draw nigh to you. Cleanse your hands, ye sinners; and purify your hearts, ye double minded.
9 Be afflicted, and mourn, and weep: let your laughter be turned to mourning, and your joy to heaviness.
10 Humble yourselves in the sight of the Lord, and he shall lift you up.

1. Self-centered living (1-3). James makes reference to some of the disorders found in the Church. His charge is that the *wars and fightings* ("fights and quarrels," TEV) *among* them are the outer reflection of "the desires which are always at war within" (TCNT) them. Their outer conflicts reveal inner problems.

The picture is not a pretty one. In spite of unprincipled self-interest, they find themselves frustrated and defeated. Taking matters into their own hands, they fail to get what they want because they do not ask God for it (2). Even when they pray, their prayers are not answered because their motives are wrong. They seek God's gifts only to consume them on their own desires (3). The petition "Bless me, Lord" is basically immoral unless with it, in word or intention, we pray, "and make me a blessing."

2. Compromise with the spirit of the world (4). The pleasure-seeking motive leads to compromise with the world. James calls these people *adulterers and adulteresses* (4), "unfaithful people!" (TEV). Flirting with the world is spiritual infidelity. This is prophetic language, strongly reminiscent of Hos. 1:2; 2:13; Jer. 5:7; 9:2; etc. They must know that morally compromising *friendship* with *the world is enmity with God.*

The world is not used here in the sense that "God so loved the world, that he gave his only begotten Son" (John 3:16). It is used in the sense of *"the world apart from God,* the godlessness of the world, the world's disregard for God, the world's resentment of the standards of God, the world's intentness on its own ways and its refusal of the ways of God" (Barclay).

The spirit of the world is very insidious. It may creep into the Church quite unrecognized. A. W. Tozer probes the consciences of Christians with a series of questions in his book *The Divine Conquest:* "What can we say then when Christian men vie with one another for place and position? What can we answer when we see them hungrily seeking for praise and honor? How can we excuse that passion for publicity which is so glaringly evident among Christian leaders? What about political ambition in Church circles? What about the fevered palm that is stretched out for more and bigger 'love offerings'? What about the shameless egotism among Christians? How can we explain the gross man-worship that habitually blows up one and another popular leader to the size of a colossus? What about the obsequious hand-kissing of moneyed men by those purporting to be sound preachers of the gospel?"[4]

Dr. Tozer answers his questions with a thought-provoking comment: "There is only one answer to these questions; it is simply that in these manifestations we see the world and nothing but the world. No passionate profession of love for 'souls' can change evil into good. These are the very sins that crucified Jesus."[5]

3. The strivings of a carnal heart (5). V. 5 is admittedly one of the most difficult in the letter. It is given as a saying of scripture. Yet there is no biblical passage that can be recognized as its source. It is possible that James is summarizing what he understands as the whole sweep of scripture.

Even the statement is difficult to interpret. Translators and commentators are divided as to what it means. A number of them take *The spirit that dwelleth in us* to be the Holy Spirit, who strives within us to keep us loyal to God. Thus Weymouth, "The Spirit which He has caused to dwell in us yearns jealously over us." Others take the verse to mean that God yearns for the complete loyalty of the human spirit He has placed within us. This is Moffatt's understanding: "He yearns jealously for the spirit he set within us."

A third possibility is suggested by the KJV rendering, to which the NEB virtually returns: "The spirit which God implanted in man turns toward envious desires." "The spirit that God placed in us is filled with fierce desires" (TEV). This is the human spirit, created by God, but corrupted by sin and controlled by the lusts of the carnal nature. This is the "flesh which lusteth against the [Holy] Spirit" (Gal. 5:17); the "carnal mind," which is "enmity against God: for it is not subject to the law of God, neither indeed can be" (Rom. 8:7).

The remedy for this condition is the *more grace* God *giveth* (6). The Greek reads literally, "He gives greater [or 'a greater'] grace." This grace is unknown to the proud and self-sufficient. It is given abundantly to the humble. This is "sanctifying grace," the greater "grace wherein we stand, and rejoice in hope of the glory of God" (Rom. 5:2).

The way to greater grace is to *submit yourselves therefore to God* (7). The word translated *submit* is *hupotasso*. It is primarily a military term. It means literally to "rank under," to be of lower rank. It means to be subject to or under obedience to. It is almost a synonym for Paul's great term *yield* or *present* (Rom. 6:13; 12:1), the New Testament words that carry the meaning we ordinarily attach to *consecrate* or *consecration*.

Thomas Barclay, who served as a missionary in Formosa many years, left a written dedication of himself that conveys the thought. It was his practice to sign it anew each year. Part of the covenant read: "This day do I surrender myself to Thee. I renounce all former lords that have had dominion over me, and I consecrate to Thee all that I have: the faculties of my mind, the members of my body, my worldly possessions, my time, my influence: to be used entirely for Thy glory, and resolutely employed in obedience to Thy commands, as long as Thou continuest me in life; with an ardent desire and humble resolution to continue Thine through all the ages of eternity.... To Thee I leave the management of all events, and say without reserve, 'Not my will, but Thine, be done.'"[6]

4. Resisting the devil (7). The sequence here is correct. We must submit ourselves to God before we can successfully resist the devil. Many have resisted the devil without submitting to God and have found that he did not flee. Our victory is in having on "the whole armour of God"

(cf. Eph. 6:10-20). Satan is a defeated foe to one who has submitted himself to God (1 Pet. 5:8-9).

5. "Clean hands, and a pure heart" (8). James parallels Ps. 24:4 in this verse: those may ascend into the hill of the Lord and stand in His holy place who have "clean hands, and a pure heart." *Clean hands* represent a life cleansed of the guilt of sins committed. *A pure heart* resolves the problem of double-mindedness. "Purity of heart is to will one thing," said Kierkegaard. As Mendell Taylor describes it, "Everything inside is on God's side."

6. The reward of true humility (9-10). James seems now to be addressing a wider audience. The first step into the Christian life is the humbling experience of repentance. The first two beatitudes are: "Blessed are the poor in spirit: for theirs is the kingdom of heaven. Blessed are they that mourn: for they shall be comforted" (Matt. 5:3-4).

There is a false humility that talks of the "poor, weak worm of the dust" and carries a "'scuse me for living" attitude. It is often a bid for attention or sympathy and masks an attitude the very opposite of what it professes. The humility God calls for is a deep recognition of human dependence upon Him. All our boasted self-sufficiency must be laid aside. When we thus humble ourselves before the Lord, *he shall lift* us *up* (10).

The Sin of Judging

James 4:11-12
> 11 Speak not evil one of another, brethren. He that speaketh evil of his brother, and judgeth his brother, speaketh evil of the law, and judgeth the law: but if thou judge the law, thou art not a doer of the law, but a judge.
> 12 There is one lawgiver, who is able to save and to destroy: who art thou that judgest another?

James comes back again to the sin of evil speaking. The word he uses is *katalalia,* literally, "to talk against" another. It is translated "backbiting" elsewhere in the KJV New Testament. Its meaning is to speak evil of someone in that person's absence, hence, "to bite behind the back" when the individual is not present to defend himself.

To speak evil of and judge another is to break the law that says, "Thou shalt love thy neighbour as thyself." One who breaks the law sets himself above the law. He actually judges it and speaks against the law itself. To judge another is to set oneself up in the place of God, the *one lawgiver, who is able to save and to destroy* (12). What is any man that he should thus presume to sit on God's judgment throne?

The Uncertain Future

James 4:13-17

> 13 Go to now, ye that say, To day or to morrow we will go into such a city, and continue there a year, and buy and sell, and get gain:
> 14 Whereas ye know not what shall be on the morrow. For what is your life? It is even a vapour, that appeareth for a little time, and then vanisheth away.
> 15 For that ye ought to say, If the Lord will, we shall live, and do this, or that.
> 16 But now ye rejoice in your boastings: all such rejoicing is evil.
> 17 Therefore to him that knoweth to do good, and doeth it not, to him it is sin.

That God has veiled the future from our eyes is in most respects a blessing. We are called upon to live but one day at a time. Planning for the future, without the reservation *"If the Lord will"* implied if not stated, is, like judging, taking to oneself the prerogatives of God. The only absolutely sure prediction we can make is that most of our predictions will be wrong!

Human life at best is a fleeting thing, like a morning cloud that appears for a while and quickly disappears (14). We do not know what the future holds. We know who holds the future. As William Barclay writes: "The true Christian way is not to be terrorized into fear, and not to be paralysed into inaction, by the uncertainty of the future, but to commit the future and all our plans into the hands of God, and always to remember that our plans may not be within the purpose of God."

V. 17 must not be taken from its context and generalized into a principle that every unrealized ideal is sin. James is simply calling attention again to the fact that it is not enough to know the right way. It is necessary to follow the right way. It is one thing to have the blueprint; it is something else to build the building. It is one thing to have the road map; it is quite another to take the journey.

James has set forth the truth about Christian living and its imperatives. His readers know what is right. Now they must do it. There are many whose sins are sins of commission. They do what they have been forbidden to do. There are many more whose sins are sins of omission. They fail to do what they have been commanded to do. Both kinds of sin are death to the soul and fall under the judgment of God.

JAMES 5

Patience and Prayer
James 5:1-20

Four topics make up c. 5. After another warning to men of wealth, the author writes of the need for patient endurance, the value of prayer, and the reclamation of those who stray.

Another Warning to the Rich

James 5:1-6

> 1 Go to now, ye rich men, weep and howl for your miseries that shall come upon you.
> 2 Your riches are corrupted, and your garments are motheaten.
> 3 Your gold and silver is cankered; and the rust of them shall be a witness against you, and shall eat your flesh as it were fire. Ye have heaped treasure together for the last days.
> 4 Behold, the hire of the labourers who have reaped down your fields, which is of you kept back by fraud, crieth: and the cries of them which have reaped are entered into the ears of the Lord of Sabaoth.
> 5 Ye have lived in pleasure on the earth, and been wanton; ye have nourished your hearts, as in a day of slaughter.
> 6 Ye have condemned and killed the just; and he doth not resist you.

James's strongest attack on the sins of the wealthy is reserved for this last chapter. It may fairly be wondered if James expected many rich people to read these words. It is more probable that his purpose is to warn humble and generally poor Christians about the utter foolishness of trusting in riches and the danger wealth poses to the character of those who possess it.

1. **Wealth is but for a day** (1-3). The temporary character of earthly treasures is the theme of these verses. On earth, said Jesus, "moth and rust doth corrupt, and . . . thieves break through and steal" (Matt. 6:19). Treasure laid up under such conditions is a poor object of trust, to say the least.

2. Even more dangerous is what money does to those obsessed with it (4-6). Mammon is a god who incites his followers to gain more wealth by any means possible. The rich withhold the wages of those who work for them. They give themselves to pleasures and wantonness. They persecute the just who are unable to resist them. The corrosion of ill-gotten gains will eat the very flesh of its holders like fire (cf. v. 3).

It is necessary to see the principle here. What counts is not what we have, but what has us. J. B. Chapman told of going to a rural church to preach during the depths of the Great Depression of the late twenties and early thirties. The people were poor and discouraged. The pastor, he said, asked him to preach from the text "The love of money is the root of all evil."

"That looks like the last problem your people would have," he replied. "They don't appear to have enough money to bother them."

"But it doesn't say, 'Money is the root of all evil,'" the pastor said. "It says, 'The *love of* money is the root of all evil.' The people don't have it, but they love it just the same."

Even those with only moderate amounts of this world's goods are constantly tempted to spend money they cannot afford to get things they do not need in order to impress people they do not like!

Patient Endurance

James 5:7-12

> 7 Be patient therefore, brethren, unto the coming of the Lord. Behold, the husbandman waiteth for the precious fruit of the earth, and hath long patience for it, until he receive the early and latter rain.
> 8 Be ye also patient; stablish your hearts: for the coming of the Lord draweth nigh.
> 9 Grudge not one against another, brethren, lest ye be condemned: behold, the judge standeth before the door.

10 Take, my brethren, the prophets, who have spoken in the name of the Lord, for an example of suffering affliction, and of patience.
11 Behold, we count them happy which endure. Ye have heard of the patience of Job, and have seen the end of the Lord; that the Lord is very pitiful, and of tender mercy.
12 But above all things, my brethren, swear not, either by heaven, neither by the earth, neither by any other oath: but let your yea be yea; and your nay, nay; lest ye fall into condemnation.

The English word *patience* is used five times in the KJV of this passage. The Greek term thus translated is *makrothumeo*. It literally means "long-tempered"—the opposite of the common expression "short-tempered." It is usually translated "longsuffering." It is self-restraint in the face of provocation. It is the quality of character that does not surrender to circumstances or go down under trial. It is the opposite of despair, and is usually associated with hope.

1. Patience waits for the harvest (7). Faith and hope combine to justify the patience with which the farmer waits for the seed to germinate, grow, and ripen into harvest. No amount of worry or fretting will speed up the harvest by as much as a single day. Each worker in the Kingdom needs to learn that it is not only work but worry that makes one weary.

2. The coming of the Lord is at hand (8-9). The return of Christ is mentioned three times in vv. 7-9. Early Christians remembered Jesus' promise that if He went away He would come again and receive them to himself (John 14: 1-3). They lived in constant readiness for and expectancy of His coming. We who live more than 1,900 years closer to the event should also be ready, for we know not the day nor the hour when the Son of Man will come again.

Grudge not (9) means, "Do not complain, murmur, or grumble." To do so is to run the risk of being judged, and the Judge is already standing at the door.

3. Our example (10-11). We are encouraged to take heart from the example of the prophets. We count them happy because they did not give up when the going was hard. The faithful endurance of Job and the outcome of his testing proves that our God is compassionate and merciful.

4. One's word as good as a bond (12). The Christian's word

should be as good as a bond. This verse is a direct reference to Matt. 5:34-37 from the Sermon on the Mount. The command here does not refer to legal oaths. It simply means that one's reputation for truthfulness should be such that when he says, Yes, it will be accepted as Yes without a confirming oath.

Prayer and Healing

James 5:13-18

> 13 Is any among you afflicted? let him pray. Is any merry? let him sing psalms.
> 14 Is any sick among you? let him call for the elders of the church; and let them pray over him, anointing him with oil in the name of the Lord:
> 15 And the prayer of faith shall save the sick, and the Lord shall raise him up; and if he have committed sins, they shall be forgiven him.
> 16 Confess your faults one to another, and pray one for another, that ye may be healed. The effectual fervent prayer of a righteous man availeth much.
> 17 Elias was a man subject to like passions as we are, and he prayed earnestly that it might not rain: and it rained not on the earth by the space of three years and six months.
> 18 And he prayed again, and the heaven gave rain, and the earth brought forth her fruit.

James gives suggestions for contrasting conditions of life. Those in trouble should pray. Those who are "in good spirits" (Weymouth) or "in a happy mood" (Williams) should sing psalms—literally, "songs of praise."

1. Sickness is a time for special care on the part of the Christian community. The sick should *call for the elders of the church* (14). These are not necessarily ministers. Lay leaders were called *elders* in the New Testament. They would be persons of faith and experience. To *pray over* is to pray about the sick. *Anointing . . . with oil* has been understood both as a religious rite and as the application of appropriate medical remedies. For example, Luke 10:34 relates the medicinal use of oil and wine in treating wounds.

It is interesting to note the use of the term *save* in relation to healing. The New Testament often uses *save* as a synonym for "heal" or "make whole." Salvation and healing are closely related. Salvation delivers from sins that destroy body and mind. It is also the gateway to physical healing for many. Dr. S. I. McMillen, a medical doctor, says, "Physicians know that about two-thirds of our physical and emotional symptoms stem from the carnal emotions of jealousy, envy, self-centeredness, resentment, anger, and guilt." He quotes Dr. William Sadler's emphasized words in the *Practice of Psychiatry: "The sincere acceptance of the principles and teachings of Christ with respect to the life of mental peace and joy, the life of unselfish thought and clean living, would at once wipe out more than half the difficulties, diseases, and sorrows of the human race."*

When sickness strikes, as it may the most sincere of God's children, many experience divine healing. Others, as Paul in 2 Cor. 12:7-10, receive sufficient grace to live adequately in spite of physical infirmities. To claim that any and all may be healed if they but have sufficient faith is to go beyond what scripture states. On the other hand, many Christians doubtless suffer needlessly because they do not follow the directions of the Bible in regard to prayer for healing.

Nor is it scriptural to attribute all sickness to sin. If sin has been the cause, the sin will be forgiven. But the conditional form of the statement clearly shows that individual instances of sickness may come from causes other than personal sin.

2. Christians are urged to confess their *faults one to another, and pray one for another, that* they *may be healed* (16). *Faults* is actually "sins" in the better Greek texts of the New Testament. This should not be taken to counsel the indiscriminate public confession of sins in the church. A sound principle is that the area of commission should be the area of confession. Secret sins should be confessed specifically to God alone. Sins against persons should be confessed to those persons, as far as this is possible. Public sins should be publicly confessed. Confession should never be used as an occasion for further injury. When in doubt, the individual should seek the counsel of godly pastors or older and more mature Christians.

3. The power of prayer is stated and illustrated. "Tremendous power is made available through a good man's

earnest prayer" (Phillips). Elijah's prayer for drouth and later for rain is a classic example. Elijah was "a man with human frailties like our own" (17, NEB). There was nothing unique about him that would account for the results he obtained through prayer. Therefore, similar power is open to men of faith today.

This is the kind of prayer that changes conditions and circumstances. It rests on the foundation of a life of devotion. Tenis Van Kooten wrote in *Building the Family Altar:* "The only ones who know how to pray on the run are those who have learned to know God in the quietness of sitting with him. You call to your friend to help you as he passes by your home. But he did not become your friend by your calling to him. Your friendship was there, you could now call to him in confidence when he passes your home. So, too, you can pray on the run, but only when you already know God through much personal fellowship with him."[7]

Reclaiming Those Who Stray

James 5:19-20

>19 Brethren, if any of you do err from the truth, and one convert him;
>20 Let him know, that he which converteth the sinner from the error of his way shall save a soul from death, and shall hide a multitude of sins.

The Epistle ends rather abruptly but on a positive note. James has condemned, throughout, laxness in the faith and practice of the Christian community. He is the foe of all unchristlike traits and attitudes.

Yet the intention of it all is not to condemn but to reclaim. His last words call for utmost concern for those who have turned aside. *The truth* is one of James's names for the gospel (1:18; 3:14), an expression John (1:17; 5:23; 8:32) and Paul (Rom. 1:18, 25, etc.) also use. James is under no illusion that a Christian can go back into sin and still be saved from death. Such erring believers must be converted—literally, "turned out of the error of his way."

The effect of reclaiming the backslider is to *save a soul from death, and . . . hide a multitude of sins.* The *multitude of sins* are not only those of the backslider, already committed, but those that would result from his influence on others.

James is one of three books in the New Testament to end without an "Amen" at the close (the others are Acts and 3 John). The abruptness of the ending may account for this. But there is also the suggestion that the problems with which James deals will never all be resolved. They will be with us until Jesus comes again.

The First Epistle of
PETER

Topical Outline of First Peter

Introduction

Salutation, 1:1-2

God's Saving Power, 1:3-12
> The Basis of Our Faith, 1:3-5
> The Trial of Our Faith, 1:6-9
> Faith as Fulfillment, 1:10-12

The Call to Holiness, 1:13—2:10
> The Supreme Motivation, 1:13-16
> The Price of Our Redemption, 1:17-21
> A Pure Love, 1:22-25
> Growth in Grace, 2:1-3
> The Sure Foundation, 2:4-8
> A New People, 2:9-10

Christian Ethics, 2:11—3:12
> The Call to a Godly Life, 2:11-12
> Duties to the State, 2:13-17
> Servants Must Follow the Servant, 2:18-25
> Duties in the Family, 3:1-7
> Duties Within the Church, 3:8-12

Christ's Example in Suffering, 3:13—4:19
> Suffering for Righteousness' Sake, 3:13-22
> The Value of Suffering, 4:1-6
> Christian Graces in Times of Trouble, 4:7-11
> The Judgment of the Church, 4:12-19

Pastors and People, 5:1-11
> Duties of Spiritual Leaders, 5:1-4
> Humility in Service, 5:5-7
> Resisting the Devil, 5:8-9
> Benediction, 5:10-11

Conclusion, 5:12-14

Introduction

It has been said that the key word to the writings of John is *love;* the key word to the writings of Paul is *grace;* the key word to the writings of James is *works;* and the key word to the writings of Peter is *faith.* This is clearly true of 1 Peter. Its major theme is faith in time of testing.

Written to encourage Christians facing persecution, 1 Peter is "the Epistle of hope" designed to strengthen the storm-tossed in every age.

Gospel Motifs in Peter

As is the case with the other General Epistles, the authorship of 1 and 2 Peter has been debated. Introductions to the standard commentaries trace the pros and cons. It is enough here to note that none of the objections seem compelling. There is good reason to hold the traditional view that these letters are the work of Simon Peter, son of Jonas, one of the Twelve.

One New Testament scholar has pointed out the parallel between the theological motifs in 1 Peter and in Peter's recorded sermons in the Acts.

1. Both stress the fact that the Old Testament has been fulfilled in Jesus. The age of the Messiah has begun. God's final word has been spoken (1 Pet. 1:3, 10-12; 4:7—Acts 2:14-16; 3:12-26; 4:8-12; 10:34-43).

2. Both emphasize the death and resurrection of Christ as the fulfillment of Old Testament prophecies and the means whereby salvation is provided (1 Pet. 1:20-21; 2:21-25—Acts 2:20-31; 3:13-14; 10:43).

3. The risen Christ is exalted to the right hand of God as the Head of a new race (1 Pet. 1:21; 2:7; 3:22—Acts 2: 22-26; 3:13; 4:11; 5:30-31; 10:39-42).

4. Christ is coming again and will judge the living and the dead (1 Pet. 1:5, 7, 13; 4:5, 13, 17-18; 5:1, 4—Acts 3:19-23; 10:42).

5. Therefore, all should repent of their sins, accept God's forgiveness and the promise of eternal life, and receive His Holy Spirit (1 Pet. 1:13-25; 2:1-3; 4:1-5—Acts 2:38-39; 3:19; 5:31; 10:42).

The Christian and Persecution

A gray shadow of persecution hangs over the Epistle of hope. The menace of Roman emperor worship can already be seen. Christians were at first subject to persecution from religious authorities. The first great bloodbath the Church had to endure came when Roman civil authorities began to require of believers the confession, "Caesar is Lord."

Pagans of whatever religious persuasion had no problem with such a statement. They were worshipers of many gods. Where there are many gods, there is always room for one more. It was relatively simple for them to add Caesar to the list.

Christians did not have this option. They were committed to the worship of one God, manifest as Father, Son, and Holy Spirit. One who said, "Jesus is Lord," could not say, "Caesar is Lord." So the issue was joined, and Rome dedicated its might for some 250 years, with periods of remission, to the extermination of a religion which would not accept the divinity of the Roman emperor.

1 Peter then becomes a commentary on the beatitude, "Blessed are they which are persecuted for righteousness' sake: for theirs is the kingdom of heaven" (Matt. 5:10). Peter's concern is that, when persecution comes, it be for righteousness' sake, not for perversity's sake.

Christian people sometimes incur opposition that they regard as persecution which really has nothing to do with their allegiance to Christ. Sometimes a cantankerous disposition is passed off as piety. Karl Barth somewhere quizzically noted that when Daniel was in the lions' den he did not twist the lions' tails! He did nothing to provoke antagonism.

Important, too, is Peter's emphasis on the importance of a radiant, victorious spirit even in the midst of trouble.

Archibald Hunter, in an eloquent sentence, describes the emotional tone of 1 Peter: "Here is no 'grey and close-lipped Stoicism' which can only 'grin and bear it'; here is a document which has caught the authentic spirit of that Master 'who for the joy that was set before him endured the cross,' which though the skies lower and the enemy press hard and heavy, glows with that hope, that buoyant expectancy, of 'an inheritance incorruptible, and undefiled, and that fadeth not away,' eternal in the heaven."

1 PETER 1

Salutation
1 Peter 1:1-2

1 Peter 1:1-2

> 1 Peter, an apostle of Jesus Christ, to the strangers scattered throughout Pontus, Galatia, Cappadocia, Asia, and Bithynia,
> 2 Elect according to the foreknowledge of God the Father, through sanctification of the Spirit, unto obedience and sprinkling of the blood of Jesus Christ: Grace unto you, and peace, be multiplied.

1. Peter uses the familiar letter form in starting his Epistle. The name and title of the writer comes first, much as it would today in a printed letterhead. He identifies himself simply as *an apostle of Jesus Christ,* a title Paul also customarily used (2 Cor. 1:1; Eph. 1:1; Col. 1:1; 1 Tim. 1:1; 2 Tim. 1:1; Titus 1:1).

The term *apostle* comes from the Greek *apo,* "from," and *stello,* "to send." It means an ambassador, a messenger or envoy, one who officially represents the sender. The term is used in two ways in the New Testament. It identifies one of the original Twelve chosen by Jesus, in which number Paul always included himself. One criterion for inclusion with the Twelve was having seen the risen Lord (Acts 1:22). The term *apostle* also applies to official messengers or spokesmen for the Church. In this secondary sense, Barnabas (Acts 14:4, 14), Andronicus and Junius (Rom. 16:7), Silas and Timothy (1 Thess. 2:6), and others (2 Cor. 8:23; Phil. 2:25, where the KJV translates "messengers"), are called apostles.

2. An ancient letter, as do ours today, next indicated the person or persons to whom it was addressed. In this case, it is *the strangers scattered* abroad. This phrase is literally "sojourners of the dispersion" or Diaspora, a term used to describe non-Palestinian Jews. References in the letter itself (1:18; 2:10; 4:3) show that Peter did not use this in a narrow sense. He used it to describe the entire Christian community in the areas he names.

3. These are *elect according to the foreknowledge of God the Father* (2). The concept of election in scripture has

been much misunderstood. It has been used in such a way as to teach a total predestination. But biblical election is according to God's foreknowledge (Rom. 8:29). Predestination properly understood is God's gracious provision for the salvation of all who savingly believe in Christ (John 3:15-16; Rom. 10:8-13; etc.). The elect are those who receive that provision.

Election is *through sanctification of the Spirit. Sanctification* is a complex theological term that stands for the inwardness of salvation—the renewal of man's moral nature in the image of God. It is the work of the Holy Spirit (Rom. 15:16; 2 Thess. 2:13) made possible by the self-giving of Christ on the Cross (Eph. 5:25-27; Heb. 13:12) according to the will of the Father (1 Thess. 4:3; Heb. 10:10). Sanctification begins in the new birth or regeneration, which is "initial sanctification." It is made complete in a subsequent crisis of faith (1 Thess. 5:23-24).

The outcome of *sanctification of the Spirit* is *obedience and sprinkling of the blood of Jesus Christ.* This is the same combination of ideas that is expressed in 1 John 1:7, "If we walk in the light . . . the blood of Jesus Christ his Son cleanseth us from all sin." *Sprinkling of the blood* is a reference to the Old Testament rite of purification for lepers. A bit of hyssop was dipped into the blood of an animal sacrifice and sprinkled on the person to be cleansed (Lev. 14:1-7; Ps. 51:7). It means cleansing, purification, freeing from pollution.

The *sanctification of the Spirit* begins and becomes entire (1 Thess. 5:23) at crisis times in the life of a believer. But it brings him into a continuing relationship with God. *Obedience* (walking in the light) is the requirement for the continued cleansing from all sin which the full work of sanctification implies. No crisis, however wonderful, can take the place of learning to walk with the Lord day by day, living by faith, prayer, Bible study, and effective witness and service in the Kingdom. The "workings of grace" must follow the "works of grace" to make them effective.

4. *Grace* and *peace* are typical expressions of greeting in

New Testament letters (Rom. 1:7; 1 Cor. 1:3; 2 Cor. 1:2; Gal. 1:3; etc.). *Grace* is the beautiful New Testament word for the undeserved favor and help of God. *Peace* is the Greek equivalent of the Hebrew greeting and benediction *Shalom.* It means not only harmony and serenity, but wholeness and health. *Grace* and *peace* are not just added; they are *multiplied,* made to abound.

God's Saving Power
1 Peter 1:3-12

Peter gives us one of the great New Testament summaries of the gospel in the opening paragraphs of his letter. It centers in three topics: the basis of our faith, the trial of our faith, and faith as fulfillment.

The Basis of Our Faith

1 Peter 1:3-5

> 3 Blessed be the God and Father of our Lord Jesus Christ, which according to his abundant mercy hath begotten us again unto a lively hope by the resurrection of Jesus Christ from the dead,
> 4 To an inheritance incorruptible, and undefiled, and that fadeth not away, reserved in heaven for you,
> 5 Who are kept by the power of God through faith unto salvation ready to be revealed in the last time.

1. This paragraph is in the form of a doxology—an ascription of praise to God: *Blessed be the God and Father of our Lord Jesus Christ* (3). *Blessed* is from *eulogeo,* literally, "to speak well of." When addressed to God, it means to praise Him, acknowledging His goodness, desiring His glory. *The God and Father of our Lord Jesus Christ* is a beautiful thumbnail description of the true and living God of the Bible. God was known in the Old Testament as the Lord who delivered His people from the bondage of Egypt. He is most characteristically known in the New Testament (2 Cor. 1:3; Eph. 1:3) as the *Father of our Lord Jesus Christ.* Through Christ, we can come to God (John 14:6). In Christ, we know what God is like. The child expressed it ungrammatically but truly: "Jesus is the best photograph God ever had took!"

2. It is God's *mercy* expressing itself in the death and *resurrection of Jesus Christ from the dead* that has be-

gotten us again unto a lively hope. Begotten . . . again is literally "regenerated." It means "born again" (John 3:3-7). It is the impartation of new and spiritual life. It initiates the "new creation" (2 Cor. 5:17, Greek), and is the initial step in personal salvation.

Like other New Testament writers, Peter puts major emphasis on the resurrection of Christ. That Christ crucified was raised from the dead by the power of God was not a theme reserved for Easter in the New Testament. It was an element in every New Testament sermon. The Cross for New Testament Christians was not a crucifix with the form of the dying Saviour affixed to it. The Cross was an empty Cross. Close by was an empty tomb. Everything the Cross meant is guaranteed by the risen Redeemer, the contemporary Christ, the living Lord of His Church.

3. We are born anew to a living *hope*. This hope is the confident expectation of *an inheritance incorruptible, and undefiled, and that fadeth not away*—"a perfect inheritance beyond the reach of change and decay" (4, Phillips). The picture is one of a treasure laid up in a safe place beyond the reach of thieves (Matt. 6:19-21).

The English word also suggests the importance of a "reservation." Two men were travelling to a convention. They arrived late. One was told with regret that there were no rooms available. The other was handed a key. When the first man asked, "How come you get a room and I don't?" the other replied, "I phoned ahead and made a reservation."

The reservation is for those *who are kept by the power of God through faith unto salvation ready to be revealed in the last time* (5). God's keeping power is given *through faith,* not through feelings. To be *kept* is taken from a military term meaning to be guarded or garrisoned. God's people are surrounded by an invisible shield. They are surrounded by heavenly hosts, much as Elisha was when threatened by the Syrian army (2 Kings 6:8-17).

There is a salvation which is an accomplished fact in the lives of those who receive the Saviour. We have been saved by grace through faith (Eph. 2:8). There is a salvation which is an ongoing process. We are being saved (1 Cor. 1:18, Greek). But there is a salvation yet to come. It is even now "nearer than when we believed" (Rom. 13:11). When Jesus comes again, He will "appear the second time without sin [or, a sin offering] unto salvation." Salvation is three-dimensional. It is free—in justification. It is full—in entire sanctification. And it is final—in glorification at the resurrection from the dead.

The Trial of Our Faith

The faith that saves and keeps will also be tried. The testing of faith is often mentioned in the New Testament. Untested faith is unsure faith. Only in the testing times does faith find its sure foundation in God's unfailing grace.

1 Peter 1:6-9
> 6 Wherein ye greatly rejoice, though now for a season, if need be, ye are in heaviness through manifold temptations:
> 7 That the trial of your faith, being much more precious than of gold that perisheth, though it be tried with fire, might be found unto praise and honour and glory at the appearing of Jesus Christ:
> 8 Whom having not seen, ye love; in whom, though now ye see him not, yet believing, ye rejoice with joy unspeakable and full of glory:
> 9 Receiving the end of your faith, even the salvation of your souls.

Christians have a right to rejoice in the keeping power of God and in the hope that is theirs in heaven. Yet they often find themselves *in heaviness through manifold temptations* (6). *In heaviness* is literally "sorrowful and made to grieve." It is the natural reaction of even a believing heart to the testings and trials that come through both the agency of others and the circumstances of life.

Three considerations serve to make the grief bearable:

First, it is only *for a season,* for a little while. One man suggested that the most comforting words in scripture are "It came to pass." Our trials are not here to stay. They soon pass by. The sky clears. The clouds are rolled back. The sun shines again, and our spirits rejoice the more for the heaviness of soul that has preceded.

Second, the negative moods, the depressed feelings, come through some necessity we may not fully understand: *if need be.* Perhaps we need to be taught not to count too much on the natural joys of life. There seems to be some deep rhythm in our emotional makeup. We cannot enjoy two mountaintop experiences without a valley between. Heights of blessing may be followed by seasons of heaviness.

Third, the trial of faith, though as by fire, results in a confirmed or proved faith that will find *praise and honour and glory at the appearing of Jesus Christ* (7). Another recurrent note throughout the New Testament is Christ's second coming. In times of fiery testing, the courage and faith of the Christian community were lifted by its hope of the Lord's return. To "comfort one another" with words about the Second Coming (1 Thess. 4:15-18) was literally "to strengthen and put heart into" each other.

The sustaining power in Christian life is love for the unseen Saviour. Although our physical eyes have never seen Him, "we love him, because he first loved us" (1 John 4:19). In this love we can *rejoice with joy unspeakable and full of glory*—"inexpressibly glorious pleasure" as Bo Reicke translates it.

On the surface, *heaviness through manifold temptations* and *joy unspeakable and full of glory* would appear to be contradictory qualities. Yet they are not incompatible. Even in the stormiest times, the child of God is sustained by a deep sense of rightness with God and the inner well-being that rightness brings.

The outcome is *the salvation of your souls* (9). This is *the end of your faith.* The term translated *end* is *telos.* It means not only "end" in the sense of termination, but "end" in the sense of completion, goal, or inner potential. The destination of the believer is not a hole in the ground and a hopeless eternity. It is participation in the victory and glory of the coming Christ.

Faith as Fulfillment

1 Peter 1:10-12

> 10 Of which salvation the prophets have enquired and searched diligently, who prophesied of the grace that should come unto you:
> 11 Searching what, or what manner of time the Spirit of Christ which

> was in them did signify, when it testified beforehand the sufferings of Christ, and the glory that should follow.
> 12 Unto whom it was revealed, that not unto themselves, but unto us they did minister the things, which are now reported unto you by them that have preached the gospel unto you with the Holy Ghost sent down from heaven; which things the angels desire to look into.

Peter sounds again one of the most consistent notes in the New Testament. The salvation brought by Christ is the fulfillment of the hope of the ages as expressed by the prophets of the old covenant. The Spirit who inspired the prophets is *the Spirit of Christ* (11). He made known *the sufferings of Christ* in the ritual of sacrifice in the Old Testament. But the Old Testament not only revealed Messiah's cross (Psalm 22; Isaiah 53); it also pictured His glory (Psalms 2; 110; Dan. 2:36-45).

This hope of the ages finds fulfillment in the gospel preached *with the Holy Ghost sent down from heaven* (12). The "age of the Spirit" had been foretold in the Old Testament (Isa. 32:13-16; 44:3-4; Joel 2:28-30; Zech. 12:10). That age had now dawned. Even angels long to understand the mysteries revealed to the people of God in the new covenant.

No one could deny the real piety evident in the lives of patriarchs, psalmists, and prophets before Christ. But their privileges were less than ours. They lived in the time of prediction. We rejoice in the fact of fulfillment. The result is a unity of the people of God throughout the ages. God has "provided some better thing for us, that they without us should not be made perfect" (Heb. 11:40). Fulfillment perfects prediction. Old Testament saints are made perfect in the reality God has provided through Christ.

The Call to Holiness
1 Peter 1:13—2:10

The second major division of Peter's first letter (1:13—2:10) is a ringing call to holiness of heart and life. It is prefaced with the word *Wherefore* (1:13). The fact of faith implies obligation. God's indicative is our imperative. Love for Him impels obedience to Him (John 14:15).

The Supreme Motivation

1 Peter 1:13-16

> 13 Wherefore gird up the loins of your mind, be sober, and hope to the end for the grace that is to be brought unto you at the revelation of Jesus Christ;
> 14 As obedient children, not fashioning yourselves according to the former lusts in your ignorance:
> 15 But as he which hath called you is holy, so be ye holy in all manner of conversation;
> 16 Because it is written, Be ye holy; for I am holy.

1. V. 13 is a preamble to what follows. In view of what Christ has done for us, we are to *gird up the loins of* our minds. The picture here is of one who tucks his coat or robe into a belt in order to free his limbs for working or running. We would be more apt to say, "Roll up your sleeves," or, "Take off your coat."

The Bible always makes it clear that "salvation is of the Lord." Yet we have a part in it too. Our responsibility is "our response to His ability." Because God has willed it so, the response is needed to make the divine ability effective.

2. We are to *be sober* in the sense of having "sound, solid, balanced judgment" (Barclay). The Holy Spirit is the Spirit of "power, and of love, and of a sound mind" (2 Tim. 1:7). This is the very opposite of the instability that is easily influenced away from the solid, central core of Christian faith into the cults and isms of the day.

3. We are to put our hope in the ultimate *grace* that will come to us when Jesus comes again. Like salvation, *grace* is a three-dimensional word. We have been saved by grace (Eph. 2:8). We have been sanctified by grace (Titus 2:11-14). We are to be glorified also by grace.

An elderly minister was nearing the end of his life. A visitor said to him one day, "I suppose as you lie here you are thinking of all the sermons you've preached, and all the good you've done in your lifetime."

"Oh, no," replied the man of God. "I long ago bundled up my sermons and good works and threw them all overboard. I'm going to swim to glory on the plank of free grace."

So shall we all.

4. Peter then gives us the *ABC*s of Christian holiness:

   a. As obedient children (14), we are to respond to God. We cannot go back to the old life. William Barclay gives an expanded translation of these words: "You must not allow your lives to be shaped by the influence of the passions which used to dominate you in the days of your ignorance." God calls His obedient children to holiness.

   b. Be ye holy (15). As He who has called us is holy, so are we to be holy. This does not mean that we are to be as holy as God is. We are still frail and fallible human beings. It means that we are to share His moral image in the measure of our capacity to share it. We are to be "partakers of the divine nature" (2 Pet. 1:4). As a single cup of water from the ocean shares the chemical properties of the whole, or as a tiny wristwatch keeps time with "Big Ben" in the tower, our finite beings are to be tuned to the purity and holiness of God.

   c. Conversation, or the whole style of lives we live, is the sphere in which we are to be holy. The Old Testament command (Lev. 11:44; 19:2; 20:26) here quoted (16) is set firmly in the arena of life, not ritual. Our holiness is more than a matter of our "standing." It is a matter of our spiritual "state." It is to reflect itself in all our conduct. The holiness of the Old Testament had a large element of the ritual and ceremonial in it. Holiness in the New Testament is spiritual and ethical (Rom. 6:19-22; 1 Thess. 4:3-8).

   It is worth noting that the call to holiness is not based on considerations of tradition, custom, or convenience. It is grounded firmly in the holiness of God. Christians may seek holiness for secondary reasons. The supreme motivation—never to be lost—is the simple fact that God is holy and those who serve Him must be like Him.

The Price of Our Redemption

1 Peter 1:17-21

> 17 And if ye call on the Father, who without respect of persons judgeth according to every man's work, pass the time of your sojourning here in fear:
> 18 Forasmuch as ye know that ye were not redeemed with corruptible

> things, as silver and gold, from your vain conversation received by tradition from your fathers;
> 19 But with the precious blood of Christ, as of a lamb without blemish and without spot:
> 20 Who verily was foreordained before the foundation of the world, but was manifest in these last times for you,
> 21 Who by him do believe in God, that raised him up from the dead, and gave him glory; that your faith and hope might be in God.

One essential ingredient of holy living is the reverent awe that is meant by the KJV use of the term *fear*. The NEB understands v. 17 as a reference to the Lord's Prayer: "If you say 'our Father' to the One who judges every man impartially on the record of his deeds, you must stand in awe of him while you live out your time on earth." This is no slavish dread of a tyrannical God. This is the deep reverence befitting men who speak the hallowed name of their God.

There is no favoritism with God. He is not impressed by airs or pretense. Credentials do not count with Him. He looks at the quality of our service in terms of the potential we have. From those to whom He has given five talents, He expects five-talent performance. From those who have two talents, He expects two-talent service. Even the man with one talent may earn the same commendation—"Well done, thou good and faithful servant"—if he uses that talent to the measure of his ability (cf. Matt. 25:14-30).

It was not *silver and gold* that redeemed us from "the empty folly of . . . [our] traditional ways" (18, NEB). It was a price beyond all calculation. It was the lifeblood of the Lamb of God, who alone can take away the sin of the world (John 1:29). God's design for man's redemption dates from before the foundation of the world, although it has only been made known in this gospel age (20). Our sharing in that redemption comes, Peter says again, through faith in God, who *raised* Christ *from the dead, and gave him glory* (21). For this reason, our *faith and hope* must be in God, not in our own merits or according to what we could deserve.

Here is another swift summary of the whole gospel. Our "hope is built on nothing less than Jesus' blood and righteousness. . . . [We] dare not trust the sweetest frame [our own feelings], but wholly lean on Jesus' name" (Edward Mote). All we have and are depends on Him who has redeemed us by His own blood.

Count Nicholas von Zinzendorf is known in church history as a great Christian leader, donor of the Herrnhut Estate, which was the European headquarters of the Moravian Brethren. But Count Zinzendorf was not always known for his devotion. He grew up as an aristocrat. He was trained for a diplomatic career in the service of the court at Dresden. Young, noble, rich, and talented, the young count had long been a professing Christian.

The real turning point in his life came when, on a trip to Paris, the Count stopped to rest his horses in Düsseldorf. There he visited the art gallery where Sternberg's picture of the Crucifixion was displayed. The artist had called his picture "Ecce Homo" ("Behold the Man") and under it had inscribed two lines: "This I did for thee; what hast thou done for Me?"

The eyes of the young nobleman met the eyes of the Saviour, and he was filled with shame and conviction. He had no answer to the question of the picture. He stood transfixed. Hours passed, the light faded, and it was nightfall when Zinzendorf left the gallery.

But a new day had dawned for him. From that time, his heart and life, his wealth and fame, all went to the service of the Saviour. "I have but one passion," he declared; "it is Jesus, Jesus only." So should it be for us all.

A Pure Love

1 Peter 1:22-25

> 22 Seeing ye have purified your souls in obeying the truth through the Spirit unto unfeigned love of the brethren, see that ye love one another with a pure heart fervently:
> 23 Being born again, not of corruptible seed, but of incorruptible, by the word of God, which liveth and abideth for ever.
> 24 For all flesh is as grass, and all the glory of man as the flower of grass. The grass withereth, and the flower thereof falleth away:
> 25 But the word of the Lord endureth for ever. And this is the word which by the gospel is preached unto you.

The piety that manifests itself in reverent awe toward God is to be evident in pure love toward others. On its subjective side, holiness is the purifying of the soul that results from *obeying the truth through the Spirit.* From a purified soul flows genuine and fervent love, the finest evidence of the Spirit within. The basis for this new divine life and the pure love it engenders is *being born again, not of corruptible seed, but of incorruptible, by the word of God, which liveth and abideth for ever* (23).

The New Testament gives a large place to *the word of God* as the divine seed that engenders spiritual life. In a different setting, Jesus spoke of the word of God as seed sown in the field from which springs the harvest (Matt. 13:3-23; Mark 4:1-12; Luke 8:4-10). John contrasts the life that results from the will of man with that which comes from the will of God (John 1:11-13). The word which is truth sanctifies (John 17:17; Acts 20:32). As we shall see, it is by the word of God we grow (2:2).

In contrast to everything human, the Word of God is eternal and unchanging. Human glory springs up as the wild flowers in the field, and is just as quickly gone. To put confidence in human wisdom alone is to trust a faulty guide. Only the Word of the Lord embodied in the gospel can give us a fixed frame of reference from which to judge the passing scene.

1 PETER 2

Growth in Grace

1 Peter 2:1-3

> 1 Wherefore laying aside all malice, and all guile, and hypocrisies, and envies, and all evil speakings,
> 2 As newborn babes, desire the sincere milk of the word, that ye may grow thereby:
> 3 If so be ye have tasted that the Lord is gracious.

Growing in spiritual maturity, Peter says, demands two kinds of action on our part. The first is negative, what we must avoid. The second is positive, what we must do. Negatives are important, but not in themselves alone. They are important because they clear the way for the positive actions that build the soul.

1. What we must avoid (1). We are to avoid five common

pitfalls that threaten Christian integrity. The original Greek term for *laying aside* is a very vivid word. It means to "strip off as one would strip off soiled garments." It is the term Paul used in Rom. 13:12 ("let us therefore cast off the works of darkness") and Eph. 4:22 ("that ye put off . . . the old man, which is corrupt according to the deceitful lusts").

a. We are to strip off *all malice.* The word for *malice* is *kakia,* "malicious and twisted conduct" (Barclay). It testifies to the demand of the new life for a radical change from old ways of living.

b. All guile is to be laid aside. The original word here means deceitfulness, being two-faced. It comes from a verb that meant to catch game with bait. Any sort of insincerity or carefully disguised motive is out of keeping with holiness.

c. Hypocrisies are to be put away. Similar to guile, "hypocrisy" is from a term applied to an actor playing a role. It soon came to be used in the bad sense, of one who hides his real character or feelings and puts on a front in order to gain some personal advantage. No objection has been raised so often against Christians as the charge of hypocrisy. It is only fair to say that hypocrisy is by no means limited to the sphere of religion. A great many people spend their lives acting a part, playing psychological games. To the extent that there is any tendency to hypocrisy in the Church, it must be stripped off as decisively as possible.

d. Envies. William Barclay writes in *Daily Bible Studies:* "It may well be said that envy is the last sin to die. . . . So long as self remains active within a man's heart there will be envy in his life." Envy was the cause of the greatest tension in the company of Christ's apostles: the 10 envied James and John in their attempt to gain preference in the Kingdom (Mark 10:41) and at the Last Supper argued over who would have seats of honor (Luke 22:24).

e. All evil speakings comes from *katalalia,* literally, "speaking against." It includes slander, malicious gossip, disparagement, and detraction. One would be hard put to find a sin that has caused more heartache and hard feelings both inside and without the Church. Nothing else destroys the unity of the body of Christ so quickly.

2. What we must do (2-3). Everything desirable and upbuilding, Peter sums up in *the sincere milk of the word. Sincere* is a one-word translation of two Greek words, *logikon adolon. Adolon* means "pure, unadulterated." *Logikon* is difficult to put into English. It is often translated "reasonable," since *logos* is the usual Greek word for reason or intelligence. Others translate it "spiritual," since *logos* also applied to the divine Reason that is the Ruler of all things. But *logos* also means "word," as it is translated in John 1:1 ff. It may therefore be used here to refer to the Word of God described in 1:24-25. All three applications are meaningful, obviously. The Word of God is both spiritual and reasonable. This does not mean that scripture is such that man's unaided reason could write it. It means that, however far the Bible may surpass reason, it is never unreasonable or out of harmony with the rational structure of reality.

The Word of God is to our souls what milk is to young bodies. Without perpetrating too serious a pun, it may be noted that children do not thrive on "skim" milk. It takes whole milk to provide all needed nutrients. Too many Christians try to subsist on "skim milk." They "skim" through the scripture without ever seeking to sound its depths. No one part of the Bible is exclusively the Word of God. It is the whole Bible that gives us God's full revelation of himself. Therefore we must neglect no part of it.

The fact that we *have tasted that the Lord is gracious* (3) whets our appetites for more. Appetites are largely acquired. One rarely hungers or thirsts for food or drink he has never tasted. *Gracious* is *chrestos,* the word used in the Greek translation of the Old Testament in Ps. 34:8, to which this is an allusion: "O taste and see that the Lord is *good.*" One of the first signs of spiritual disease is loss of appetite for the things of God. A good appetite goes with robust health, both physical and spiritual.

The Sure Foundation

1 Peter 2:4-8

> 4 To whom coming, as unto a living stone, disallowed indeed of men, but chosen of God, and precious,
> 5 Ye also, as lively stones, are built up a spiritual house, an holy priesthood, to offer up spiritual sacrifices, acceptable to God by Jesus Christ.
> 6 Wherefore also it is contained in the scripture, Behold, I lay in Sion a chief corner stone, elect, precious: and he that believeth on him shall not be confounded.
> 7 Unto you therefore which believe he is precious: but unto them which be disobedient, the stone which the builders disallowed, the same is made the head of the corner,
> 8 And a stone of stumbling, and a rock of offence, even to them which stumble at the word, being disobedient: whereunto also they were appointed.

In a change of metaphors, Peter now speaks of individual Christians as living stones from which is built a spiritual temple founded on the "chief corner stone." This is one of Paul's favorite illustrations (1 Cor. 3:10-11), and he uses the same Old Testament quotations (2:6—Isa. 28:16 [cf. Rom. 9:33 and Eph. 2:20]; 2:8—Isa. 8:14 [cf. Rom. 9:33]).

1. The Foundation. The gracious or good Lord is *a living stone, disallowed indeed of men, but chosen of God, and precious* (4). These words summarize the quotations from Isa. 28:16 and Ps. 118:22 found in vv. 6-7. The Foundation chosen and provided by the Father, precious in His sight, was rejected by men. Jesus himself used Ps. 118:22 as relating to his rejection by the rulers of His people: "Did ye never read in the scriptures, The stone which the builders rejected, the same is become the head of the corner: this is the Lord's doing, and it is marvellous in our eyes?" (Matt. 21:42; Mark 12:10-11; Luke 20:17).

The One whom men rejected, God has highly honored. He is the *chief corner stone* (6). The entire structure of the Church and the Kingdom rests upon Him. Those who believe *on him shall not be confounded*—made ashamed or "be disappointed," as Weymouth translates it.

But the *corner stone* is also *a stone of stumbling, and a rock of offence* (8) to those who are *disobedient* and unbelieving. The same gospel that is the word of life to those who believe it is the sentence of death to those who reject it (John 3:17-20; 2 Cor. 2:15-16). The phrase at the end of v. 8—*whereunto also they were appointed*—has been misleading to some. Those who are *disobedient* are destined to *stumble;* they are not destined to be disobedient.

2. The building. Those who receive Christ as their Saviour, thus acknowledging the precious Cornerstone which God has laid, in turn become *lively stones* and *are built up a spiritual house, an holy priesthood, to offer up spiritual sacrifices, acceptable to God by Jesus Christ* (5). Paul uses the same metaphor in Eph. 2:20-22. The Temple of God in Jerusalem was the visible sign of God's presence with His people. That structure of stone and wood was long ago destroyed. Yet God is not without a temple on earth. His temple is now the Church, a spiritual structure wherein are offered *spiritual sacrifices.* These *spiritual sacrifices* are the consecrated lives of the people of God: "I beseech you therefore, brethren, by the mercies of God, that ye present your bodies a living sacrifice, holy, acceptable unto God, which is your reasonable ['spiritual,' ASV] service" (Rom. 12:1).

A New People

1 Peter 2:9-10

> 9 But ye are a chosen generation, a royal priesthood, an holy nation, a peculiar people; that ye should shew forth the praises of him who hath called you out of darkness into his marvelous light:
> 10 Which in time past were not a people, but are now the people of God: which had not obtained mercy, but now have obtained mercy.

Peter picks up the idea of the holy priesthood he had mentioned in v. 5. Christians are not only the living stones that make up the temple of God; they *are a chosen generation, a royal priesthood, an holy nation, a peculiar people* (9). God still has a temple on earth; also, He still has a chosen people in whom the spiritual ideals never fully realized in national Israel have now become real. Like Paul (Rom. 2:25-29; 4:16-17; Gal. 3:16-17) and the writer to the Hebrews (cc. 8—10), Peter views the Church as the fulfillment of God's covenant with Israel.

The "peculiarity" of God's people is not oddity or strangeness. The Greek term, *peripoiesin,* actually means "for one's own possession." *Peculiar* means unique, distinctive, God's personal property. As in Titus 2:14, where the peculiarity of God's people is their zeal for good works, here Peter identifies the distinctiveness of the Christian profession as showing *forth the praises of him who hath called you out of darkness into his marvellous light.*

The wonder of grace is that it has taken a people who *in time past were not a people,* strangers to *mercy,* and has constituted them *the people of God,* recipients of His mercy and grace (10). *People* in the Greek New Testament is *laos,* from which we derive the English words "laity" and "layman." The point is that all God's people are a royal priesthood. The sharp distinction between clergy and laity to which we are accustomed is not found in the New Testament. There, the people of God are all ministers (servants). God "appointed some to be apostles, others to be prophets, others to be evangelists, others to be pastors and teachers. He did this to prepare all God's people for the work of Christian service, to build up the body of Christ" (Eph. 4:11-12, TEV).

Christian Ethics
1 Peter 2:11—3:12

While the note of obligation has not been missing entirely in Peter's discussion thus far, the major emphasis has been doctrinal and theological. Now, much in the manner of Paul, Peter turns from doctrine to ethics, from the "believing side" of the gospel to the "behaving side." His transition, *Dearly beloved, I beseech you as strangers and pilgrims* (2:11), is almost the same as that of Paul at a similar point in Romans (12:1).

Theology and ethics, doctrine and duty, are never far apart in the New Testament. The interaction is a two-way street. Belief inevitably affects behavior. On the other hand, behavior has its reflex action on belief. The two are like the wings of a flying bird, or the legs of a man when he walks. Both are essential, and "what therefore God hath joined together, let not man put asunder."

The Call to a Godly Life

1 Peter 2:11-12

> 11 Dearly beloved, I beseech you as strangers and pilgrims, abstain from fleshly lusts, which war against the soul;
> 12 Having your conversation honest among the Gentiles: that, whereas they speak against you as evildoers, they may by your good works, which they shall behold, glorify God in the day of visitation.

In general terms, Peter reiterates the Christian obligation to be "holy in all manner" of life (1:15). He warns against yielding to the desires of the flesh (Greek, *sarx*). While "flesh" has come to mean "physical" or "bodily" to us, it is a much broader term in New Testament ethics. Paul lists among the "works of the flesh" 12 out of 17 sins that have no bodily or physical basis at all: e.g., idolatry, witchcraft, quarrelling, a contentious temper, envy, fits of rage, selfish ambition, dissension, party intrigues, etc. (cf. Gal. 5:19-21, NEB). Paul pictures the tension between "flesh" and "the Spirit" as hindering the believer "so that what you will to do you cannot do" (Gal. 5:17, NEB; cf. Rom. 7:18-24). This strife goes on until "the flesh with the affections and lusts" is "crucified" (Gal. 5:24; cf. Rom. 6:6).

Abstention *from fleshly lusts* is for the sake of good conduct (the meaning of the KJV, *conversation honest,* 12) before *the Gentiles*—literally, "among the nations." "Good conduct" carries the thought of a manner of life which is winsome and attractive. Although falsely charged by ungodly neighbors with evil, Christians may vindicate their profession by consistent and godly lives. "The best argument for Christianity is a real Christian. . . . The strongest missionary force in the world is a Christian life" (Barclay).

The *good works* of the Christian community will be acknowledged even by their adversaries *in the day of visitation.* The ordinary meaning of this latter phrase would be "in the day of judgment" when Christ returns. But Ronald Knox understands it to mean the visitation of God in mercy and forgiveness toward those who are convinced by the godly lives of Christian neighbors and thereby turned to the Lord. It is this outcome that glorifies God and vindicates the gospel.

Duties to the State

1 Peter 2:13-17

> 13 Submit yourselves to every ordinance of man for the Lord's sake: whether it be to the king, as supreme;
> 14 Or unto governors, as unto them that are sent by him for the punishment of evildoers, and for the praise of them that do well.
> 15 For so is the will of God, that with well doing ye may put to silence the ignorance of foolish men:
> 16 As free, and not using your liberty for a cloak of maliciousness, but as the servants of God.
> 17 Honour all men. Love the brotherhood. Fear God. Honour the king.

Peter follows his general exhortation with specific applications. He turns first to the Christian's responsibility toward civil government, a passage paralleled in Rom. 13:1-7. Christians are to be law-abiding citizens.

It is perhaps worth noting that at this time in New Testament history, the Christian Church was tolerated by civil authorities. The persecutions that had come had been inspired by religious leaders rather than by civil governors. This is most clearly seen in Acts, where the authority of civil government is pictured as clearly on the side of the Church and against the accusations of religious leaders.

All this was to change, shortly and dramatically, when Nero launched his bloodbath of persecution against the Christians in Rome. There are intimations of this coming change here in 1 Peter. But for the present, at least, the Church could look to the state for protection against the unlawful actions of those who opposed Christianity on purely religious grounds.

1. Like Paul, Peter thinks of obedience to lawfully constituted civil authority as a matter of Christian conscience—*for the Lord's sake* (13; "for conscience sake," Rom. 13:5). It assumes, of course, that there is no direct conflict between the requirements of civil government and man's obligation to his God. When such a conflict arose, as it did soon after in the claim that the Roman emperor was "Lord" or "God," all Christians followed the principle Peter had stated 30 years before when ordered not to preach in the name of Christ—"We ought to obey God rather than men" (Acts 5:29; cf. 4:19-20).

2. Peter's concern here is the same as expressed in v. 12: *that with well doing ye may put to silence the ignorance*

of foolish men (15). The New Testament reverses most human evaluations of life. The worldly life is thought to be "sophisticated" and "smart." Actually, it is the result of ignorance and foolishness. The bridesmaids who were prepared to meet the bridegroom were "wise." Those who were not prepared were "foolish" (Matt. 25:1-11). The Old Testament had said the same: "The fear of the Lord is the beginning of wisdom" (Prov. 1:7; 9:10; cf. 1 Cor. 1:17-29).

3. Christians are *free*. But they must not abuse their liberty and make it a rationalization for misconduct (16). Liberty is not license. Freedom always implies responsibility. As the belligerent, fist-swinging roughneck was reminded, "Your freedom to swing your fists ends where my nose begins." The highest expression of Christian freedom is, contradictory though it may seem, to become *the servants of God*.

4. Christians are also to *honour all men* (17) in the sense that they recognize that man is made in the image of God. People are never to be "used." They are ends in themselves, never the means to serve the ends of others. Christians are to *love the brotherhood*. While we honor all, our attitude toward our fellow Christians is to be closer and warmer. There is a "tie that binds our hearts in Christian love."

Christians are to *fear God*, not with slavish dread, but with reverence and awe.

Christians are to *honour the king*. This does not mean an unceasing barrage of negative criticism poured out against the institutions of society—police, the courts, congress, or parliament—or the persons holding high office —the mayor, the governor, the president, the queen. Unfortunately, this particular command is honored more in the breach than by observance on the part of some who make high claims for their biblical orthodoxy.

Servants Must Follow the Servant

1 Peter 2:18-25

> 18 Servants, be subject to your masters with all fear; not only to the good and gentle, but also to the froward.

19 For this is thankworthy, if a man for conscience toward God endure grief, suffering wrongfully.
20 For what glory is it, if, when ye be buffeted for your faults, ye shall take it patiently? but if, when ye do well, and suffer for it, ye take it patiently, this is acceptable with God.
21 For even hereunto were ye called: because Christ also suffered for us, leaving us an example, that ye should follow his steps:
22 Who did no sin, neither was guile found in his mouth:
23 Who, when he was reviled, reviled not again; when he suffered, he threatened not; but committed himself to him that judgeth righteously:
24 Who his own self bare our sins in his own body on the tree, that we, being dead to sins, should live unto righteousness: by whose stripes ye were healed.
25 For ye were as sheep going astray; but are now returned unto the Shepherd and Bishop of your souls.

1. From the duty of all Christians in relation to government, Peter turns to a particular class of believers. *Servants* (18) were actually slaves. There were said to have been as many as 60 million slaves in the Roman Empire, many of them prisoners of war. Large numbers of these became Christians. While the principles of Christianity finally destroyed the institution of human slavery, New Testament writers worked within the realities of the human situation in which they lived.

The life of a slave was always a reflection of the character of his master. A kind and particularly a Christian master might make the life of his slaves reasonably tolerable (cf. Philemon). A *froward* ("crooked" or "perverse") master could make life for his slaves a hell on earth.

Even slaves who suffer the indignities and mistreatment of a harsh master—particularly when they take care to serve well—may be heartened by the example of Christ. No one suffered more and deserved it less. We suffer *with* Christ, but He *suffered for us, leaving us an example, that ye should follow his steps* (21).

What applied to slaves in the first century applies to God's servants in all generations. The term Peter used for *example* is particularly vivid. It was a term that described the writing in a copybook. Children learned to write by imitating the writing that was inscribed at the top of the page. So are we to trace in our own lives the attitudes and actions of our divine Exemplar, who left His footprints for us to follow.

2. In a beautiful description of the sacrificial life and death of Jesus in vv. 22-24, Peter's thought is controlled by Isaiah 53. His reference to servants reminded him of the "Fourth Servant Song" of the Book of Isaiah (52:13—53:12). Six references to Isaiah 53 are made here:

a. Jesus *did no sin* (Isa. 53:9). That the example of Jesus was a sinless life makes impossible any humanistic application of this truth. A man came to his pastor with a direct challenge: "I don't appreciate your preaching about the cross of Christ. You should preach Jesus as an Example for us to follow."

The minister replied, "All right. The first point in the example of Jesus is that He did no sin. Can you take that first step?"

The man was honest. "No," he said, "I guess I can't take even the first step."

b. Jesus was without *guile* (Isa. 53:9). *Guile* is the word we have already met in v. 1. It is deceit, two-facedness, "to catch game with bait." Jesus was the most transparently honest Man who ever lived.

c. Jesus *was reviled* without retaliation (Isa. 53:7). "He was oppressed, and he was afflicted," Isaiah said, "yet he opened not his mouth: he is brought as a lamb to the slaughter, and as a sheep before her shearers is dumb, so he openeth not his mouth."

d. Jesus *bore our sins in his own body* (Isa. 53:6, 12). He is "the Lamb of God, which taketh away [literally, 'bears away'] the sin of the world" (John 1:29). The majesty and mystery of the Cross is the fact that "Christ died for our sins" (1 Cor. 15:3), so that through His atoning death we might have life.

e. By His *stripes ye were healed* (Isa. 53:5). No greater statement of vicarious suffering has ever been written than Isaiah 53 and Peter's parallel here. Christ suffered in our stead, and through His resurrection life we are healed—both spiritually and physically.

f. We *were as sheep going astray* who have *now returned unto the Shepherd and Bishop of* our *souls* (25; Isa. 53:6). The comparison here is frequently used in the

Bible. Psalm 23 is the leading Old Testament passage at this point, as John 10 is the leading New Testament passage.

With the idea of Christ as Shepherd, Peter joins another truth. Christ is the *Bishop of* our *souls.* The Greek word here is *episkopos.* It literally means overseer and has been translated "Guardian" (NEB) and one "who keeps watch over" (Knox). This is the only place in the New Testament where this particular term is applied to Christ. It is often used of Christ's ministers (Phil. 1:1; 1 Tim. 3:1; Titus 1:7) and identified with the function of "elders" in Acts 20:17, 28 (KJV, "overseers").

1 PETER 3

Duties in the Family

1 Peter 3:1-7

> 1 Likewise, ye wives, be in subjection to your own husbands; that, if any obey not the word, they also may without the word be won by the conversation of the wives;
> 2 While they behold your chaste conversation coupled with fear.
> 3 Whose adorning let it not be that outward adorning of plaiting the hair, and of wearing of gold, or of putting on of apparel;
> 4 But let it be the hidden man of the heart, in that which is not corruptible, even the ornament of a meek and quiet spirit, which is in the sight of God of great price.
> 5 For after this manner in the old time the holy women also, who trusted in God, adorned themselves, being in subjection unto their own husbands:
> 6 Even as Sara obeyed Abraham, calling him lord: whose daughters ye are, as long as ye do well, and are not afraid with any amazement.
> 7 Likewise, ye husbands, dwell with them according to knowledge, giving honour unto the wife, as unto the weaker vessel, and as being heirs together of the grace of life; that your prayers be not hindered.

Peter continues this great ethical section with an admonition to wives and husbands.

1. The wife's place (1-6). Peter is concerned that Christian wives so live that unsaved husbands will be won. Here is another testimony to the power of example and influence. Husbands who *obey not the word* may be won *without the word . . . by the conversation* (manner of life) *of the wives* (1). This would not minimize the spoken witness.

But in the confines of the home, it would avoid any suggestion of nagging and in the end be more effective than words.

Peter's directions regarding women's attire are similar to those of Paul in 1 Tim. 2:9-10. In each case, stress is put on the inwardness of true beauty. The form of the statement is the familiar New Testament form of contrast. Jesus said, "Labour not for the meat which perisheth, but for that meat which endureth unto everlasting life" (John 6:27). This does not forbid one to work for his daily bread. It simply stresses the importance of spiritual food. So outward adorning is less important than the incorruptible *ornament of a meek and quiet spirit, which is in the sight of God of great price* (4).

An example of godly conduct is Sarah's subjection to Abraham (6). A wife who follows such an example need not be *afraid with any amazement,* a phrase Knox translates, "Let no anxious thoughts disturb you."

2. The husband's duty (7). Husbands likewise must live with their wives in understanding and consideration. They must treat their wives with special respect as "the weaker sex." Christian couples are *heirs together of the grace of life*—"God's gift of life eternal" (Barclay). They must therefore keep things right between themselves if they are to have things right between them and God. Failure in proper consideration in the home will result in hindered prayers.

Duties Within the Church

1 Peter 3:8-12

> 8 Finally, be ye all of one mind, having compassion one of another, love as brethren, be pitiful, be courteous:
> 9 Not rendering evil for evil, or railing for railing: but contrariwise blessing; knowing that ye are thereunto called, that ye should inherit a blessing.
> 10 For he that will love life, and see good days, let him refrain his tongue from evil, and his lips that they speak no guile:
> 11 Let him eschew evil, and do good; let him seek peace, and ensue it.
> 12 For the eyes of the Lord are over the righteous, and his ears are open unto their prayers: but the face of the Lord is against them that do evil.

From the family in the home, Peter turns to the larger

family of God in the Church. While the words here would apply to all human relationships, they have special application to relationships within the household of faith.

Christians are to be *of one mind* (8), literally, "of one disposition" rather than of one opinion. Their ruling sentiment is to be compassionate understanding. The Greek word is *sympatheis,* "feeling with," the source of our English word "sympathy." Christians are to *love as* brothers, *philadelphoi,* and be kindly and *courteous.* If treated wrongly, they are not to retaliate but rather "return good for evil." This kind of magnanimity of spirit is possible because they live in the consciousness that they are destined for eternity and God will make up to them for all they suffer by reason of their relationship to Him (9).

Peter emphasizes this last point with a lengthy quotation from Ps. 34:12-16. This psalm describes the kind of character God desires in those who serve Him. The point of the quotation is the need for living with a forgiving spirit, trusting God to vindicate the right and reward the righteous.

One can only regret that so much of modern church life falls so far short of the pattern set forth here. A local church animated by the spirit of unity, sympathy, brotherly love, kindness, courtesy, and forgiveness would be the most attractive group on earth. Yet we cannot have in the church what does not characterize us as individuals. May we strive with all that is in us to exemplify this kind of life.

Christ's Example in Suffering
1 Peter 3:13—4:19

This section reminds us again of the cloud of threatened persecution that hung over the believers to whom Peter wrote. While we may not experience the suffering that comes from human opposition, "all that will live godly in Christ Jesus shall suffer . . ." (2 Tim. 3:12). Suffering is the common lot of man. No one can avoid it completely. What matters is not that we suffer, but how we take it.

So Peter's words apply to our lives as they did to men of his day.

Suffering for Righteousness' Sake

1 Peter 3:13-22

> 13 And who is he that will harm you, if ye be followers of that which is good?
> 14 But and if ye suffer for righteousness' sake, happy are ye: and be not afraid of their terror, neither be troubled;
> 15 But sanctify the Lord God in your hearts: and be ready always to give an answer to every man that asketh you a reason of the hope that is in you with meekness and fear:
> 16 Having a good conscience; that, whereas they speak evil of you, as of evildoers, they may be ashamed that falsely accuse your good conversation in Christ.
> 17 For it is better, if the will of God be so, that ye suffer for well doing, than for evil doing.
> 18 For Christ also hath once suffered for sins, the just for the unjust, that he might bring us to God, being put to death in the flesh, but quickened by the Spirit:
> 19 By which also he went and preached unto the spirits in prison;
> 20 Which sometime were disobedient, when once the longsuffering of God waited in the days of Noah, while the ark was a preparing, wherein few, that is, eight souls were saved by water.
> 21 The like figure whereunto even baptism doth also now save us (not the putting away of the filth of the flesh, but the answer of a good conscience toward God,) by the resurrection of Jesus Christ:
> 22 Who is gone into heaven, and is on the right hand of God; angels and authorities and powers being made subject unto him.

1. The Christian response to suffering (13-17). The question of v. 13 seems out of place if we take *harm* to mean temporal damage. But the point here is that no essential evil can come to the man who is passionately devoted to the good. Suffering cannot damage his soul. Evil cannot penetrate his spirit. When he suffers for righteousness' sake, God adds the compensating blessing that makes it all worthwhile. The reference to the eighth beatitude ("Blessed are they which are persecuted for righteousness' sake: for theirs is the kingdom of heaven"—Matt. 5:10) is clearer in the original, for Peter uses the same Greek word *makarios,* "happy" or "blessed."

Sanctify the Lord God in your hearts (15) is translated, "In your hearts be consecrated to Christ as Lord" (Williams), or, "Have reverence for Christ in your hearts, and make him your Lord" (TEV). The idea is to put Christ in first place as the true Lord of life.

We are also to be ready to answer any who ask about

the *reason of the hope that is in* us and to answer "with modesty and respect" (NEB). This is the most effective kind of witnessing. It puts the initiative on the other. He can but listen when what he is told is in answer to a question he has asked.

Such witnessing is possible only if believers live in *good conscience,* depending more on their winsome attitudes and good lives to answer false accusations than on their words (16). Always, of course, it is understood that the Christian's suffering is that which comes on him, not for his misconduct, but in spite of his good life (17). Some of us suffer more for our foolishness' sake than we do for righteousness' sake. Such suffering goes without reward. It is no more than we deserve.

2. Christ's suffering for us (18-22). Peter gives another great summary of the meaning of Christ's atoning death. He suffered for us, *the just for the unjust, that he might bring us to God* (18). He was put to death physically, but made alive by the Spirit—a point Paul also emphasizes (Rom. 1:4; 8:11).

a. Vv. 19-20 have given rise to much debate. Together with 4:6; Acts 2:27; and Eph. 4:8-10, this is the New Testament source of what is called the doctrine of "the descensus." It is preserved in a phrase in the Apostles' Creed, "He descended into hell"—or as it should be translated, "Hades," the place of the dead.

To properly understand these passages, we must remember that Jesus used two terms both of which are translated "hell" in the KJV, but which are quite different in meaning. One is *gehenna* (Matt. 5:22, 29, 30; 10:28; 18:9; etc.), the place of fiery torment to which the finally rebellious are consigned. The other is *hades* (Matt. 16:18; Luke 10:15; 16:23; also Rev. 20:13-14), the unseen realm of the dead.

Behind the Greek term *hades* is a Hebrew Old Testament term, *sheol. Sheol* is translated in the KJV 31 times by "grave," 31 times by "hell," and three times by "pit." Contemporary translations usually just transliterate it and print it as "Sheol."

While interpretations of the biblical data differ, the general teaching is that "sheol" or "hades" was the intermediate state in which the dead existed. The righteous dead there awaited the crucifixion and resurrection of Jesus. The wicked dead there await the final resurrection and judgment of all at the great white throne of Rev. 20:11-15.

In the interval between His crucifixion and His resurrection, it is implied that Jesus descended into the place of the dead and there proclaimed His victory over sin and death. He then "led captivity captive" (Eph. 4:8), taking the righteous dead with Him to heaven. The resurrection of Christ appears to have put an end to the waiting of the righteous in Hades. The wicked, however, still await the last great judgment, after which "death and hell *[hades]*" shall be "cast into the lake of fire. This is the second death" and comes to all whose names are not "written in the book of life" (Rev. 20:14-15).

In this Church age, those who die unsaved go to *hades*. It is for them a place of torment, although not their eternal state. Those who die in the Lord go immediately into His presence (Luke 23:43; 2 Cor. 5:1-8; Phil. 1:21-24; 1 Thess. 5:9-10). Even for the righteous dead, the eternal state has not been fully realized and will not be until the resurrection of the dead. But there is no indication of "soul sleeping" between death and the resurrection. For the Christian, "to be absent from the body" is "to be present with the Lord" (2 Cor. 5:8).

b. As Noah and his family had been saved by being brought to safety through the water of the Flood, we are brought to spiritual salvation through the water of baptism. Peter makes it clear that the mere application of water is not sufficient. Our problem is not *filth of the flesh* (21) such as water could wash away. Our problem is spiritual. Baptism is "the pledge of a good conscience to God" (Barclay).

The word translated *answer* in the KJV is *eperotema*. This was a business and legal term. It was the pledge of one signing a contract that he would fulfill all its terms.

Baptism is defined as "the sign and seal of the new covenant of grace" (*Manual*, 1972, p. 308).

c. It is *the resurrection of Jesus Christ* (21) that makes our salvation possible. He now has *gone into heaven, and is on the right hand of God* (22) making intercession for us (Heb. 7:25-26). *Angels and authorities and powers* are *made subject unto him.* While the New Testament recognizes that there are "principalities and powers" still in rebellion against Christ (Eph. 6:12), their defeat is certain (Col. 2:10-15). "Wherefore God also hath highly exalted him, and given him a name which is above every name: that at the name of Jesus every knee should bow, of things in heaven, and things in earth, and things under the earth; and that every tongue should confess that Jesus Christ is Lord, to the glory of God the Father" (Phil. 2:9-11).

1 PETER 4

The Value of Suffering

1 Peter 4:1-6

> 1 Forasmuch then as Christ hath suffered for us in the flesh, arm yourselves likewise with the same mind: for he that hath suffered in the flesh hath ceased from sin;
> 2 That he no longer should live the rest of his time in the flesh to the lusts of men, but to the will of God.
> 3 For the time past of our life may suffice us to have wrought the will of the Gentiles, when we walked in lasciviousness, lusts, excess of wine, revellings, banquetings, and abominable idolatries:
> 4 Wherein they think it strange that ye run not with them to the same excess of riot, speaking evil of you:
> 5 Who shall give account to him that is ready to judge the quick and the dead.
> 6 For for this cause was the gospel preached also to them that are dead, that they might be judged according to men in the flesh, but live according to God in the spirit.

Vv. 1-2 are Peter's parallel to Paul's teaching in Rom. 6:4-6, 10-11. Christ's suffering for us was His death on the Cross. It is a suffering and death He calls us to share (Matt. 16:24). When by our identification with Christ and His cross we become dead to sin (Rom. 6:1-2), we can live no longer therein. We no longer live in the flesh (our humanity apart from God) but in the Spirit (Rom. 8:9). Consecration and the renewing of our minds have brought us into the "good, and acceptable, and perfect, will of God" (Rom. 12:1-2).

These Christians have given "enough time in the past" to "lives . . . spent in indecency, lust, drunkenness, orgies, drinking parties, and the disgusting worship of idols" (3, TEV). That they have ceased these ways is cause for surprise to their heathen acquaintances. But those same unsaved people will *give account to him that is ready to judge the quick* (living) *and the dead* (5).

Peter's words about preaching *the gospel . . . to them that are dead* (6) has been the occasion for much speculation. It has been made the basis for theories of a "second chance" after death, particularly for those who had not heard the gospel during their lifetimes. It is at least possible, however, that Peter thinks of those who were by that time dead but who had heard the gospel while they lived —either in prospect, from the lips of prophets, or during the early years of Christian preaching. Death has claimed their bodies as a consequence of racial sin; but they live in the Spirit, sharing the eternal life of God.

There is no salvation apart from Christ. But Christ is "the true Light, which lighteth every man that cometh into the world" (John 1:9). Christ may have more ways of coming to men than we know about. Certainly the Judge of all the earth will do right (Gen. 18:25). His judgment will be by the law written in men's hearts as well as by the law inscribed in the Scriptures (Rom. 2:12-16). This in no way lessens the missionary imperative of the Church. But it does affirm the justice and love of God.

Christian Graces in Times of Trouble

1 Peter 4:7-11

> 7 But the end of all things is at hand: be ye therefore sober, and watch unto prayer.
> 8 And above all things have fervent charity among yourselves: for charity shall cover the multitude of sins.
> 9 Use hospitality one to another without grudging.
> 10 As every man hath received the gift, even so minister the same one to another, as good stewards of the manifold grace of God.
> 11 If any man speak, let him speak as the oracles of God; if any man

> minister, let him do it as of the ability which God giveth: that God in all things may be glorified through Jesus Christ, to whom be praise and dominion for ever and ever. Amen.

Much of the New Testament urges Christian duties on the basis that *the end of all things is at hand* (7). There can be little doubt that early Christians expected the Lord's return during their own lifetimes. Some have claimed that in this they were "mistaken."

What we may overlook, however, is the fact that the Bible often expresses as near or even as having already happened what is absolutely certain. That is, "imminence" (nearness) is often logical rather than chronological. This is clearly seen in the so-called "prophetic present" of the Old Testament. A prime example is Isa. 9:6-7, where the birth of Messiah over 700 years later is reported as having already occurred. A New Testament example is Rom. 8:30, where Paul proclaims the glorification of God's people as an accomplished fact. He is so certain of it that he can speak of it as already having taken place.

Yet for us today Peter's words take on new meaning. We are 1,900 years closer to the end than when the apostle wrote. What was the basis for exhortation then is even more important now. In view of the soon coming of Christ, some important Christian imperatives emerge:

1. *Be ye therefore sober, and watch unto prayer* (7). Seriousness of purpose and prayerful watchfulness are called for. Carelessness and irresponsibility are a betrayal of the faith we profess.

2. "Above all, love each other intensely, for love draws a veil over many a sin" (8, Barclay). The essence of godliness is *agape,* God's kind of love. It is forgiving love, and thereby covers a *multitude of sins.*

3. "Extend ungrudging hospitality towards one another" (9, Weymouth). The duty of hospitality to fellow Christians was especially important in New Testament times, when Christians were so often cut off from normal family ties that might have afforded them hospitality. It is no less important today as a means of encouraging the kind of

relationships that can serve as bridges for personal witnessing. "Hospitality evangelism" has many values in our day also, when home ties tend to be so weak.

4. The exercise of spiritual gifts (10-11). This is Peter's abbreviated list of the *charismata,* the spiritual gifts about which Paul writes in 1 Corinthians 12 and Rom. 12:6-8. Spiritual gifts are much more numerous than the single listing in 1 Cor. 12:8-11 would tend to indicate. Peter mentions two of the most universal: speaking for God, and serving (11).

Every man hath received at least one *gift.* There is no definite article, *the,* in the Greek. Paul speaks of "eternal life through Jesus Christ our Lord" as "the gift *[charisma]* of God" (Rom. 6:23). All Christians are to that degree "charismatic."

While the exercise of gifts may differ in degree as well as in kind, there is little doubt that Peter has underlined two that are practically universal. All Christians can *speak as the oracles of God* (11) when they express the truth God sets forth in His Word. All Christians can render some service *(minister).* All gifts are to be used to help one *another, as good stewards of the manifold grace of God* (10). *Manifold* means many-colored, varied, and beautiful in its expression. The end of it all is *that God in all things may be glorified* (11).

The Judgment of the Church

1 Peter 4:12-19

> 12 Beloved, think it not strange concerning the fiery trial which is to try you, as though some strange thing happened unto you:
> 13 But rejoice, inasmuch as ye are partakers of Christ's sufferings; that, when his glory shall be revealed, ye may be glad also with exceeding joy.
> 14 If ye be reproached for the name of Christ, happy are ye; for the spirit of glory and of God resteth upon you: on their part he is evil spoken of, but on your part he is glorified.
> 15 But let none of you suffer as a murderer, or as a thief, or as an evildoer, or as a busybody in other men's matters.
> 16 Yet if any man suffer as a Christian, let him not be ashamed; but let him glorify God on this behalf.
> 17 For the time is come that judgment must begin at the house of God: and if it first begin at us, what shall the end be of them that obey not the gospel of God?
> 18 And if the righteous scarcely be saved, where shall the ungodly and the sinner appear?

19 Wherefore let them that suffer according to the will of God commit the keeping of their souls to him in well doing, as unto a faithful Creator.

Peter comes back again to the inevitability of suffering. *The fiery trial* should not be thought of as *some strange thing* (12). Rather it should be looked upon as participation in Christ's sufferings to which an ultimate *glory* is attached. "If so be that we suffer with him, that we may be also glorified together. For I reckon that the sufferings of this present time are not worthy to be compared with the glory which shall be revealed in us" (Rom. 8:17-18).

It is important that the reproach that comes be *for the name of Christ* (14), and not for wrongdoing on our part (15). There is a strange listing of sins in v. 15. The danger that Christians might be busybodies *in other men's matters*—prying when they should be praying, nosey and meddling—is not hard to see. Even the *evildoer* ("mischief-maker," RSV) may be motivated aright—his harmdoing the result of blundering ignorance rather than ill will.

But to warn Christians against any one of them being *a murderer, or . . . a thief* is not easy to understand. Peter may use these words in a figurative way. "Ye have heard that it was said by them of old time, Thou shalt not kill; and whosoever shall kill shall be in danger of the judgment: but I say unto you, That whosoever is angry with his brother without a cause shall be in danger of the judgment" (Matt. 5:21-22). "Whosoever hateth his brother is a murderer: and ye know that no murderer hath eternal life abiding in him" (1 John 3:15). "Will a man rob God? Yet ye have robbed me. But ye say, Wherein have we robbed thee? In tithes and offerings" (Mal. 3:8).

Whatever be the case, the very extremes—from murder to being a busybody—show that God does not "grade" sins. There are no "big" sins or "little" sins, no mortal or venial sins, in His sight. The Christian must utterly destroy sin or sin will utterly destroy him.

The time is come that judgment must begin at the

house of God (17). Peter here uses an important word. It is *kairos*. It means not just any time, but a crisis time, a decisive moment. If judgment begins at the house of God, there is no hope for those who *obey not the gospel of God. If the righteous* are saved with no margin of human merit that they can claim, "what will happen to the impious and the sinner?" (18, Barclay). "So even those who suffer, if it be according to God's will, should commit their souls to him—by doing good; their Maker will not fail them" (19, NEB).

1 PETER 5

Pastors and People
1 Peter 5:1-11

The last chapter of 1 Peter deals with the respective obligations of spiritual leaders and members of the Church.

Duties of Spiritual Leaders

1 Peter 5:1-4

> 1 The elders which are among you I exhort, who am also an elder, and a witness of the sufferings of Christ, and also a partaker of the glory that shall be revealed:
> 2 Feed the flock of God which is among you, taking the oversight thereof, not by constraint, but willingly; not for filthy lucre, but of a ready mind;
> 3 Neither as being lords over God's heritage, but being ensamples to the flock.
> 4 And when the chief Shepherd shall appear, ye shall receive a crown of glory that fadeth not away.

As one among them, Peter addresses the *elders* (1). The word is *presbuteros*. In New Testament usage, it means simply an officer or recognized leader in a Christian church. The office did not necessarily mean full-time Christian service, although 1 Tim. 5:17 indicates that at least some elders were paid (where the KJV "honour" should be translated "pay"). There would be more than one in a local group, and they were "ordained" to their office (Acts 14:23; Titus 1:5). They administered the financial affairs of the church (Acts 11:30) and with the apostles were final authorities in church affairs (Acts 15:2; 16:4; 21:18-25).

Peter emphasizes the spiritual function of the elders. They are to *feed the flock of God* (2), literally, "to shepherd the flock." This they do by *taking the oversight thereof,* in which the verb is *episkopountes,* other forms of which are elsewhere translated "bishop." They are to do this "not as though it were forced upon you but of your own free will" (Goodspeed). They are to do it "not from the motive of personal profit but freely" (Williams).

Neither are elders to exercise their office as "little tin gods" (3, Phillips), but as true examples. Those who serve as worthy under-shepherds *shall receive a crown of glory that fadeth not away* (4), to be given them *when the chief Shepherd shall appear.*

Humility in Service

1 Peter 5:5-7

> 5 Likewise, ye younger, submit yourselves unto the elder. Yea, all of you be subject one to another, and be clothed with humility: for God resisteth the proud, and giveth grace to the humble.
> 6 Humble yourselves therefore under the mighty hand of God, that he may exalt you in due time:
> 7 Casting all your care upon him; for he careth for you.

The *younger,* whether in point of years or spiritual office and maturity, are to be subject to leadership. This is not easy. Most people would rather lead than follow. A girl, applying for entrance to an exclusive girls' school, found on the questionnaire, "Are you a leader or a follower?" With much hesitation, she checked "follower," thinking her chances of entrance would be dim. She received an almost immediate acceptance with a note, "We have accepted 1,650 leaders. It will be good to have at least one follower among them."

All personal relationships are to be marked by humility because *God resisteth the proud, and giveth grace to the humble* (5)—a quotation from the Greek version of Prov. 3:34, also cited in Jas. 4:6. Verse 6 is a memory of Luke 18:14, "Every one that exalteth himself shall be abased; and he that humbleth himself shall be exalted." The secret of Christian serenity is *casting all your care upon him; for he careth for you* (7).

Resisting the Devil

1 Peter 5:8-9

> 8 Be sober, be vigilant; because your adversary the devil, as a roaring lion, walketh about, seeking whom he may devour:
> 9 Whom resist stedfast in the faith, knowing that the same afflictions are accomplished in your brethren that are in the world.

Sobriety and vigilance are important *because your adversary the devil, as a roaring lion, walketh about, seeking whom he may devour* (8). It has been said that young lions, sharp of teeth and claw and quick of limb, hunt silently. It is the old lions whose teeth are broken, whose claws are blunt, and whose limbs are stiff that roar when they hunt, hoping thereby to paralyze their prey with fright and make it an easier catch. For that reason, Christians are to *resist* the devil, assured, as James said, that he will flee from them (Jas. 4:7).

Benediction

1 Peter 5:10-11

> 10 But the God of all grace, who hath called us unto his eternal glory by Christ Jesus, after that ye have suffered a while, make you perfect, stablish, strengthen, settle you.
> 11 To him be glory and dominion for ever and ever. Amen.

The body of the letter closes with a beautiful benediction. *Make you perfect* here does not use *teleios*, the ordinary Greek word for "perfect." The word is *katartisei*. Its first meaning is to mend, as of the nets of fishermen (Mark 1:19). It means to equip or furnish. One of the by-products of suffering is to be equipped or furnished to help others who suffer (2 Cor. 1:3-4). Suffering likewise strengthens, establishes, and settles those who endure it with trust in *the God of all grace*.

Conclusion
1 Peter 5:12-14

1 Peter 5:12-14

> 12 By Silvanus, a faithful brother unto you, as I suppose, I have written briefly, exhorting, and testifying that this is the true grace of God wherein ye stand.
> 13 The church that is at Babylon, elected together with you, saluteth you; and so doth Marcus my son.
> 14 Greet ye one another with a kiss of charity. Peace be with you all that are in Christ Jesus. Amen.

The conclusion of 1 Peter indicates the name of the scribe: *Silvanus* (12) or Silas. He sends greetings from *the church that is at Babylon* (13), a Christian code-name for Rome. Mark, whom Peter here calls his son and whose gospel is widely recognized as a transcript of Peter's own preaching, was also present.

Christians are to greet each other with the *kiss of* love, and a final benediction invokes peace upon all who *are in Christ Jesus* (14). So, in an age of turmoil and trouble, the final word is *peace*.

The Second Epistle of
PETER

Topical Outline of Second Peter

Introduction

Salutation, 1:1-2

Piety and Christian Growth, 1:3-21
    Necessary Additions to Faith, 1:3-7
    Values in Christian Maturity, 1:8-11
    A Necessary Reminder, 1:12-15
    Our Sure Word of Truth, 1:16-21

Warning Against False Teachers, 2:1-22
    The Danger of Heresy, 2:1-3
    The Lessons of History, 2:4-11
    Modern Balaams, 2:12-16
    The Tragic End, 2:17-22

Christ's Second Coming, 3:1-16
    The Doubters, 3:1-7
    The Day of the Lord, 3:8-10
    The Moral Dynamic, 3:11-16

Conclusion, 3:17-18

Introduction

The importance of maturity in the sanctified life is the central theme of 2 Peter. Faith takes hold of the promises of God and makes us "partakers of the divine nature," delivering us from "the corruption that is in the world through lust" (1:4-5).

But faith cannot live alone. To faith must be added the graces that make for maturity in holy character. We must "grow in grace, and in the knowledge of our Lord and Saviour Jesus Christ" (3:18).

Peter or Another?

2 Peter is one of the shorter books of the New Testament and at the same time has the dubious distinction of being the most debated. A number of New Testament scholars think some other person than Simon Peter was the author.

The pros and cons of the argument can be found in any New Testament introduction or critical commentary. It is sufficient to say here that there is no compelling reason to deny the complete accuracy of the first line of the letter: "Simon Peter, a servant and apostle of Jesus Christ, to those who through the righteousness of our God and Savior Jesus Christ have received a faith as precious as ours" (1:1, NIV).

Apart from the arguments of scholars is the fact that there is nothing in 2 Peter to motivate a forger to attach Peter's name to it. It teaches nothing contrary to what we know Peter taught; it introduces no novelty in Christian doctrine; it contains nothing a forger might wish to validate by attaching an honored name to his writing.

Keeping the Faith

New Testament writers were concerned both to establish their readers in the true faith and to warn against accepting false doctrines. This concern is particularly evident in 2 Peter.

Just as there were false prophets in Old Testament times, Peter foresees the danger of heresy in Christian circles. Particularly is he concerned about doctrines that excuse sin and immorality on the part of those who profess the name of Christ.

Peter knows well the lure of any teaching that permits carnal men to "eat their cake and have it too"; to live by the lusts of the flesh while claiming final salvation through Christ (2:12-19). But he makes it clear that those who fall for such teaching are worse off than if they had never heard the gospel (20-22).

The Day of the Lord

Not only right doctrine, but the approaching end of the age points to the need for "spotless" and "blameless" lives (3:14, NIV).

2 Peter 3 is one of the great definitive passages in the New Testament describing the second coming of Christ. Peter sets it squarely in the context of true doctrine and right living. For him, truth about the second coming of Christ is not the basis for speculation but for righteousness, steadfastness, and Christian maturity. So should it be for us all.

2 PETER 1

Salutation
2 Peter 1:1-2

2 Peter 1:1-2
> 1 Simon Peter, a servant and an apostle of Jesus Christ, to them that have obtained like precious faith with us through the righteousness of God and our Saviour Jesus Christ:
> 2 Grace and peace be multiplied unto you through the knowledge of God, and of Jesus our Lord,

The salutation of Peter's second letter is very much like the salutation of 1 Peter. He adds to the title *apostle of Jesus Christ* that of *servant*. Paul (Rom. 1:1; Phil. 1:1), James (1:1), and Jude (1) also took *servant* as a title. When used of service to men, *servant* (literally, "slave") was a term of subjection. When used of service to God, it was a term that implied high honor.

The letter is addressed to those who *have obtained like precious faith* (literally, "faith of equal value") *with* the apostle and his companions. This faith is "in the righteousness of our God and Savior Jesus Christ" (RSV). The KJV here obscures Peter's clear affirmation of the deity of Christ. Jesus Christ is both "God and Savior."

That *grace and peace be multiplied* to his readers is Peter's wish both here and in the salutation of 1 Peter (1:2). That such multiplication is to come *through the knowledge of God, and of Jesus our Lord* is a characteristic note of 2 Peter (1:3, 5-6, 8; 2:20; 3:18). It is worth noting that *knowledge* here, as usually in the Bible, carries the idea of "acquaintance with" rather than mere "knowledge about." It is not merely the product of the mind's activity or apprehension; it is given through the Holy Spirit's teaching (John 14:26; 16:13-15).

Piety and Christian Growth
2 Peter 1:3-21

Necessary Additions to Faith

2 Peter 1:3-7
> 3 According as his divine power hath given unto us all things that per-

> tain unto life and godliness, through the knowledge of him that hath called us to glory and virtue:
>
> 4 Whereby are given unto us exceeding great and precious promises: that by these ye might be partakers of the divine nature, having escaped the corruption that is in the world through lust.
>
> 5 And beside this, giving all diligence, add to your faith virtue; and to virtue knowledge;
>
> 6 And to knowledge temperance; and to temperance patience; and to patience godliness;
>
> 7 And to godliness brotherly kindness; and to brotherly kindness charity.

1. Peter is deeply concerned for the maturity of his Christian friends. He clearly recognizes that the Christian life is not a matter of human attainment. It is by God's *divine power* that we are *given . . . all things that pertain unto life and godliness* (3). His *promises* likewise are *given unto us* that we *might be partakers of the divine nature, having escaped the corruption that is in the world through lust* (4). Conversion and cleansing are the work of God—"works of grace" we call them.

2. But Peter is the apostle of Christian growth. It was he who described the coming of the Holy Spirit at Pentecost, not as a goal or end to be reached, but as a starting point or beginning of a life of Christian commitment (Acts 11:15). We must build on the foundation of faith a firm superstructure of Christian character. We are to do this with *all diligence* (5), with utmost earnestness, care, and zeal. Seven qualities are listed as important additions to the foundation of experiential faith:

a. Virtue (arete) is moral excellence in general, and courage in particular. It suggests the active side of faith as it ventures undaunted into life.

b. Knowledge (gnosis) Barclay defines as "that knowledge which enables a man to decide rightly and to act honourably and efficiently in the day-to-day circumstances and situations of life." It is practical wisdom.

c. Temperance (egkrateia) is self-mastery or self-control. Paul lists this among the "fruit of the Spirit" (Gal. 5:23). It represents the control of the spirit over the body, the disciplines of humanity so necessary for effective living.

d. *Patience (hupomone)* is endurance or steadfastness. It "is the brave and courageous acceptance of everything that life can do to us, and the transmuting of even the worst event into another step on the upward way" (Barclay).

e. *Godliness (eusebeia)* is a word for which we have no exact English equivalent. It implies an attitude that does what is thought to be well pleasing to God. "Piety" is sometimes used to translate this term.

f. *Brotherly kindness (philadelphia)* is usually translated "brotherly love" (e.g., in Rom. 12:10; 1 Thess. 4:9; Heb. 13:1). Christians constitute a brotherhood in the Spirit and are to regard their fellow disciples as children of the same Father.

g. *Charity (agape)* goes beyond brotherly love in that it embraces those for whom there may be no natural affection. *Caring* may be the nearest English word we have to the meaning of *agape*. We can care for and be committed to the well-being of those we may not be fond of. While the English term *charity* now misses far the meaning of *agape* love, it is instructive to recall that it comes from *caritas,* the Latin term that does mean "caring."

Values in Christian Maturity

2 Peter 1:8-11

> 8 For if these things be in you, and abound, they make you that ye shall neither be barren nor unfruitful in the knowledge of our Lord Jesus Christ.
> 9 But he that lacketh these things is blind, and cannot see afar off, and hath forgotten that he was purged from his old sins.
> 10 Wherefore the rather, brethren, give diligence to make your calling and election sure: for if ye do these things, ye shall never fall:
> 11 For so an entrance shall be ministered unto you abundantly into the everlasting kingdom of our Lord and Saviour Jesus Christ.

Peter lists five values to be gained by adding to faith the qualities listed in vv. 5-7.

1. Fruitfulness (8). To be neither *barren nor unfruitful* would better be translated "neither idle nor unproductive" (Goodspeed). Peter shares his Master's concern that His people bear fruit (John 15:1-6). Their productive activity must be *in the knowledge of our Lord Jesus Christ.* Busy-

ness for busy-ness' sake is no part of God's plan for His people.

2. Vision (9). To fail to grow is to become blind and shortsighted. In both the strict and the adapted sense, "Where there is no vision, the people perish" (Prov. 29:18).

A missionary told of returning to the church she had attended as a girl. In the Sunday school classroom hung a motto made of letters pasted on a cardboard background: "Where there is no vision, the people perish."

The passing years had taken their toll of the congregation. The church had lost ground. Its members were discouraged and defeated. Morale was low.

Brooding over the problems she found, the missionary went into the little classroom she had known so well as a child. The motto was still on the wall, but the paste under the first letter had dried and the letter had dropped away. The motto now read, "here there is no vision, the people perish."

"This," she said, "is the problem. Here there is no vision, and the work languishes."

3. Remembrance (9). Failure to add to faith results in forgetfulness of what Christ has done for our redemption. Our greatest safeguard as Christians from the peril of ingratitude and insensitivity is a keen recollection of the price paid for our salvation.

4. Stability (10). To have the qualities to be added to faith results in stability: *if ye do these things, ye shall never fall* (10). Christian security is never the automatic thing it has sometimes been represented to be. On the other hand, it is not a matter of doubt. God has made abundant provision for His people so that they need never fall.

5. Entrance (11). The promise of glory is not by a narrow margin, "scarcely saved." "You will be given the full right to enter the eternal Kingdom of our Lord and Savior Jesus Christ" (11, TEV).

A Necessary Reminder

Christian nurture is always "precept upon precept; line upon line." Lessons learned may need to be relearned.

Peter had heard this from the lips of his Lord. "Feed my lambs," Jesus had said (John 21:15; "sheep," vv. 16-17). This is an unending task. Sheep fed one day are ready to eat again the next day.

2 Peter 1:12-15

> 12 Wherefore I will not be negligent to put you always in remembrance of these things, though ye know them, and be established in the present truth.
> 13 Yea, I think it meet, as long as I am in this tabernacle, to stir you up by putting you in remembrance;
> 14 Knowing that shortly I must put off this my tabernacle, even as our Lord Jesus Christ hath shewed me.
> 15 Moreover I will endeavour that ye may be able after my decease to have these things always in remembrance.

It is important to *be established in the present truth* (12). All God's truth is timeless and timely. Yet some aspects of truth are more needed at some periods in the life of the Church. Important aspects of *the present truth* for our times center about the person and work of the Holy Spirit, and the return of Jesus Christ to this earth.

Peter's statement about the approaching end of his life (14) reminds us of Paul's parallel in 2 Tim. 4:6-8. John Wesley said of his people, "They die well." Only one who has walked with God can have such confident serenity as death draws near. Both Peter and Paul regarded the earthly life as living in a *tabernacle* or tent (cf. 2 Cor. 5:1ff.). At best it is temporary. Our true home is "on the other side."

Our Sure Word of Truth

2 Peter 1:16-21

> 16 For we have not followed cunningly devised fables, when we made known unto you the power and coming of our Lord Jesus Christ, but were eyewitnesses of his majesty.
> 17 For he received from God the Father honour and glory, when there came such a voice to him from the excellent glory, This is my beloved Son, in whom I am well pleased.
> 18 And this voice which came from heaven we heard, when we were with him in the holy mount.
> 19 We have also a more sure word of prophecy; whereunto ye do well that ye take heed, as unto a light that shineth in a dark place, until the day dawn, and the day star arise in your hearts:
> 20 Knowing this first, that no prophecy of the scripture is of any private interpretation.
> 21 For the prophecy came not in old time by the will of man: but holy men of God spake as they were moved by the Holy Ghost.

Our Christian faith, experience, and hope are not based on *cunningly devised fables* (16) but on *a more sure word of prophecy* (19), or "the word of prophecy confirmed" (Greek).

Peter and his fellow apostles were *eyewitnesses of* Christ's *majesty* on the Mount of Transfiguration (cf. Matt. 17:1-8; Mark 9:2-10; Luke 9:28-36). Here Moses, representing the Law, and Elijah, representing the Prophets, were subordinated to the Son, the supreme and final revelation of God.

This supreme and final revelation is like a light shining in the dark, the dawn of a new day marked by the beauty of the morning star (19). While truth is a very personal possession, it is a possession we have as part of a shared venture. *Scripture is* not *of any private interpretation* (20). There is no such thing as a "private truth," apart, of course, from a true report of personal experience. Truth is shared. One who claims a truth he alone can see is like the proud mother's report of her son marching with his unit in the parade: "They're all out of step but Johnny!"

The prophetic word of the Old Testament was not by the will of man—the product of human intellect. The keynote of prophetic preaching was always "Thus saith the Lord." "Men they were, but, impelled by the Holy Spirit, they spoke the words of God" (21, NEB).

2 PETER 2

Warning Against False Teachers
2 Peter 2:1-22

The Danger of Heresy

2 Peter 2:1-3

> 1 But there were false prophets also among the people, even as there shall be false teachers among you, who privily shall bring in damnable heresies, even denying the Lord that bought them, and bring upon themselves swift destruction.
> 2 And many shall follow their pernicious ways; by reason of whom the way of truth shall be evil spoken of.

> 3 And through covetousness shall they with feigned words make merchandise of you: whose judgment now of a long time lingereth not, and their damnation slumbereth not.

The importance of true prophecy reminded Peter of the danger of false teachers. False teachers in Christendom are like the false prophets in Old Testament times. They speak words not from the true God. They introduce heresies that are destructive. They even deny *the Lord* who *bought them,* not by disavowing His cause, but by professing it while all the time teaching what undercuts it.

False teachers always seem to find followers (2). It is never safe to judge the truth of a new religious fad by the number of adherents it wins. The particular heresy here described was a form of gnosticism—possibly that extreme that "persuaded people that, being now redeemed by Christ and living in the spirit, they could disregard moral scruples and live as they wished as far as their everyday lives were concerned" (A. R. C. Leaney). The result of following teachings such as this was that *the way of truth* was *evil spoken of* (2). The deepest wounds Christianity bears are those suffered in the house of professed friends. There is a sting in the cynical remark of George Bernard Shaw to the effect that "the trouble with Jesus Christ was that He had disciples," sometimes very unworthy.

The motive of the false teachers is *covetousness*—"greed for money" (NEB). With rare exceptions, cult leaders profit personally from their activities—some of them far beyond reason. "They will trade on your credulity with sheer fabrications" (NEB). But the God of truth will not be mocked. The judgment of such false teachers is at hand.

The Lessons of History

2 Peter 2:4-11

> 4 For if God spared not the angels that sinned, but cast them down to hell, and delivered them into chains of darkness, to be reserved unto judgment;
> 5 And spared not the old world, but saved Noah the eighth person, a preacher of righteousness, bringing in the flood upon the world of the ungodly;
> 6 And turning the cities of Sodom and Gomorrha into ashes condemned them with an overthrow, making them an ensample unto those that after should live ungodly;

> 7 And delivered just Lot, vexed with the filthy conversation of the wicked:
> 8 (For that righteous man dwelling among them, in seeing and hearing, vexed his righteous soul from day to day with their unlawful deeds);
> 9 The Lord knoweth how to deliver the godly out of temptations, and to reserve the unjust unto the day of judgment to be punished:
> 10 But chiefly them that walk after the flesh in the lust of uncleanness, and despise government. Presumptuous are they, selfwilled, they are not afraid to speak evil of dignities.
> 11 Whereas angels, which are greater in power and might, bring not railing accusation against them before the Lord.

Peter chooses three well-known examples of sin and its punishment to illustrate the certain fate of false teachers and their followers.

1. The fall of angels (4). The origin of evil in the universe is cloaked in obscurity. The hints that are given in scripture point to the creation of Satan and his demons as powerful angelic beings. Through pride or ambition, Satan and those associated with him rebelled against God. The result was that they were expelled from heaven.

Hell (*tartarus,* used only here in the New Testament) and *chains* (the better Greek manuscripts have "pits") *of darkness* describe the sphere within which fallen angels operate, destined as they are for final judgment and everlasting fire (Matt. 25:41). Rebels against the greatest light, they are doomed to the deepest darkness.

2. Men before the Flood (5). The generation before the Flood, rejecting the witness and work of Noah, was also doomed by turning from the truth. Only here is Noah described as *a preacher of righteousness,* although the account in Gen. 6:8-9 reports that Noah was "perfect in his generations" and "found grace in the eyes of the Lord." Only seven besides Noah *(the eighth)*—his wife and three sons and their wives—were saved.

3. Sodom and Gomorrha (6-11). The character of Lot shows up better here than in the Genesis record. Lot was "shocked by the dissolute habits of the lawless society" (7, NEB). Two different Greek words in this passage are both translated *vexed* in the KJV. In v. 7, the word is *kataponoumenon,* "oppressed," literally, "worn down by toil." In v. 8, the word is *ebasanizen,* "tormented." The

wearing effect of exposure to evil finally became torment to Lot.

Too many of us allow ourselves to become accustomed to evil until it no longer shocks us. Alexander Pope's well-known lines trace this danger:

> *Vice is a monster of so frightful mien,*
> *As to be hated needs but to be seen;*
> *Yet seen too oft, familiar with her face,*
> *We first endure, then pity, then embrace.*

A terrible picture is drawn of those who reject the truth. They are "abandoned to sensuality" (10, Weymouth). They despise authority (Goodspeed). They are daring, defiant, seeking to please only themselves. While the exact meaning of the evil speaking here described is obscure, the characterization of these false teachers is clear enough. They "rush in where angels fear to tread," with no restraint of modesty or self-control.

Modern Balaams

2 Peter 2:12-16

> 12 But these, as natural brute beasts, made to be taken and destroyed, speak evil of the things that they understand not; and shall utterly perish in their own corruption;
> 13 And shall receive the reward of unrighteousness, as they that count it pleasure to riot in the day time. Spots they are and blemishes, sporting themselves with their own deceivings while they feast with you;
> 14 Having eyes full of adultery, and that cannot cease from sin; beguiling unstable souls: an heart they have exercised with covetous practices; cursed children:
> 15 Which have forsaken the right way, and are gone astray, following the way of Balaam the son of Bosor, who loved the wages of unrighteousness;
> 16 But was rebuked for his iniquity: the dumb ass speaking with man's voice forbad the madness of the prophet.

These are blazing words, written in holy wrath. False religions condemn true faith without even bothering to understand it (12). The fruits of their own corrupt teachings will destroy them. They lead their followers to sensuality and evil (13-14). The mark of their apostasy is that they *cannot cease from sin*. There is no power of moral uplift in error.

Again Peter comes back to the *covetous* motivations of cult leaders. They are like *Balaam,* the Babylonian prophet who attempted to defeat the people of God with his incantations (Numbers 22 ff.) and whose evil advice (Num. 31:16) lured many Israelites to their deaths. In the New Testament, Balaam is the symbol of preaching for money, and religion without moral standards (Jude 11; Rev. 2:14). Balaam's donkey (Num. 22:28) was a better guide than his master!

The Tragic End

The theme of inescapable judgment runs all through this chapter. Whatever the fate of those who have never had opportunity to know the truth, Peter had no doubt at all about the fate of those who had the truth and corrupted it.

2 Peter 2:17-22

> 17 These are wells without water, clouds that are carried with a tempest: to whom the mist of darkness is reserved for ever.
> 18 For when they speak great swelling words of vanity, they allure through the lusts of the flesh, through much wantonness, those that were clean escaped from them who live in error.
> 19 While they promise them liberty, they themselves are the servants of corruption: for of whom a man is overcome, of the same is he brought in bondage.
> 20 For if after they have escaped the pollutions of the world through the knowledge of the Lord and Saviour Jesus Christ, they are again entangled therein, and overcome, the latter end is worse with them than the beginning.
> 21 For it had been better for them not to have known the way of righteousness, than, after they have known it, to turn from the holy commandment delivered unto them.
> 22 But it is happened unto them according to the true proverb, The dog is turned to his own vomit again; and the sow that was washed to her wallowing in the mire.

The cultists described here preyed chiefly on the church—people who had escaped the defilement of sin (20). They had *known the way* (21). Both false teachers and their followers are included in this description. It would be far better never to know Christ than to know and betray Him and die in apostasy.

Vv. 20-22 is one of a score of passages that warn Christians against turning back to the old life. To argue that such are not actually converted is to go directly against the sense of this whole passage. While the washed pig returning to the mire is not mentioned elsewhere in the Bible, the dog going back to its vomit is used in Prov. 26:11 to describe the fool who returns to his folly.

The whole passage is reminiscent of the parable of the house swept and beautified but left empty and occupied by seven demons worse than the one originally cast out (Matt. 12:43-45).

2 PETER 3

Christ's Second Coming
2 Peter 3:1-16

2 Peter 3 is one of the key New Testament passages dealing with the return of Christ. It stands as a clear witness against the idea that the New Testament Church gradually gave up its teaching about the Second Coming when Jesus did not return as soon as expected.

The Doubters

2 Peter 3:1-7

> 1 This second epistle, beloved, I now write unto you; in both which I stir up your pure minds by way of remembrance:
> 2 That ye may be mindful of the words which were spoken before by the holy prophets, and of the commandment of us the apostles of the Lord and Saviour:
> 3 Knowing this first, that there shall come in the last days scoffers, walking after their own lusts,
> 4 And saying, Where is the promise of his coming? for since the fathers fell asleep, all things continue as they were from the beginning of the creation.
> 5 For this they willingly are ignorant of, that by the word of God the heavens were of old, and the earth standing out of the water and in the water:
> 6 Whereby the world that then was, being overflowed with water, perished:
> 7 But the heavens and the earth, which are now, by the same word are kept in store, reserved unto fire against the day of judgment and perdition of ungodly men.

Instead of giving heed to false teachers, the readers are urged to be mindful of the teachings of faithful instructors in the way of truth. Far from voicing novelties, Peter is recalling to their minds what was taught by both prophets in the Old Testament and the apostles in the New.

Much Old Testament prediction about the Messiah was not specifically fulfilled in Christ's first advent. Some of its remainder is being fulfilled in the "new Israel," the Church. But there are other Old Testament teachings concerning the Messiah that point to the end of human history and the passing of time into eternity.

The apostles in the New Testament likewise freely predicted a second appearance of Christ on earth. Jesus himself had clearly taught, "I will come again" (John 14:3; cf. Matt. 16:27; 24:1—25:46; Mark 13:3-37; Luke 17:20-37; 21:5-38). At His ascension, the disciples were told, "This Jesus, who was taken up from you into heaven, will come in the same way as you saw him go into heaven" (Acts 1:11, RSV). And every writer in the New Testament—Paul, Peter, James, Jude, and John—echoed the same truth over and over.

Like all Bible truths, this one is met with skepticism by some. People who are living for themselves apart from Christ *(walking after their own lusts,* 3) do not welcome the truth that Jesus is coming again. Their argument is that "everything remains exactly as it was since the beginning!" (4, Phillips). Such an argument is simply not true. "They deliberately ignore this fact, that . . . the world that then existed was deluged with water and perished" (5-6, RSV). Without previous warning and without precedent, an entire generation was swept away. That those living before the Flood did not believe it was coming did not save them as the water rose.

The connection between the Flood and Christ's return has been made by Jesus himself (Matt. 24:38-39; Luke 17:26-27). Jesus also connected His coming again with the destruction of Sodom and Gomorrha, a judgment executed by fire rather than water (Luke 17:28-32). The same word of God that had warned people before the Flood (Gen. 6:3, 7 ff.) now warns of destruction by *fire* (7).

The Day of the Lord

2 Peter 3:8-10

> 8 But, beloved, be not ignorant of this one thing, that one day is with the Lord as a thousand years, and a thousand years as one day.
> 9 The Lord is not slack concerning his promise, as some men count slackness; but is longsuffering to us-ward, not willing that any should perish, but that all should come to repentance.

> 10 But the day of the Lord will come as a thief in the night; in the which the heavens shall pass away with a great noise, and the elements shall melt with fervent heat, the earth also and the works that are therein shall be burned up.

The day of the Lord is a very common Old Testament phrase to describe the end times. It was almost always connected with God's intervention in the affairs of men. Peter's point here is that delay is not denial. That Jesus tarries is itself an expression of His long-suffering and mercy. The eternal God is not limited by man's calendars. However it seems to us, God *is not slack* (slow). He is never too soon, but He is never late.

Some Bible students have been concerned with timetables and calendars for Christ's return. The wide differences among them testify to the limited success of their efforts. The Lord has told us enough about the future to whet our appetites, but not enough to satisfy our curiosity.

That day will come unexpectedly. It will be the end of earthly history within the time span that began with creation (Gen. 1:1). It will introduce a new eternal order involving "new heavens and a new earth, wherein dwelleth righteousness" (13).

The Moral Dynamic

2 Peter 3:11-16

> 11 Seeing then that all these things shall be dissolved, what manner of persons ought ye to be in all holy conversation and godliness,
> 12 Looking for and hasting unto the coming of the day of God, wherein the heavens being on fire shall be dissolved, and the elements shall melt with fervent heat?
> 13 Nevertheless we, according to his promise, look for new heavens and a new earth, wherein dwelleth righteousness.
> 14 Wherefore, beloved, seeing that ye look for such things, be diligent that ye may be found of him in peace, without spot, and blameless.
> 15 And account that the longsuffering of our Lord is salvation; even as our beloved brother Paul also according to the wisdom given unto him hath written unto you;
> 16 As also in all his epistles, speaking in them of these things; in which are some things hard to be understood, which they that are unlearned and unstable wrest, as they do also the other scriptures, unto their own destruction.

The "So what?" of the Second Coming is clear in Peter's mind: "What sort of persons ought you to be in lives of holiness and godliness?" (11, RSV). With *new heavens and a new earth* (13) "to look forward to, do your utmost to be found at peace with him, unblemished and above reproach in his sight" (14, NEB).

Peter's attitude toward Paul reflects the bigness of the man. Although Paul had "withstood him to the face, because he was to be blamed" (Gal. 2:11), Peter did not hold animosity or a grudge. He admits that Paul's writings contain some things difficult to understand, but contends for their value. Bible writers are completely unself-conscious regarding the inspiration of their pages. They spoke better than they knew, as Peter says of the prophets of the Old Testament (1 Pet. 1:10-12).

Conclusion
2 Peter 3:17-18

2 Peter 3:17-18

17 Ye therefore, beloved, seeing ye know these things before, beware lest ye also, being led away with the error of the wicked, fall from your own stedfastness.
18 But grow in grace, and in the knowledge of our Lord and Saviour Jesus Christ. To him be glory both now and for ever. Amen.

A final warning and a lifetime program complete Peter's letter. The warning is against the influence of *the wicked* (17; literally, "the lawless"). This would include both the false religionists of c. 2 and those who *wrest* the *scriptures* to *their own destruction* (16).

Peter, the great apostle of crisis at Pentecost, is just as strong on the importance of growth in the Christian life (18; cf. Acts 11:15; 2 Pet. 1:5-11). There is nothing here about growing *into* grace. One cannot grow plants *into* his garden. This is an exhortation to growth *in* grace.

With growth in grace and as the chief means to it must go growth in *the knowledge of our Lord and Saviour Jesus Christ*. Some have wrongly separated grace and knowledge, and have supposed them to be incompatible. Peter will hear nothing of such a separation. Jesus is the Source of both "grace and truth" (John 1:17). *To him be glory both now and for ever. Amen.* And amen!

Reference Notes

HEBREWS

1. H. Orton Wiley, *The Epistle to the Hebrews* (Kansas City: Beacon Hill Press, 1959), p. 53.

2. Charles R. Erdman, *The Epistle to the Hebrews: An Exposition* (Philadelphia: The Westminster Press, 1934), p. 36.

3. Johannes Schneider, *The Letter to the Hebrews,* trans. William A. Mueller (Grand Rapids, Mich.: William B. Eerdmans Publishing Co., 1957), p. 18.

4. William Barclay, *The Epistle to the Hebrews,* "The Daily Bible Study" (Philadelphia: The Westminster Press, 1955), p. 19.

5. William Neil, *The Epistle to the Hebrews,* "Torch Bible Commentaries" (London: SCM Press, Ltd., 1955), p. 42.

6. W. E. Vine, *An Expository Dictionary of New Testament Words* (London: Oliphants, Ltd., 1958), 3:223.

7. Barclay, *Hebrews,* p. 53.

8. F. F. Bruce, *Commentary on the Epistle to the Hebrews* (Grand Rapids, Mich.: Wm. B. Eerdmans Publishing Co., 1964), p. 59.

9. F. B. Meyer, *The Way into the Holiest* (New York: Fleming H. Revell Co., 1893), p. 48.

10. Schneider, *Hebrews,* p. 33.

11. Meyer, *Way into the Holiest,* p. 56.

12. Schneider, *Hebrews,* pp. 34-36.

13. William Temple, *Christus Veritas,* p. 217; quoted by Leon Morris, *The Lord from Heaven* (Grand Rapids, Mich.: Wm. B. Eerdmans Publishing Co., 1958), p. 50.

14. Barclay, *Hebrews,* pp. 38-39.

15. Quoted by Thomas Hewitt, *The Epistle to the Hebrews,* "The Tyndale New Testament Commentaries" (Grand Rapids, Mich.: Wm. B. Eerdmans Publishing Co., 1960), p. 103.

16. R. Gregor Smith, "Perfect," *A Theological Word Book of the Bible,* edited by Alan Richardson (London: SCM Press, Ltd., 1950), p. 167.

17. Alexander Purdy, "The Epistle to the Hebrews" (Exegesis), *The Interpreter's Bible,* edited by George A. Buttrick (Nashville: Abingdon Press, 1955), 11:684.

18. Wiley, *Hebrews,* p. 286.

19. Schneider, *Hebrews,* p. 84.

20. E. C. Wickham, *The Epistle to the Hebrews,* "Westminster Commentaries" (London: Methuen and Co., Ltd., 1910), p. 71.

21. Barclay, *Hebrews,* p. 120.

22. Wiley, *Hebrews,* p. 320.

23. Wickham, *Hebrews,* p. 82.

24. Wiley, *Hebrews,* p. 333.

25. Norman Snaith, *Hymns of the Temple* (London: SCM Press, Ltd., 1951), p. 44.

26. Meyer, *Way into the Holiest,* p. 136.

27. Neil, *Hebrews,* p. 116.

28. Andrew Murray, *The Holiest of All,* p. 423; quoted by Wiley, *Hebrew,* p. 387.

29. Barclay, *Hebrews,* p. 173.

30. In his book of sermons on *The Parables of Jesus* (Nashville: Broadman Press, 1970).

31. Erdman, *Hebrews,* p. 114.

32. Barclay, *Hebrews,* pp. 183-84.

33. Schneider, *Hebrews,* p. 116.

34. *Ibid.*

35. *Ibid.,* p. 118.

36. Wiley, *Hebrews,* p. 395.

37. Barclay, *Hebrews,* p. 207.

38. *Ibid.,* p. 218.

39. Neil, *Hebrews,* pp. 13-14.

JAMES

1. Archibald Hunter, *Introducing the New Testament* (Philadelphia: The Westminster Press, 1946), p. 167.

2. E. Stanley Jones, *The Reconstruction of the Church—On What Pattern?* (Nashville: Abingdon Press, 1970), p. 55.

3. Bruce Larson, *No Longer Strangers* (Waco, Tex.: Word Books, Publishers, 1971), pp. 52-53.

4. A. W. Tozer, *The Divine Conquest* (Harrisburg, Pa.: Christian Publications, Inc., 1950), p. 118.

5. *Ibid.,* p. 119.

6. *Prairie Overcomer,* published by Prairie Bible Institute, Three Hills, Alberta, Canada, n.d.

7. Tenis Van Kooten, *Building the Family Altar* (Grand Rapids, Mich.: Baker Book House, 1969), p. 142.

Bibliography

(Books referred to in the text or especially recommended for supplemental reading)

Barclay, William. *The Epistle to the Hebrews.* "The Daily Bible Study." Philadelphia: Westminster Press, 1955.

———. *The Letters of James and Peter.* 2nd ed. "The Daily Bible Study." Philadelphia: Westminster Press, 1960.

Bowman, John Wick. "The First and Second Letters of Peter," *The Layman's Bible Commentary.* Edited by Balmer H. Kelley. Richmond: John Knox Press, 1959.

Bruce, F. F. *Commentary on the Epistle to the Hebrews.* Grand Rapids, Mich.: Wm. B. Eerdmans Publishing Co., 1964.

Cargill, Robert. *The Parables of Jesus.* Nashville: Broadman Press, 1970.

Cochrane, E. E. *The Epistles of Peter.* Grand Rapids, Mich.: Baker Book House, 1965.

Cullman, Oscar. *Christology of the New Testament.* Philadelphia: Westminster Press, 1959.

Erdman, Charles R. *The Epistle to the Hebrews: An Exposition.* Philadelphia: Westminster Press, 1934.

———. *The General Epistles: An Exposition.* 1st ed. Philadelphia: Westminster Press, 1918.

Hewitt, Thomas. *The Epistle to the Hebrews.* "The Tyndale New Testament Commentaries." Grand Rapids, Mich.: Wm. B. Eerdmans Publishing Co., 1960.

Hunter, Archibald. *Introducing the New Testament.* Philadelphia: Westminster Press, 1946.

Hunter, Archibald M., and Homrighausen, Elmer G. "The First Epistle of Peter," *The Interpreter's Bible,* Vol. XII. Edited by George Arthur Buttrick, *et al.* New York: Abingdon-Cokesbury Press, 1957.

Jones, E. Stanley. *The Reconstruction of the Church—On What Pattern?* Nashville: Abingdon Press, 1970.

Larson, Bruce. *No Longer Strangers.* Waco, Tex.: Word Books, Publishers, 1971.

McNab, Andrew. "The General Epistle of James," *The New*

Bible Commentary. Edited by F. Davidson, *et al.* Grand Rapids, Mich.: Wm. B. Eerdmans Publishing Co., 1953.

Meyer, F. B. *The Way into the Holiest.* New York: Fleming H. Revell, 1893.

Neil, William. *The Epistle to the Hebrews.* "Torch Bible Commentaries." London: SCM Press, Ltd., 1955.

Paine, Stephen W. *The First Epistle of Peter.* "The Wycliffe Bible Commentary." Edited by Charles F. Pfeiffer and Everett F. Harrison. Chicago: Moody Press, 1962.

Poteat, Gordon. "James" (Exposition), *The Interpreter's Bible.* Edited by George A. Buttrick, *et al.* Vol. 12. New York: Abingdon-Cokesbury Press, 1951.

Purdy, Alexander. "The Epistle to the Hebrews" (Exegesis). *The Interpreter's Bible.* Edited by George A. Buttrick. Vol. 11. Nashville: Abingdon Press, 1955.

Reicke, Bo. "The Epistles of James, Peter, and Jude," *The Anchor Bible.* Edited by William Foxwell Albright and David Noel Freedman. Vol. XXXVII. New York: Doubleday and Doran, 1964.

Ross, Alexander. "The Epistles of James and John," *The New International Commentary on the New Testament.* Grand Rapids, Mich.: Wm. B. Eerdmans Publishing Co., 1954.

Schneider, Johannes. *The Letter to the Hebrews.* Translated by William A. Mueller. Grand Rapids, Mich.: Wm. B. Eerdmans Publishing Co., 1957.

Smith, R. Gregor. "Perfect," *A Theological Word Book of the Bible.* Edited by Alan Richardson. London: SCM Press, Ltd., 1950.

Snaith, Norman. *Hymns of the Temple.* London: SCM Press, Ltd., 1951.

Stibbs, Alan M. *The First Epistle General of Peter.* "Tyndale New Testament Commentaries." Edited by R. V. G. Tasker. London: Tyndale Press, 1959.

Strachan, R. H. "The Second Epistle General of Peter," *The Expositor's Greek Testament.* Grand Rapids, Mich.: Wm. B. Eerdmans Publishing Co., n.d.

Tasker, R. V. G. "James," *The Tyndale New Testament Commentaries.* Edited by R. V. G. Tasker. Grand Rapids, Mich.: Wm. B. Eerdmans Publishing Co., 1957.

Temple, William. *Christus Veritas.* Quoted by Leon Morris,

The Lord from Heaven. Grand Rapids, Mich.: Wm. B. Eerdmans Publishing Co., 1958.

Tozer, A. W. *The Divine Conquest.* Harrisburg, Pa.: Christian Publications, Inc., 1950.

Van Kooten, Tenis. *Building the Family Altar.* Grand Rapids: Baker Book House, 1969.

Vine, W. E. *An Expository Dictionary of New Testament Words.* Vol. 3. London: Oliphants, Ltd., 1958.

Wickham, E. C. *The Epistle to the Hebrews.* "Westminster Commentaries." London: Methuen and Co., Ltd., 1910.

Wiley, H. Orton. *The Epistle to the Hebrews.* Kansas City: Beacon Hill Press, 1959.